B
U
P

Deborah Carè · Chiara Paolino
Marcello Smarrelli

INNOVATING BUSINESS WITH ART

The Fondazione Ermanno Casoli Method

Foreword by
Ariane Berthoin Antal

Photo credits: Ramiro Chavez/White Balance, p. 141; Michele Alberto Sereni, p. 143, 145; Daniele Alef Grillo, p. 147; Marco Tedeschi and Fabrizio Carotti, p. 151; Francesco Ciavaglioli, p. 153; Emanuele Colombo, p. 157; Eva Bialkowska, p. 161; Maurizio Esposito, p. 163; Ramiro Casto Xiquez, p. 171; Cristina Leoncini, p. 173; Stefano Menconi, p. 177.

Cover: Cristina Bernasconi, Milan
Typesetting: Laura Panigara, Cesano Boscone (MI)
Translator: Andrew Spannaus for Language Solutions for Business - London.

Original edition: *Innovare l'impresa con l'arte,*

English extended edition

EGEA S.p.A.
Via Salasco, 5 - 20136 Milano
Tel. 02/5836.5751 – Fax 02/5836.5753
egea.edizioni@unibocconi.it – www.egeaeditore.it

First edition: October 2021

ISBN Domestic Edition	978-88-99902-86-5
ISBN International Edition	978-88-31322-37-9
ISBN Digital International Edition	978-88-31322-46-1
ISBN Digital Domestic Edition	978-88-238-8343-7

Print: Logo s.r.l., Borgoricco (Padua)

Table of Contents

Foreword

by *Ariane Berthoin Antal*[*]

The relationship between art and business has existed for centuries, and probably in Italy longer than any other country, but scholars only quite recently started turning their attention to this relationship. Over the past two decades researchers have uncovered a growing variety of ways of bringing the arts into the world of business (as well as other kinds of non-arts-based organizations) and they have examined the effects of different approaches.

The outcomes of this research have interested diverse audiences, including policy makers, managers, and the artists themselves, as well as social scientists. Each of these groups have different stakes in the research: policy makers want to know whether it is worth funding such initiatives; managers want to know whether they can achieve their organization's objectives more effectively by bringing in artists; artists want to benefit from an external perspective on their new kinds of artistic activities; and researchers seek more insights into organizational processes and the effects of innovative initiatives on organizational outcomes.

The literature that has emerged over the past decades varies in tone: at one end of the spectrum there are instrumental publications highlighting how the arts can serve organizations better, and at the other end are those deploring all engagement of the arts in the world of business and organizations. In between these two positions are publications that try to conceptualize the new ways in which arts and organizations are relating to one another, using different theoretical lenses and varying degrees of empirical richness.

---

[*] WZB Berlin Social Science Center.

Unlike many research areas, the field of arts and business has not been dominated by Anglo-Saxon writers and organizations. The experimentation and the research have been spread across different cultures and continents, and they have been written about in different languages. The cross-fertilization of ideas and practices nevertheless depends on the availability of translations, which is why this English edition of the Italian book published in 2018 by Deborah Carè, Chiara Paolino, and Marcello Smarrelli is so important.

Innovating Business with Art adds significant value to the field of arts and business in several ways. First, it contributes to the intellectually vibrant stream of research that combines conceptualization with rich empirical material. The authors take a reflective stance on the phenomenon, consciously avoiding the temptation of slipping into one of the two extremes that either instrumentalizes or deplores the engagement of arts and business. Furthermore, in every chapter they provide useful guidance on how to maintain this posture. They examine closely the many artistic interventions that the Ermanno Casoli Foundation has enabled in Italy and in other countries, looking and listening for elements from each unique situation that can be formulated into a systematic and replicable "prototype" that other artists and organizations could adjust to suite their own specific context. Second, their analysis is multileveled: they emphasize the essential involvement of people by listening to the perspectives and experiences of employees, artists and managers; they consider the consequences for the organizations; and they address the implications for society. For all three levels, the authors have selected powerful quotations from their interviews, so the experience comes alive for the reader. Third, the English edition of this book contains an additional chapter that "benefits" (if one can dare to apply this word to such a terrible period) from the pandemic, because the authors used the time to reflect again and dig deeper into the past cases, and some artists and organizations found new ways to work under the restrictions that Covid-19 imposed on society. Their findings enrich our understanding and offer new avenues for future work, in which I sincerely hope that the next generation of researchers will tread with courage and curiosity alongside artists, workers, managers, engaging organizations like those described in this book. May they also have the good fortune of working with as generative and far-sighted a partner as the Fondazione Ermanno Casoli.

Introduction to the international edition

As authors with a very diverse approaches and affiliations, we started the first edition of this book (at that time published in Italian, our own language), thinking about how to communicate a methodology and 'thought through' way to organize artistic interventions in the workplace, the method and the ethos of the Fondazione Ermanno Casoli (FEC).

In our view how the FEC approached including arts into business life deserved to be decoded for a wider audience of managers, artists and communities, so that art could be implemented in the company setting more systematically in our country. At that time, in 2018, we recognized that four main patterns could be used to interpret the experience of the FEC, revolving around the power of art to shape and co-evolve with the identity of a company, to create other sources of organizational learning and change, to guide innovation, and to enforce a different view of individual and company's performance.

After almost three years and the chance to translate the book, we could not help thinking about how the Covid-19 pandemic has changed our world, and the workplace especially, constraining us to be somehow half (or less) of ourselves: split among our offices, our houses, the open and closed schools, sometimes unfortunately the hospitals and the swab centers. In this context, thinking about what art could do in this divided world appeared as an important question to us and to the FEC, which, during the pandemic, did not stop its operations and organized one artistic intervention in Italy and prepared a second one in Mexico. Thus, the occasion of translating the book and to realize this international edition has created for the authors the opportunity to write an additional chapter, the final one, where we reflect about the role of art in business during the pandemic times and analyze the most recent experiences of FEC.

In the following pages, for the first 5 chapters, the reader finds the translation of the book we originally wrote in Italian in 2018, starting from the Introduction, where we described the pillars of this method we wanted to decode and understand, to the proper chapters, each dedicated to a different topic, from organizational identity to company performance, and to a specific set of artistic interventions organized and carried out by the FEC in different companies.

In the sixth chapter, the new one, we discuss what art could do for the workplace and the workplace for art, in these difficult times of absence of employees from offices and shopfloors, and of constrained interactions.

What we observe is the power of art to reconnect the individual, and the local stories of workers and artists, to a wider context of values, in order to produce meanings and interpretations of the pandemic. As in the words of the Casoli family and of the FEC's board: '*in these challenging times, the FEC became a place to stay more focused on the local territories, wherever they are. The FEC became more and more the occasion to attempt a reconnection between the people and workplace when a relationship seemed not to be possible anymore*'. Through the last chapter, a desire to keep together humanities and business thinking, employees' rationality, emotions and wellbeing, company performance and social care emerge as a possibility. A possibility that deserves the authentic involvement of artists, workers, managers, researchers, and their social communities to consolidate in these times.

Introduction

The Desire to Discuss Innovation and Method

This book aims to analyze a way of working. Not to exalt it, but to describe it with the hope that we can discuss a "method" through which art can enter business, a method that is conscious and structured, not a random encounter or one linked to a fad. The heart of the book brings together some of the main interventions that various artists have created in companies thanks to the Ermanno Casoli Foundation (hereafter the "FEC"). Yet the authors of this book will not provide only a description of how artists can work in a business – with its management, employees, spaces, brand, and products – but they try to provide the reader with a theoretical framework in which to situate a series of experiences: those in which artists create works of art together with a company, so that it is possible to take a deeper and more conscious look at the collaboration between art and organizational life.

So why speak of "innovation" and the FEC "method" in the title of the book? The word method recalls the possibility to structure an activity in a formal and stable way, to give continuity to one's actions, to have a benchmark to understand and evaluate them, and thus to have the opportunity to present them legitimately to the relevant communities. The FEC has the goal of promoting the entry of contemporary art into companies in order to stimulate processes of renewal of the ways of working, and of perceiving the environment and work relationships, according to a systematic and replicable approach.

To understand how the goal of innovation and method can coexist with contemporary art and how they coexist in this book, it is important to use these introductory pages to present some of the fundamental traits of the FEC and its initiatives. Starting in the introduction, we will cite certain artistic interventions that the artists have carried out with the FEC, with the goal of intriguing the reader and encouraging further investigation that will take place in the the following chapters chapters and the final project summaries.

The FEC was created in memory of Ermanno Casoli, the founder of Elica, an art lover and an artist himself, whose personality can be found not only in the name of the Foundation, but also in some of the characteristics of its identity and positioning. The FEC is not only linked to the figure of Ermanno Casoli, but also to the Elica company, its principal supporter and the location where it most often has the opportunity to experience the interventions with the artists before promoting them in other companies, always sharing the distinctive values that the two identities have in common.

Those values that link FEC, Elica, and Ermanno Casoli can be summarized thanks to some apparently conflicting conceptual dimensions: experimentation and replicability; the refinement of processes and the involvement of people.

Experimentation and replicability

The concept of experimentation implies the idea of searching, of going beyond current knowledge through application and empirical trial. The work with art that the FEC has encouraged in companies is a complex process, that implies a dialogue between the artist and the company, able to inaugurate a new way of seeing, feeling, and operating, that may be destabilizing, but whose meaning all of the employees are able to reconstruct.

Think of a project like *I Saettatori* (The Darters) by Francesco Barocco, where the artist and Elica employees are involved in the experimentation of a technique and the realization of a work. This involvement takes place both in company and cultural places, allowing the employees to have multifaceted experiences in different contexts and play different roles. Or consider *Teste* (Heads), in which the artist Francesco Arena organizes a series of encounters with Elica employees in a preparatory phase, to arrive at a composition that is complex, consisting of different ideas, tools, and artifacts, that range from photographs to sculptures, and ultimately to an installation conceived to change, disappear, and be reborn in a new form over time. This inclination to seek challenges and experiment was also a characteristic of Ermanno Casoli. His daughter Cristina Casoli, president of the FEC, tells us:

> My father was not born an entrepreneur; he was a veterinarian satisfied with what he did, but he wasn't afraid to completely change his profession and daily routine. When he married my mother, he jumped into this new "enterprise" of founding a business that made hoods [...] so we saw him go from being a veterinarian to fiddling with a hand drill to make the hoods himself.

Experimentation is a value that the FEC shares with Elica, a "laboratory" and "incubator" in which to try to develop interventions of various kinds that involve artists. The company, despite maintaining its identity as a place of production, through the presence of art and artists intends to develop laterality of thinking and reflection, as explained by Francesco Casoli, the chairman of Elica:

> In the company there is a constant presence of people who apparently have no link with industrial production, such as artists, architects, and art historians. But this presence is voluntary, intentional. It is important to have agents to destabilize norms and procedures, able to create that discontinuity that is decisive to be competitive in the market.

In the authors' intentions, the concept of experimentation must be accompanied by that of replicability. Replicability implies the possibility for an activity or artifact to be reproduced multiple times. In our common understanding, it seems to be an oxymoron to associate replicability with experimentation. In this case, replicability indicates the FEC's desire to work with artists and companies to understand what happens from their encounters and create a "prototype" that, with all of the adjustments necessary for different contexts, becomes replicable in other company settings. This is done with the hope that the art itself, in time and through a more structured approach, will become an occasion for innovation and change with respect to the numerous other "metaphors," training tools and management consulting. The possibility to replicate derives from the opportunity, guaranteed by the Foundation's structure, to construct long-term relationships with artists, to understand their methods of work and how they can satisfy, more or less effectively, the needs of the companies that open their doors to an intervention with contemporary art.

Replicability and experimentation are thus very close concepts in the life of the FEC and Elica. If we think of one of the first workshops, *Dal progetto all'oggetto* (From the Design to the Object, 2008) carried out by Ettore Favini, Christian Frosi, and Nico Vascellari, we can comprehend this association. At the center of the intervention created by the three artists is the theme of design as a fundamental methodological passage in the development of both a work of art and an industrial product, but also of the elaboration of new concepts and new emotional categories. Therefore, design thinking is not typical only of the creative process, but of any solid process of research and study, including in areas different from art. This entails an awareness that the two processes – art and production – are not so far apart, when they are distinguished by a rigorous procedures and methods. Francesco Casoli in describing the relationship between Elica, the FEC, and the world of art, says:

> It is fundamental to communicate to the world of industrial production that those who make art and creativity their life, spend their energy systematically in searching. This connection is relevant so that those who work in traditional processes can accept with more awareness the entry of art into their work situation.

Respecting the originality of the work, the artistic process, and the needs of the company that request it, the goal of the FEC is to form an attachment with artists and companies that do not have a dogmatic and rigid approach, searching for an alternative method of working. The FEC, in turn, studies and articulates this method to make the organizational part replicable and transform the inevitable conflicts and misunderstandings that can arise in the encounter between art and companies into elements of value.

The refinement of the processes and the involvement of people

The refinement of a process implies the fact that it is designed with advanced and precise criteria, so as to be as effective as possible. To "refine" also implies the ability to learn what can be modified and improved, establishing a connection, as a "third period," with the phases of experimentation and replication described previously. A distinctive characteristic of the FEC's approach is that of creating complex artistic interventions that require different timings and techniques with respect to the traditional way of introducing art into companies, with artifacts and "intermediate" events that find meaning in the concluding phase of the work. Among the best examples is what was created by the work of Francesco Barocco, that we have already cited above, with *I Saettatori* at Elica in 2011, working around the artistic practice of engraving, its history, its concepts, and its techniques, involving the company's employees in an experience that transformed their status from that of "pupils" to that of "artists," and ultimately to "art historians," guides and mentors of other colleagues, borrowing the categories of the artistic world to revive their company spaces. Getting to the heart of business questions to reflect on the theme of economic exchange, *L'intelligenza del caso* (The Intelligence of Chance) – the workshop created by Cesare Pietroiusti again at Elica – was structured through the creation of artifacts produced with paper, wine and smoke, but also with concepts such as the exchange and duration of the work of art, to set in motion a dynamic of reflection that took shape during the activities and continued afterwards thanks to the continued presence of the works at the company. These are only two examples of how the planning of an artistic intervention can reach such advanced levels, as regards both the concepts on which to reflect, and the processes through which to convey them.

Experimenting and maintaining memory allows the FEC to always make improvements and continuously renew the artistic interventions, so that this innovative contribution can reach the Foundation's stakeholders and above all the employees of the companies with which it interacts. In fact, together with the refinement of the artistic intervention, at the moment of its entry into a company, the FEC seeks to involve as many people as possible in the intervention, with the goal of generating new ways of thinking and feeling in a large part of the organization.

Although the FEC has also carried out activities for more limited populations, the interventions usually foresee the involvement of a large number of people, even the employees of an entire factory, joined together in interfunctional professional groups without any hierarchical distinction. This desire for involvement contains a goal functional to the well-being and performance of the people who work in the company. As Francesco Casoli says:

> Our goal is to engage the largest number of employees, and since the company is multinational, we should also attempt to reach with art the different nations

> and continents in which we operate. If laterality of thinking must become a widespread skill, it is important to systematically reach many organizational populations.

This goal of engagement also reflects the spirit of Ermanno Casoli, that emerges in the words of his daughter Cristina:

> When my father painted a picture he never created it only for himself, closed in a studio; to the contrary, he made sure that many others contributed to his painting. He was a man who loved having people around him to give a hand or even only to ask a question.

In the chapters that follow, the authors, alternating between theoretical rationalization, illustration of practice, and artistic treatment, will attempt to explain this "method" of work and its implications for generating innovation at different levels of companies, trusting that a critical debate will be triggered, with a growing presence of artists and contemporary art in companies.

1 An Overview

1.1 Why write and read a book on contemporary art, innovation, and business life

Since the publication of the book by Lotte Darsø, *Artful Creation. Learning* Tales of Arts in Business (2004), the discussion of the relationship between art and management has been enriched with many different contributions. Managerial theories have been used to interpret artistic phenomena and careers (Montanari, Scapolan and Giannecchini, 2016); the artistic sector has been the subject of a study to examine the role of traditional business (Soda, Usai and Zaheer, 2004); and more often, management has been called on to "restore the health" of the world of art, at times with questionable results (Zan, 2002). In recent years, though, it has become possible to interpret the spheres of art and management on the same level. The relationship is one in which management cannot be the panacea for problems in the art system (especially those linked to governance), and art cannot generate only a "sense of belonging" or "creativity," but must become a way for companies to reflect on more complex and profound concepts.

Therefore, the issue of the relationship between art and business is not new, but has changed considerably, and the actors who operate in the area between these two worlds have changed, thanks above all to the birth of foundations that support the promotion of art. The aim of this book is not so much to document these changes, but to provide a key for interpretation linked to the concepts of "innovation" and "renewal." It is a book in which research, managerial practice and artistic knowledge aim to work together to contribute to the debate, to better understand how art and business interact, to provide information, and direction, so that this interaction is increasingly fruitful for the world of companies and the system of art.

The lens of innovation is understood here in a broad, not technical sense, to understand how art can lead to a different way of learning and reflecting on the information that is received within a company space and how it can lead to a new way of seeing and conceiving one's products, spaces, processes and artifacts.

This book aims to understand the "new" potential that is generated by the entry of art into business and observes it on multiple organizational levels, from the individual to the company as a whole, concentrating on contemporary art in particular. A work of contemporary art often entails the use of common objects or practices drawn from daily life, reconsidered in a new context or with a different fundamental motive. The artisanal aspect is often undervalued with respect to the conceptual aspect of the work. Creating the art, and thus carrying out the process, takes on new importance, becoming in some cases the crucial element of the work itself; even non-finished art is considered as the chance product of a creative process. Chance takes on a different dimension when we follow unwritten criteria linked to the spontaneous alternation of objects reconsidered through the eyes of the artist (Vettese, 2012). This procedural and conceptual character, the freedom of action, the possibility to alternate noble materials and ancient techniques with tools and practices from daily life and work, makes contemporary art a particularly versatile and effective medium to support renewal in companies.

If we were to summarize the reasons for writing, but above all for reading this book, we could use the following titles:

- *A false myth: art is a "formative" metaphor that is easy to use especially in training.* The use of contemporary art is increasingly frequent in training, not only for managers. It is so widespread that art now seems to have become a tool in and of itself, more than a conceptual and material universe that enters the company, with points of both contact and deviation. In this book we will present complex examples of interaction between art and business. This complexity resides in the choice of the artist, in how the artist's philosophy does or does not adapt to a company's history or needs, and in how intermediaries play a crucial role in supporting companies to understand how art can not just provide responses, but help discuss and propose new ways of feeling and thinking. According to the authors' perspective, art comes into companies not only during official training sessions, and in doing so, appeals to a system of concepts and a way of learning of its own, which requires consciousness in order not to banalize its significance.

- *The need for a connection to the contemporary world.* In this book we will stress the importance of connecting contemporary art to the current time of the company (in terms of the economic, social, and cultural events that will most likely influence the life of businesses). For the authors, it is important to create a relationship between contemporary art and the need to compose or recompose relationships, taking into account the pressing need to restore a sense of solidarity and future in companies. We aim to present evidence and theories of how contemporary art, if introduced properly and consciously, can be a way to bring these needs to light and encourage a positive response to them.
- *The importance of organizational theories to explain both the positive and problematic role that art can have for people, processes, and spaces.* For a long time, the essential studies that investigated the relationship between art and management referred to institutionalist or neo-institutionalist theory. In many other cases, though, the relationship between art and companies, that is interesting per se, found itself being a-theoretical, presenting mostly empirical evidence without a clear key for interpretation. Currently, however, there are many theoretical currents that can help construct meaning, and thus guide managerial practice on the relationship between art and business: from organizational literature on spaces to that on values, materiality, and professional and personal identities. In this book we have tried to give more space to the latter approaches, aiming to offer an original perspective to interpret artistic interventions in companies.
- *The need to accumulate data and information.* The world of research and the world of business need to test theories and accumulate evidence on the functioning of the art system and on how it interacts with the business system. "Theorization-data collection-advancement of theories-renewal of practice" is the only cycle through which it is possible to initiate a reflection on managerial practice

that is truly informative on the possible courses of action or problematization of existing ones. This book has also been written with the hope that in Italy companies will increasingly be open to collaborative initiatives with museums, foundations and universities, so that they can finally work together. This way, for example, there would be a better understanding of the ability to trace the positive effects of the entry of art into companies to a general, not episodic purpose, highlighting the most problematic aspects of this process that can naturally emerge, of which there is little discussion.

- *The importance for companies of generating new organizational spaces, internally and at their boundaries.* Art allows a company to experience a public dimension more, since it brings an artistic intervention and/or work of art inside the company, that is relevant for the general public due to its cultural, entrepreneurial, social, but also political implications, if foreseen by the artist's intervention and philosophy. This mixture obligates the art system and the entrepreneurial system to confront forms of governance of their mechanisms of functioning that are different than usual, implying the participation of a variety of actors that go from local entities to schools, to the surrounding community in a broad sense.

To be coherent with these motivations, the book is structured so as to introduce in each chapter a theoretical organizational matrix approach, that can be suitable to discuss the artistic interventions organized by the FEC for the companies that have collaborated with it and to draw working implications that are useful for both the managerial and the artistic community. The interventions are reinterpreted to provide an interpretation in light of theory, to derive guidelines useful for understanding and planning artistic interventions in companies.

1.2 What subjects the book addresses and why

In this book, we have chosen to address four major themes, that allow for interpreting how contemporary art and business interact with and influence each other on different levels: the individual dimension of the worker and that of the group, and the definition of products, processes, and organizational spaces, that also generates implications for the concept of competitive advantage for a business. Adding to the development of these four themes is a fifth part that uses a more historical-artistic approach to analyze the works cited in the book.

Below is a more detailed illustration of the reasons that have led the authors to address each theme, and a summary of the implications each can have for the managerial and artistic communities that wish to experiment with, or have already experimented with, the entry of contemporary art into companies.

1.2.1 *Personal and organizational identity*

The concept of personal and professional identity allows for a reference to how contemporary art can activate a new or renewed perception of oneself at work with respect to one's group of reference and organization. The identification with the organization is linked to the motivation and emotional link that people construct with their company and is thus fundamental to trigger positive and effective work behaviour. This chapter analyzes how an artistic intervention can provide the opportunity to generate a process of positive identification for the individual and the company. The construction and reconstruction of work identity is addressed by highlighting how art can first generate a "break" and then a "mending" to create a richer perception of the self and a premise for more effective work behaviour. The implications for planning an artistic intervention include, for example, how to connect to the company's history (its past identity) to its future (the desired state). This connection ensures that the artistic intervention is located in a context and a narrative desired jointly by the company and the artist. The times and types of interventions are also briefly discussed to highlight how the processes of identification imply the need to have time available with one's employees: if the aim is to provoke a reflection on how people define themselves in relation to the company, it is necessary for those people to have the perception that they will be able to begin that discussion. The artistic interventions to which we refer always include a component of conceptual elaboration that follows the artist's material production step by step. The artist, starting from the philosophy that characterizes their work and in line with their modus operandi, proposes a path that starts from a solid theoretical and content basis on which the participants are to reflect, to then proceed with a practical phase in which the thoughts materialize in the shared work. In this delicate equilibrium, the material execution is never a purely technical exercise, but the exact re-presentation of the practice linked to the artistic production, the same that the artists follow every day in their atelier. It is their routine, their daily activity, what mannerist artists defined with a very appropriate term, their "vexation." As such, the material production supports and helps both the understanding of the work of art and the figure of the artist, demythologizing them, bringing them closer, to the point of putting them on a level of comparison and empathy with the figure of the worker and what they produce.

1.2.2 *Learning through art*

The fact that art can be adopted as a formative "metaphor," especially for the managerial population, is one of the subjects addressed the most in the literature. In this book, we discuss the theme of learning through art to integrate a reflection on the approaches most traditionally associated with it in training (those linked to aesthetics and aesthetical knowledge) with the approaches more centered on active learning and thus on training design techniques that put the learner at the center. The goal is to demonstrate that art activates a broad range of learning processes that are not to be underestimated. This range goes from the activation of the five senses of the learner and their more inductive decision-making mechanisms, to the method of discussing errors, to the exercise of dissonance and divergent thought during the training intervention. In terms of implications, there is a discussion of the abilities that an artistic intervention can help develop and how that intervention should be designed for this development of skills to be plausible. In particular, we refer to how art is not just another training metaphor, but can have a role of "recomposition" of some relationships in a company. Thus, artistic activity in training should be adopted from the standpoint of facing an important challenge linked to an opportunity to restore relationships or generate dialogue on strategic issues, that can also potentially create divisions, provided they are discussed in depth.

1.2.3 *Process and product innovation*

The concept of art is associated with that of innovation, but this connection is more often made intuitively rather than empirically. In fact, there is still no evidence that artifacts and artistic processes generate a change in the company's products and practices, while there is more solid evidence of how the object and the underlying design process have a broad impact on innovation in the company at various levels. Therefore, in this book we have decided to address the question of artifacts and materiality as factors that allow for overcoming some barriers that hinder the exchange of information, and to look at the artistic process as an organizational mechanism that can support not only the integration of information, but also a structured and ideational decision-making process in a new way that is functional to the company's long-term goal. The work of art per se can become the occasion for integrating and generating knowledge; the artistic intervention, the materials and objects that are produced, can be the opportunity to rethink one's routines, how one's usual work materials are interpreted and how decisions are made. The result of the introduction of art and the artist into a company can be new organizational practices, a new way of conceiving the company spaces and artifacts, and a new habit of looking to the company's future and its goals. The theoretical discussion in this chapter is based on the literature linked to artifacts, materiality, organizational spaces and their relationship with innovation. From an empirical standpoint, the analysis is supported by the discussion primarily of two artistic interventions organized by the FEC for Elica, that had a significant impact on the process of creating prototypes and on the design of the final product. In terms of implications, the conditions are clarified in which the work of art and the intervention of artists in companies can generate a new way of integrating and generating knowledge and producing innovation, taking into consideration the viewpoint of both the company and of the artists.

1.2.4 *Competitive advantage and openness to other worlds*

For a long period of time, management has tried – and still tries today - to quantify the impact that organizational practices have on individual and company performance. This need, although legitimate, has recently been tempered in part by studies of a more qualitative and critical nature that look at how the quantification of results and thus the performance of some investments can be limiting, at times leading company decision-makers to use information that is partial or not fully representative of reality. This trend is reflected in studies that deal with the "value" of artistic interventions for the company and its competitive advantage. In the last chapter, we will first of all illustrate the need to evaluate the process and the interim results after having introduced art in the company, rather than concentrating on the need to produce a single, final indicator. These intermediate results refer first of all to the contribution that the investment in contemporary art can make to the company with regard to all of the stakeholders, from employees to the surrounding community, to other companies in the area. Together with this important clarification, we will also analyze the data from two studies that use different indicators to quantify the advantages that can derive from an investment in art. Lastly, we will offer a sort of "canvas" with which managers can organize a measurement plan in their specific situations.

1.2.5 *Summaries of the artistic interventions*

The book ends with summaries of the artistic interventions cited, that are useful for a more detailed understanding of the philosophy, the path followed by the artist and the meaning of the work of art. To this end, they are aimed at the managerial community in order to provide elements to define the meaning of the choices made by the companies that have collaborated with the FEC, in terms of artists and interventions. The summaries are also aimed at the artistic community to provide context for the meaning of the interventions conducted in companies, how they are connected to the questions that the artist explores in a general sense and to what point the artist's philosophy and the company's work philosophy can overlap or collide.

1.3 Encouraging and problematizing the use of art in companies

This is the right moment for mutual contamination between art and management: through increasing creativity, social engagement and innovation, the managerial community can approach the world of art and understand its advantages to permit experimentation in companies. At the same time, art, through its work with the professional communities that belong to the business world, can effect social change and stimulate discussion of its concepts and tools.

To understand the reasons underlying this new, broad collaboration between the managerial and artistic communities, we can make use of the concept of "mess" (Cook, 2009): managers and artists have greater trust in the potential of the relationship between their worlds and thus decide to explore a "messy area" (Cook, 2009). The meeting with the artist and his work defines a space in which the employees are immersed in a process of individual and group understanding, able to disturb all of the effects of the *knowing* process, understood as the ability to understand what is happening. The disturbance phase can be followed by a shift that allows for starting over from the time of the break with daily habits, in order to create something new, at times reaching consciousness of a need for change.

The principle that guides the authors of this book is that the creation of this *messy area*, in which art and management meet, can be of primary interest for improving the quality of people's work life, and of the processes and results with which the company works. In particular, in the chapters of this book we will discuss the following categories of benefits that the use of art in companies can generate:

- *Stimulate the ability for recomposition of relationships between businesses, employees and society.* Some managers are interested in finding partnerships with potential co-creators of a new, better society, to mend the typical social rifts in business life. The involvement of artists plays a very important role in this context: it could be the opportunity to allow them to take part in the creation of a new society in which to rethink the role of businesses, citizens, workers and artists themselves.
- *Support the management of "innovation."* For some time now, in managerial literature there has been a discussion of the importance of innovation and how it takes place. It is no longer only about continuous or disruptive innovation, but above all the ability to respond creatively to emerging problems, making use of available resources. The artist sows something new with his interpretation of reality, while the manager understands this new point of view and reorients it to make it suitable for their own business and processes. A key role is played here by improvisation, the ability to respond to a problem at the same time it arises, spontaneously, through a mechanism of seeking and creating a solution immediately. More than planning-then-doing, when an artist is present we should speak of

listening-and-observing-then-doing. This new ability to think and structure the decision-making process is one of the results that the encounter between contemporary art and management can produce.

- *Generate lower experimentation costs.* It is not only testing new product and process ideas that is important, but also deciding (and having the privilege today to decide) what ideas to produce and testing them. The artist's contribution to company life can be that of orienting the decision-making process towards certain product/process categories and giving the company and the employees involved in the artistic and managerial reflection an opportunity to experiment with these ideas during the artistic intervention, at least in terms of analogy.
- *Assist the management of uncertainty and the creation of a long-term connection.* Establishing a relationship with the organizational population that is not only transactional, but also affective, is a renewed need. This is why the managerial community has attempted to use training and communication metaphors that are always closer to the individual dimension. The most powerful metaphors are those involving art, because they allow for continuous adaptation by way of a natural innovation of thought that takes place through the experimentation of the artistic process and the creation of the work.

It thus becomes important to explicitly identify the areas of risk potentially linked to the entry of art into the organizational world. These risks, as we will see from the practical examples presented in the various chapters, often derive from an underestimation of the scope of the artistic intervention in the company's life, from unclear goals, the lack of careful planning, or an inappropriate choice of the artist with whom to collaborate. Those "dangers" can be summarized as follows:

- *Possible source of distraction.* The organizational environment and the daily activities that are carried out within it can be slowed down by the intervention of an artist within the company. The disruption of routine entails a series of advantages (as we have seen in this introductory chapter and will see in more detail later), that must, however, be compared with the enthusiasm for a practice that is far from the company's normal mode of operation. Yet this enthusiasm risks becoming a source of distraction from work, especially when it is interpreted as an activity to be carried out sequentially and according to a criterion of specialization, rather than variety of knowledge.

- *"Overcoming Aesthetic Muteness"* (Taylor, 2002). The literature speaks of *muteness* to describe the inability of the members of an organization to define what represents an artistic intervention for them, based on a background that is completely different than that of the artist. In this case we speak of a true silence with respect to the question of aesthetics within organizations. Some people could feel demotivated, with the prejudice of not being able to understand the meaning of a work of art, of being involved in something distant from them or that in any event distracts from the duties they are to perform during working hours. Moreover, not having clarity on the result and practical advantage of the artistic project can generate a feeling of frustration, insecurity and thus distrust.
- *Strengthening of stereotypes.* The encounter between different worlds and people could enhance the perception of differences, feeding new stereotypes. This regards not only the artist and members of the organization, but also the internal differences between members of the organizational population. A contemporary art intervention requires deep physical and mental involvement, that usually implies a period of time in which the artist remains at the company and an adequate planning period. This is an opportunity for sharing, that could lead to the strengthening of preconceptions rather than their elimination. Instead of encouraging collaboration and collective engagement, an artistic intervention could thus risk triggering mechanisms of defense and closure, based on the lack of receptiveness to the emotional and cognitive openness that this experience requires.
- *Still little clarity.* The expectations nourished by managers in regard to the use of art in their organizations are very high. However, what is still not very clear is how to make these artistic interventions effective from the standpoint of training. Most of the existing publications on the subject regard people very close to the artistic project (such as the manager, sponsor, or trainer), and thus sometimes the viewpoint tends to be considered too "internal" with respect to the phenomenon.

In the chapters that follow, we will attempt to contribute to defining the conditions that allow for avoiding these risks, illustrating the technical characteristics of the artistic interventions of the FEC for the companies it works with, the process through which they are organized, and the concepts through which it is possible to rationalize into managerial language what happens through artistic interventions. This way, the reader can construct their own idea of how to plan the artistic experience so that it is perfectly consistent with the current state of the respective company, the future direction to be taken and the organization's values.

In addition, the book has been written by collecting the experiences of employees and artists in relation to each of the themes touched on, thus offering additional, different points of view than those of the people who are usually consulted when exploring artistic interventions in companies.

1.4 The activities of the FEC and their treatment in the book

The goals and origins of the FEC have already been outlined in the introduction. Below we provide a detailed list of the artistic interventions that the FEC has carried out over time within Elica and other companies, so that the reader will have a guide to understand how they are contextualized with respect to the themes analyzed.

As promised, the activity of the FEC in support of contemporary art and its role in innovating business practices takes place through four fundamental projects: the Ermanno Casoli Prize, E-STRAORDINARIO and the children's version E-STRAORDINARIO for Kids, FEC for Factories, and Elica Corporate Collection.

1.4.1 *The Ermanno Casoli Prize*

The Prize is conceived as a commission granted by the FEC to an artist, who is invited to design and create a work of art for a company, with the active participation of the people who work there. The goal is to promote the production of works of art that are created within a training program in which contemporary art is a tool for knowledge of reality and a powerful metaphor for the development of an open and innovative way of thinking, entailing a variable period of residency of the artist at the companies involved.

Table 1.1 Winners of the prize and position of the artistic interventions in the book

Title	Artist	Year	Position in the book and subject to which it refers
Pelusa (Fluff)	Jorge Satorre	2021	Chapter 6; artistic intervention cited to understand how artistic interventions can connect the individual stories of the employees to the spaces and materials of the workplace, especially during emergencies.
Gentile come un ritratto	Matteo Fato	2020	Chapter 6; artistic intervention cited to explore how the artist can involve employees during a crisis time, as the Pandemic is, by keeping together their individualities and the identity of the company.
The Relay	Patrick Tuttofuoco	2019 - special 20th anniversary edition	Chapter 6; artistic intervention cited to reflect upon how art at the workplace can explore the relationships that characterizes and brings together communities.
Mass age, message, mess age (Elica 2018)	Elena Mazzi	2018	Chapter 6; artistic intervention cited to explore how art produces and disrupts meanings at the workplace and the relavance of this action in crisis times.
VITRIOL	Andrea Mastrovito	2016	Chapter 3; artistic intervention analyzed for the discussion of the effective design of a training course considering the various facets (cognitive, emotional and relating to professional development).
Disguise	Yang Zhenzhong	2015	Chapter 3; artistic intervention cited as an example of the ability to structure a multisensorial training process.
The Game	Danilo Correale	2013-2014	Chapter 2; artistic intervention analyzed to illustrate how art in companies is able to effectively guide processes of identification, considering all of the characteristics of a process of discussion of professional identity and its implications.
Rock-Paper-Scissors	Anna Franceschini	2012	Chapter 2; artistic intervention cited as an example of how art in companies establishes a relationship between personal, professional and territorial identities
I Saettatori	Francesco Barocco	2011	Chapter 3; artistic intervention cited to illustrate the concept of "physical" and "conceptual" actions in learning and the opportunity for a multisensorial approach to training through art.
Teste	Francesco Arena	2009	Chapter 2; artistic intervention cited as an example of how art can effectively influence the dynamics of identification.

Thus the Prize is assigned to those artists who show particular sensitivity for relational and social themes in their research, and for the practice of sharing artistic work.

We provide here the list of artistic interventions and artists who have received the prize, together with a description of their placement in the book in relation to the concepts examined.

1.4.2 *E-STRAORDINARIO and E-STRAORDINARIO for Kids*

Since 2008, the FEC has been working to bring contemporary art to the business world as a teaching and methodological tool through a cycle of workshops in which internationally renowned artists work to create a work of art with the employees of a company, assisted by a curator and a trainer. That platform takes the name of E-STRAORDINARIO. Each company that embraces this particular training methodology contributes to expanding a sort of diffused museum, whose collection consists of all of the artworks created during the workshops. In the wake of the success and popularity of this project, the FEC also involved the children of the employees of Elica, and subsequently of other companies, creating E-STRAORDINARIO for Kids. This is also a workshop, but the participants are children who actively enter the artist's creative process, with the conviction that contemporary art plays a very important role in the education of children.

Table 1.2 lists the projects that have been cited or analyzed in the book based on their coherence with the book's philosophy and goals.

1.4.3 *FEC for Factories*

FEC for Factories is an original mode of interaction between art and business that brings contemporary art into the heart of production systems. The artists are invited to participate in the phases that precede the creation of an industrial product, sharing the process with designers, technical personnel, marketing specialists, prototypers and specialized laborers. The goal is to rethink the genesis of the product inventing new languages to design it, produce it and speak of it.

Table 1.2 E-STRAORDINARIO projects and their position in the book

Title	Artist	Year	Position in the book and subject which they refer
The Wishful Map #4	Pietro Ruffo	2016	Chapter 5; artistic intervention cited to illustrate how contemporary art contributes to competitive advantage through the management of *stakeholders*.
The Wishful Map #3	Pietro Ruffo	2016	
The Wishful Map #2	Pietro Ruffo	2015	
The Wishful Map #1 Pocket Museum	Pietro Ruffo	2015	
Esercizi di stile #2	Diego Marcon	2016	Chapter 4; artistic intervention cited to understand the role of the artifact, even when the artist's philosophy is more focused on the theme of language.
Esercizi di stile #1	Diego Marcon	2015	
Hand#4	Francesca Grilli	2019	Chapter 6; artistic intervention cited to understand how art can bring a comprehension based on an aesthetic experience and of the interpretation of the body at the workplace.
Hand #3	Francesca Grilli	2017	Chapter 3; artistic intervention cited as an example of the meaning of the aesthetic approach to organization.
Hand #2	Francesca Grilli	2017	
Hand #1	Francesca Grilli	2015	
Condominium	Margherita Moscardini	2013	Chapter 5; artistic intervention cited to illustrate how contemporary art contributes to competitive advantage through the involvement of *stakeholders*.
Filming the process #2	Marinella Senatore	2012	
Filming the process #1	Marinella Senatore	2011	
Opera	Grzegorz Drozd	2010	Chapter 3; artistic intervention cited as an example of the meaning of the aesthetic approach to organization.
L'intelligenza del caso	Cesare Pietroiusti	2009	Chapter 3; artistic intervention cited to illustrate the importance of art and to discuss error and its value in daily and professional life.
Ricordare è conoscere	Francesco Arena	2009	Chapter 2; artistic intervention cited in the description of *Teste*.
Dal progetto all'oggetto	Vascellari, Favini, Frosi	2008	Chapter 4; artistic intervention cited to illustrate the contribution of art to decision-making and ideational processes.
Mini Italia Kobra (E-STRAORDINARIO for Kids)	Marcello Maloberti	2014	Chapter 5; artistic intervention cited to illustrate how contemporary art can also extend to company welfare practices.

Table 1.3 FEC for Factories projects and their position in the book

Title	Artist	Year	Position in the book and subject to which it refers
Sillage	Ettore Favini	2015	Chapter 3; project analyzed to illustrate how contemporary art can involve different senses and thus favor a process of memory and learning. Chapter 4; artistic intervention analyzed to illustrate how art in companies can guide process and product innovation.
Middle-Earth. A Journey inside Elica	Fabio Barile, Francesco Neri	2014	Chapter 2; artistic intervention cited as an example of how art in companies can stimulate a reflection on company identity, both locally and globally.
Aspiranti Aspiratori	Sissi	2012	Chapter 2; artistic intervention cited to illustrate how art can influence the ideation and renewal of product identity. Chapter 3; artistic intervention cited to illustrate how art can create cognitive dissonance, that facilitates learning and training. Chapter 4; intervention analyzed to illustrate how art in companies can guide process and product innovation.
Aspiranti Aspiratori-China	Sissi	2013	Aspiranti Aspiratori exhibit at the Aike-Dellarco Gallery of Shangha and the MAMbo Museum of Bologna. Chapter 4; intervention analyzed to illustrate how art in companies can guide process and product innovation.
Less than air	Andrea Nacciarriti	2010	Chapter 4; artistic intervention cited to understand the relationship between contemporary art and process and product innovation.
Pescecappa x Pescetrullo	Gaetano Pesce	2009	Chapter 4; work cited to understand the relationship between artistic interventions and process and product innovation.

1.4.4 *Elica Corporate Collection*

The Elica art collection is essentially derived from the collection of works created through the initiatives described above. The works are carefully preserved in the common spaces of Elica (hallways, coffee room, offices, outside areas). Very often they are truly site-specific interventions; the goal is to create an *artful* workplace, able to continually inspire those who go there during working hours.

1.5 Methodological note

This book is written to open up a structured area of discussion and provide a theoretical rationalization of the relationship between contemporary art and companies when a relationship is established between them through an artistic intervention. The goal is to construct an interpretation of that work to make it in a certain sense replicable, or at least adaptable to different organizational contexts. Thus, all of the chapters begin with a theoretical reflection and conclude with the implications for the management and implementation of an artistic intervention in the company, and are accompanied by interviews with artists and employees. The story of the artistic interventions and the works produced are the protagonists of both brief examples within the chapters, useful to illustrate a concept, and a true analysis, that is useful to clarify the contents introduced.

The explanation and discussion of the theoretical part takes place through the analysis of a work or initiative, organized by the FEC, through which we attempt to clarify the artistic process and the implications for the organization, with quotes from the interviews conducted.

1.6 Glossary of main terms

We provide below a sort of glossary of the most important or frequently used terms, that can be a guide for the sharing of common terminology among the members of the artistic community and the business community. The terms, provided in order to stress the areas of meaning that they express, have been chosen because they represent the most interesting concepts for the purpose of this book. Note that not all of the specific terms present in this book are illustrated here, because many of them have been defined and contextualized in the respective chapters, and it was not considered necessary to further emphasize them here.

In particular, to define the entry of works of art, installations, and performances into companies, we draw on the terminology developed by Ariane Berthoin Antal (2016) and by Barry and Meisiek (2010), referring to the concept of *artistic intervention* and its various forms:

- *Artistic intervention*. A process through which typical practices and artifacts from the world of art enter the context of a company. These interventions can vary in terms of time, scope and connection with the company: some are very extended over time and involve multiple techniques, while others can last for just a few days (or even a few hours) and be represented by a single art form. The choice of the term "intervention" is very precise and intended to be neutral. Intervention is to be considered with respect to the Latin *inter-venire*, and thus with the meaning of involving someone or something in a situation, to alter the course of events (Sköldberg et al., 2016).

We will now explain in detail all of the types of artistic interventions that can be implemented within organizations. In this book, given that we have preferred the analysis of projects such as those organized and sponsored by the FEC (i.e. usually with a long duration, that often imply the use of various techniques for the creation of artifacts, that can vary greatly, produced together with the artists) the decision was to use the term *artistic intervention* more often, rather than one of its other forms. This way we aim to support the intention of seeing the entry of art into companies as a broad and substantial process, able to include multiple cases as indicated below, and structure itself in the time and space it requires.

- *Corporate collection*. Introduction of works of art in business settings. Previously, and often today as well, these are associated with a decorative intent and a personal interest by a senior manager or entrepreneur who is an art enthusiast; more recently, corporate collections have taken on very different characteristics, with the awareness on the part of collectors of a possible "training" intent, aiming at the communication and stimulation of reflection that the collection can generate (Barry and Meisiek, 2010; Sköldberg et al., 2016). The collection can in fact be produced and exhibited to stimulate questions and reflections with respect to existing perspectives. Through a logic of innovation, more than of the aesthetics of spaces, new ways of looking at the organization are thus proposed through the works presented.
- *Artist-led intervention*. Managers can bring the artists, and not only their works, directly into companies. Like with corporate collections, these interventions contribute to catalyzing new perspectives, looking at routines in new ways, through the contamination between ordinary (routine) and diversity (the presence of the artist and

changes to routine). In this type of intervention the artists can work on the differences and similarities between their way of working and the organization's practices in order to determine the way and need for applying art in the company's work processes.

- *Artistic experimentation*. This is the expression of oneself based on what is learned through the artist, and thus a personal change of the work context, in a mechanism of artistic experimentation. When organizations begin to familiarize themselves with the language of art and the figure of the artist, the next step is direct experimentation by its members. Artistic experimentations are very effective because they allow for implementing creative processes through experience. The practical approach to art makes it less mysterious, no longer the province of a select few, but to the contrary, it becomes something to be learned and cultivated (Barry and Meisiek, 2010; Sköldberg et al., 2016).
- *Organizational studio*. The terrain for experimentation through art in a business context. In general, the studio is a physical space within the company that becomes a place of continuous research, and thus innovation. Characterized by a legitimized language of its own, its own structure and characteristic processes, it is different from the rest of the company (in the way indicated above), yet physically close to it (inside of it); it entails the separation of the members of the organization from the company routine and often involves the figure of a facilitator to allow the two worlds to communicate and understand each other.

Having defined all of the types of artistic interventions that can be implemented in an organization and that are useful for understanding the meaning of this book, we now move on to listing the concepts that recur frequently in the subsequent chapters:

- *Sensebreaking, sensegiving, sensemaking* (present in particular in Chapter 2). The processes of construction and attribution of sense refer to a conception of reality, as constructed through the interactions of the members of an organization. In particular, the idea of sensebreaking and sensemaking is that these processes of searching for sense are induced by an event, something that workers recognize as being able to generate consequences for their work life. In particular, during sensemaking there is an attempt to construct a meaning of these events, a meaning that can be accepted, ignored, or fought. The concept of sensegiving, on the other hand, refers to when the organization attempts to influence the process of construction of meaning in a particular direction. These concepts are used widely in Chapter 2, to understand how a work of art can play a role in stimulating a new construction of meanings that workers, by participating in the artistic intervention, attribute to their professionalism and their role in the company.

- *Context shifting* (present in Chapters 2 and 3). This concept refers to the fact that by "practicing" the observation and experimentation of artifacts and artistic processes, the members of an organization develop the capacity to "see more" and "see differently" as regards their organizational contexts, becoming capable of expressing concepts and competences that they previously withheld or were unable to express. The book provides various examples in which the experimentation of the artistic process led the employees of the companies involved to see their roles and work differently thanks to the activation, during the artistic intervention, of the ability to establish an analogy between the artistic activity experienced and their way of working.
- *Aesthetic knowledge, aesthetic reflexivity, aesthetic workplace* (Chapter 3). In general, the term aesthetics deals with the knowledge that is created through our experiences with the senses, knowledge that is different from "intellectual" knowledge, that in turn can be described as guided by a desire for clarity, objective truth and the pursuit of an instrumental goal. Thus defined, aesthetics also includes how thoughts, reasoning and sentiments that are created around these sensory experiences influence our cognition. Aesthetic knowledge thus implies the involvement of the senses and a focus on experience. In this book, the expression is used to refer to how the artistic interventions discussed almost always have this very complex sensory and experiential component and how this can favor learning within the organization. So the approach followed is not purely "aesthetics for its own sake": aesthetics informs the design and execution of the formative interventions based on art, but art is not considered as the only medium to capture and communicate the experience perceived, the affective dimension and the tacit

knowledge that is elicited. All of this is conceived also to reach a more functional goal for the organization, such as the development of certain/specific skills or greater well-being for the employees. Aesthetics is thus a useful category to describe the type of knowledge and affective and cognitive processes that artistic interventions produce. But it is still true that in the narrative of the book, this subjectivity is accompanied by a moment of rationalization that is more functional for the organizational goals.

- *Artifact* (Chapters 3, 4, and 5). The term is used with reference to the material production that the artistic project entails; used as such, it aims to reference the broader meaning that literature gives to the original term *organizational artifact*. In this sense, the artifact represents something that is able, for example, to preserve organizational memory, to influence the processes of construction of identity and generate critical thinking. The work of art is thus defined by this potential to "represent" or "stimulate reflection" on memory, knowledge and organizational identity.

2 Art and Identity: How Art Guides and Innovates Identification Processes to Generate More Effective Behavior

The goal of this chapter is to understand how artistic interventions in companies contribute to the integration of personal, professional and organizational identity, and to generate more functional behavior for personal and company life. The experience of the FEC allows us to empirically analyze the various facets of this relationship between art and identity, drawing some conclusions.

We will focus in particular on illustrating how the FEC's experience with the artist Danilo Correale in *The Game – una partita di calcio a tre porte* (The Game – A three-goal soccer game) helps understand the different phases and moments through which an artistic intervention can generate changes in the identity of an individual and how these transformations can lead to a richer view of one's personal and work self: art can act as a bridge in a dynamic process of contact between personal and professional identity, that are sometimes distant due to the nature of the work or the contingent moment being experienced by the company.

The chapter concludes with a series of managerial implications that can be helpful to recognize the effects of an artistic intervention in identification processes and to plan this intervention in a conscious manner.

2.1 The interaction between art and management: the role of the concept of identity and its relationship with art

The introduction of art into a company derives from the encounter of the artistic community and the managerial community, which both have basic assumptions, norms, languages, and thus very different identities.

For now, the concept of identity can be summarized as a set of qualities, convictions, values, motivations and experiences, in regard to which people define themselves and identify their similarity to a given group.

Starting from different identities, the managerial and artistic communities can collaborate for different reasons: for example, a manager or entrepreneur can decide to introduce art into their organization in order for it to influence creativity, people's sense of imitative, and thus their leadership, or to stimulate innovation and communication, or also to facilitate teamwork.[1] Artists can decide to contribute to a change, using their work to influence the ways of acting and conceptual categories of an organizational population, and to leave a "different" mark in the world of art.[2]

---

[1] For details on the capabilities that art can generate in a company, see Chapter 3.

[2] There exist many historically recognized episodes that demonstrate the frequent meeting between patrons (the holders of resources to invest in culture) and artists, a relationship based on telling the story of contemporary society through the use of images. Today's society is closer than ever to the culture of images, thanks to what is now public and continuous sharing of images in public. To start, E.H. Gombrich (1999) spoke about an artist's ability to generate *new questions* through images, allowing them to take on a social function, more than a technical one. The social function of images is an issue that has always been at the center of criticism, in continuous evolution, and certainly worthy of mention in this chapter. Certainly through painting and sculpture, but also with installations, videos, environmental and public art, performances and recent contributions of technology better 'constitute' I think, to avoid the repetition of represent/representation the modes of representation of the images characterizing contemporary art. A mechanism of continuous *discovery* exists associated with images and their historical value (Gombrich, 1999); in this context, art can be considered an indicator of the society in which it is represented, as an "expression of the humanity" of that period, and thus as Haskell (1993) explains that the art of every period is both the most complete and the most reliable expression of the national spirit in question, it is something like a hieroglyphic [...] in which the secret essence of the nation declares itself, condensed, it is true, dark at first sight, but completely and unambiguously to those who can read these signs thus a continuous history of art provides the spectacle of the progressive evolution of the human spirit. Images, just like text, have an enormous value in terms of historical documentation of a society. Art has always had this ability to inspire, seduce and corrupt at the same time, all elements able to narrate something in regard to the transformation of humanity, and thus not so much a change of technical capabilities, but rather always a new expression of a different vision of the world.

Artists thus accept finding themselves working in a very different environment than usual – for hours, days, or sometimes entire months – and measuring themselves with new values, processes and ways of thinking (Skolberg, Woodilla and Antal, 2012). The two worlds, that of art and that of management, can very often be considered distant: on the one hand there is *art pour l'art* (Cousin, 1845; Gautier, 1835), and on the other a vision of art for the use of "business" (Friedman, 2007). The two parties negotiate to find a point of contact for the identities and norms, to create common ground (Paolino, Bissola and Imperatori, 2016).

It is this meeting of the managerial and artistic worlds that makes it possible for art to be a powerful distinctive instrument in companies. However, learning processes are needed for both sides, that are possible and effective only if they are based firmly on the maintenance and enhancement of one's own initial identity (Straub, 2009). The dialogue between art and management is thus a crucial moment through which the worlds of business and art relate to each other, thanks to the joint work of artists and employees. Art creates images, through which people are able to add their own thoughts and thus reach their own view of the world. The work environment represents a business and social space and thus art allows the people who populate the company to reassess their position through a collective, ethical, identitarian, and thus social gesture.

To provide some examples, we can observe how, thanks to particular projects created by the FEC for Elica, art is able to interact with corporate identity, that is communicated to the outside through the company's image; with the local and thus social identity of the company, linked to the territory in which it operates; and lastly, with the identity of the product that it proposes to its customers.

In this regard, think of the photographs of Fabio Barile and Francesco Neri – taken for the project *Middle-Earth. A Journey inside Elica* – that tells the story of the company and its operations on a global scale, and describes the identity of the company as a mobile concept, a background based on relationships that can be created, even at great distances. *Middle-Earth. A Journey inside Elica* is in fact a commission aimed at producing a photographic campaign in three Elica facilities around the world: Querétaro (Mexico), Shengzhou (China), and Fabriano (Italy), with the goal of depicting the complexity of a multinational corporation that goes beyond the simple definition of "company." It is a world formed by the people who work there, each with their own precious identity, investigated without any rhetoric by the lens of a camera. The shots show the faces, workspaces, and landscapes that characterize the locations where the factories are located, documenting the continuous interaction and close dialogue between the photographers, the people and the environment.

The nature of the organization is described here as a mobile entity that is always reunited with the city of Fabriano, where it was all born, and thus what we could define as a local identity. Fabriano, the historic headquarters of the Elica company, has a complex and variegated identity, that today more than ever needs to be rethought. *Rock-Paper-Scissors* (Anna Franceschini, 2012) is another meaningful example of this dialectic, that tells a story of the natural scenery, industrial history, and culture and popular traditions of Fabriano. To create the video work (the winner of the 13th edition of the Ermanno Casoli Prize in 2012) – conceived according to the combinatory rules of Chinese rock-paper-scissors suggested in the title – the artist chose to spend a long period of time at the company's premises and in the surrounding territory. Her artistic residency served to gather all of the information, impressions and images that characterize the identity of the territory and of the company, that in the final work overlap and mix incessantly, with some moments of unstable and temporary equilibrium.

Rock-Paper-Scissors not only tells the story of an object and a phenomenon, but above all of its most intimate and hidden nature. The artist herself speaks of her work as "an investigation on human existence, the view of a place made by men but lacking their presence, a moment suspended in time through which it is easier to perceive its soul, the *genius loci*."

The collective work *Duemila disegni da portare via* (2009) (Two thousand drawings to take away) by Cesare Pietroiusti, created with the active participation of approximately sixty employees, also speaks of Elica. During the training activity, entitled *L'intelligenza del caso* (The Intelligence of Chance) in which issues relating to causality and error were investigated, the artist invited the participants to produce two thousand drawings using candle smoke (smoke as an element at the center of the production of extractor hoods) and wine (Rosso Conero, typical of the Marches region), elements that provoke unexpected, unpredictable and uncontrollable effects on paper (the point of excellence of the manufacturing industry in Fabriano), that once installed on a large wall within the company became and represented a collective gesture with a strong sense of identity.

This type of story contributes to strengthening the sense of belonging to the company by linking it to its territory and redefining its identity.

But art is also able to generate interaction between the company's image and the product identity, rethinking it completely and in entirely new ways.

Indeed, when we shift to interpreting the relationship between art and product, it is interesting to note how the artistic intervention allows for discovering and giving a new identity also to the company's final product, not only in terms of image.

FEC for Factories, for example, encourages rethinking the product starting from revisiting its genesis by artists. In 2012, the FEC produced a complex project for Elica entitled *Aspiranti Aspiratori* (Aspiring Aspirators) with the artist Sissi, whose focus was the concept of the purification purification of air. To do this, the artist experienced the company for a year, thanks to an artistic residency that took place inside of the premises. In order to develop a relationship of mutual exchange between the artistic process and the business process, Sissi wanted her atelier to be built inside the Prototype Laboratory of the Elica headquarters in Fabriano, thus giving life to a working space understood as a protected and limited space, but at the same one open to all interactions, which she named, in a singular but significant way, "Cubator." Here, in fact, the company's employees watched the birth and growth of the artist's work, that were air purifiers for all purposes, becoming participants and accomplices in this genesis. Through this delicate process of contamination and exchange, drawings, collages, sculptures and above all thoughts, were born. The story invented by Sissi, that has the flavor of a mythological tale, narrates the genesis of a family of ten *Aspiranti Aspiratori*, ten potential figures (products) that aspire to become air purifiers, each with a well-defined identity and a name that indicates a key concept, consistent with its form and its function.

Of the ten *Aspiranti Aspiratori* designed, three were then produced: the *Capillare*, the *Continentale* and the *Riflettente*, chosen by the company's employees and by the public that visited the exhibit during the *Fuorisalone* of Milan Design Week in 2012, through a casting (from which the video-animation that tells the story of their birth takes its name). In this case, the artistic intervention completely rethinks the concept of purification, at the same time providing unexpected ideas to describe the identity of a new product using different materials, that are also useful for the innovation of other products.[3]

[3] See Chapter 5 on the relationship between art and product innovation.

In order for this renewal to take place and for art to be able to influence or challenge the identity of a company, a territory, or a product, it is important for the philosophy and the identity of the artist to overlap with those of the company, the territory and the product itself. In the case of Elica, we find an enterprise that sees experimentation and continuous innovation as fundamental characteristics of its identity. The artistic interventions that the FEC organized with Elica seek to discuss and support the concept of contamination, integration of knowledge and research.

In addition to the examples already cited, we recall that the Elica showroom in Shanghai was inaugurated with an exhibit by the Chinese artist Yang Zhenzhong (winner of the 15th edition of the Ermanno Casoli Prize in 2015), while for the birth of Elica France an event was organized at the Italian Institute of Culture in Paris – characterized by a complex and sophisticated arrangement generating a dialogue with the historic Hôtel de Galliffet – produced by the stARTT architecture and territorial transformation studio. This is another way to communicate to the public the identity of a company strongly oriented towards design but in a constant exchange with contemporary art and architecture, an identity in which research and product innovation have "cultural" roots (Carè, 2016).

Contemporary art thus represents a fundamental process through which a company can better interpret the processes of identification and by which work, territorial and product identities emerge and take on importance. But why is it important to deal with "identity?" Why can an artistic metaphor be preferable to others to understand how these processes of construction of the individual and professional selftake place?

2.2 Art and identification processes

Being able, as an organization, to interpret how employees construct their professional identity implies understanding how and when a sense of unity with the company is constructed – that sense of being part of a larger group that shares values and results, with people adopting them as their own. This perception of "correspondence" between the self at work and the company implies the opportunity to have a relationship between the organization and employee that is not only transactional. Thanks to the processes of identification, that is, to this process of recognition of a correspondence between one's own characteristics and those of the organization, the relationship between employee and company extends to an affective dimension, in which a sense of responsibility and "ownership" is expressed towards the company and what happens to it and in it.

In addition to this affective dimension, the work on processes of construction of identity is fundamental because it leads people to share a common "map" of the company's past, present, and potential resources. This common "canvas" is essential for proper orientation in work life, to understand the organization's basic expectations, but also to understand how to reorganize the available resources creatively when necessary. Sharing an identity means participating in a code of professional norms, that is not so detailed as to be prescriptive, but deep enough to tell us where to find information and how to be creative in recombining it. Thus identity is not only the source of construction of an affective connection with the organization, but also of cognitive references, that are useful for both orienting and accepting standards and being creative (Paolino, 2017).

If we think of the complexity of linking the identity of members of an organization with that of a product and a territory, we also understand the echo that this affective and cognitive connection can generate for the community of employees and consumers through the respective collectivity or the artifacts that the company produces and hosts.

From a managerial standpoint, therefore, developing awareness and governing the processes of identification of employees with their profession, company, and more broadly with the social community of reference, allows for:

- Having awareness and being able to intervene in the construction of the affective connection between employee and company. The dynamic of identification is useful to understand how the sense of "unity" and overlapping of the individual and company spheres is created, broken and then reconstructed. This dynamic is important in light of the fact that the connection, i.e. the affective motivation towards one's company, is generally interpreted as one of the predictors of a relationship between employee and company based on the alignment of the respective beliefs and the sharing of what behavior is the most effective and functional for individual well-being and business results.

- Sharing a knowledge set that is able to give us basic information on how to behave during difficult or unexpected situations. The common "map" of references, resulting from the process of identification with one's own organization, allows employees to know how to orient themselves in the company more automatically, that is, how to find the resources available to address a problem or an emerging situation. The sharing of this basic information is the precondition for all creative behavior in the company.
- Strengthening a process of construction of the self, linking it to a broader group: one's organization. Thus, seizing the opportunity that changes linked to the "micro" dynamics of one's profession, - such as the relationship between the boss and the team - can be traced to this broader relationship with the company.

Why should contemporary art be a better metaphor than others to stimulate, interpret and guide this process of identification? Artistic interventions have some peculiarities that make them particularly suitable to understand and influence identification processes. The combination of the most recent studies on organizational identity and the interviews conducted at Elica and in other companies that have collaborated with the FEC over the years, allows for identifying some dimensions to explain the efficacy of artistic interventions, such as those organized by the FEC:

- An artistic intervention is able, especially by analogy, to provide workers with a "third-party" perspective on what they are doing, offering the opportunity to see their work routine and their meaning from a point of view outside of the company's values. This additional vision of one's own role and how to work is useful to understand one's expectations, re-insert them into the context, and rapidly and intuitively trace them to the identity of the company and the historical moment it is experiencing.
- An artistic intervention immediately communicates the *fit*, i.e. the correspondence between the person and the company, allowing for activating dynamics of reuniting or construction of a sense of one's potential detachment. Contemporary art, in particular, despite working through all mediums (that in certain cases are so simple as to paradoxically be closer to some daily work practices) is able to create an initial sense of disorientation. This break requires us to immediately

reflect on how the organization for which we work, when it offers or sponsors an artistic intervention, is the company in which we can identify, thanks to (and sometimes despite!) the fact that it orients its operations in such an innovative way to dialogue with contemporary art. This dynamic can be implemented with even more strength, for example, when the art in the company uses the company's own prototypes, products, places and people to structure its action. In this case, the choice of materials and the company stories selected for the artist's intervention become a means to celebrate certain ways of working and use them as an example of the correspondence between expected behavior and that actually implemented.
- An artistic intervention, especially when it is detailed and pervasive in the story and space of the company, is able to construct part of the organizational memory. The works of art produced and collected thanks to commissions, training interventions and prizes, can communicate and recall how organizational identity evolves over time. The change or constancy in the type of works collected or interventions with artists can in fact be interpreted as a change in the organization's strategic orientation. Contemporary art thus becomes the medium to reflect on one's own development in time and to construct its meaning.

The sections that follow will illustrate in more detail the concepts of personal and professional identity. The role of contemporary art in the construction of identities will be highlighted through the extracts of some interviews conducted at Elica and at the companies that have collaborated with the FEC. The chapter will conclude by focusing on *The Game – una partita di calcio a tre porte*, the project by Danilo Correale, the winning artist of the 14th edition of the Ermanno Casoli Prize, and how his artistic intervention can be considered an effective tool for interpretation and contribution to the revisitation of personal, professional and company identities.

2.3 The concept of personal and professional identity

The concepts of individual, professional, social and organizational identity co-exist in every business context and mutually feed each other. Everything that characterizes human beings defines identity. It is thus a concept in continuous transformation: it can refer to the meanings attributed by the self for the self (*who am I?*) or for others (*who are we?*), and is thus negotiated based on repeated social interactions: how we see each other and how we want to be seen (Goldie, 2012; Ashforth, 2010).

Individual identity is constructed on personal identity, defined with respect to the intrinsic characteristics of the individual, based on distinctive factors, together with social, relational and role identity, constructed with respect to the definition of the individual seen by others, based on factors of similarity (Burke and Stets, 2009).

Professional identity, on the other hand, can be seen as a relatively stable and durable constellation of qualities, convictions, values, motivations and experiences, in terms of which people define themselves within a certain professional role (Schein, 1978). Professional identity refers to the role held in the workplace, and thus to the sum of attributes, values, beliefs, reasons, and experiences that characterize an individual with respect to their profession. This process of identification in one's profession is made more intense by some transversal factors, such as: feeling part of something, satisfying the need for affiliation, giving meaning to one's being in the context of the company, and lastly, freely expressing oneself (Ashforth, 2010).

During his working life, an individual passes from one role to another; the term "career" refers precisely to a sequence of different experiences in time, which certainly entails a change in roles. The innovation of professions takes place through the modification of professional identity, as described by the theory of work-role transition (Nicholson, 1984; Arthur, Hall and Lawrence, 1989). This theory helps to correctly guide interactions between people and social systems within the organization. The redefinition of goals, behavior, routine and informal networks automatically entails necessary changes to the professional identity of the individual. The transition to a new role certainly brings personal development – that is implemented through changes in small daily duties, but also with the disruption of the known network – and professional development (of the role), that involves variations in one's way of working, but also a total rethinking of organizational goals in relation to the role. The presence of a greater level of perceived novelty with respect to the work performed entails significant personal growth through the assimilation and exploration of the new role.

Art can teach respect for one's professional identity, and help employees and management construct a sense of change of this identity and of how it is connected to the strategic changes experienced by the company.

For example, the creation of a corporate collection, in the most prominent cases, already follows the logic mentioned above in its capacity to stimulate questions and reflections about the identity of the company, its professional groups, and how they evolve. Management sees the presence of art in the organization as a new form of expression of corporate culture and the changes the culture is experiencing; it gives people the opportunity to connect the evolution of their role and their professionalism with the change the company experiences, as related by the changes in the collection.

Artist-led interventions and artistic experimentations represent anything but a "classic" collection formed by acquisitions; they entail an active involvement of employees in artistic expression, working in close contact with the artists, sharing ideas and practices. The interest of many contemporary artists has moved towards describing economic and managerial processes: managers involve the artists to allow the members of the organization to look at the company processes and their work identity through a different lens. To understand the scope of an intervention of this type, think of what happened at Elica with the *Aspiranti Aspiratori* project (see further discussion in Chapter 5). As has already been described, Sissi was invited to operate within the factory to propose her own personal idea of the future air purifier, using materials typical of the company's prototyping process but in a completely innovative way, accompanying the items with unusual materials such as textiles and working on technical designs creatively and spontaneously. This way the artist overturned and gave new light and instability to the work routine, stimulating a new interpretation of the materials used, the professional identities involved and the products themselves.

The process of change triggered thanks to an artistic collaboration can thus accompany the individual towards an "updated" role, and thus the transition to a new professional identity. As reported by the Elica employees involved in some artistic interventions, "art creates the space and time to mend yourself," with reference to how art contributed to making people's presence in the company an opportunity for reflection, in which individual work and personal experience can be reunited with that of the company. We can speak of a dimension of care for oneself and one's individuality within a business context in which routines, deadlines and daily difficulties of various types can lead to alienation and separation from one's passions: "Art makes it possible to carve out a slower professional moment [...] just like, after making a lot of effort in your work, you find time to rebuild yourself personally. Art helps rebuild yourself professionally."

Thanks to the artistic experience, it becomes possible to understand the psychological and social processes of the situation within the company; individuals can construct a professional image that thus allows them to identify positively with the company (Pratt, 2000). Individuals and groups become more aware of significant details, errors, and develop a greater propensity to share their skills, perceiving a new freedom of action (Barry, 2010).

2.4 How art transforms professional identity

If we look in detail at the process of transformation of professional and personal identity, this changes when the personal self is perceived as different than the role held in the company. As soon as the perception of the gap, or better, the sense of a lack of coherence between the two identities becomes high, the individual seeks to balance them, implementing a transformation of the individual or personal identity and seeking another identity that tends to make up for the perceived deficiencies. Alternatively, the literature speaks of dis-identification (Kreiner and Ashforth, 2004), that means the definitive split of personal identity from professional identity, implying the choice to live two separate identities rather than attempt a recomposition. Both of the strategies, of identification and dis-identification, in any event aim to maintain the perception of coherence.

Just when professional identity seems to clash with personal identity, art acts as a very important resource to remain linked to the company's soul. Art can accompany the split or revisitation of individual and professional identity towards reconciliation.

Think of *Teste* (Heads) by Francesco Arena (Ermanno Casoli Prize 2009), a work created as the conclusion of a long and complex process, conceived by the artist, on the methods and mechanisms that regulate and transmit memory. Three workshops preceded the definition and production of the final work and served to stress that no gesture is wasted and that the actions and thinking of each individual, joined together, contribute to creating the great tale of history; to understand how the look we give others returns to us deformed, expanded and crystallized in concepts and stories; to reflect on the relationship of the individual with the internal dynamics of a working group. Starting from these assumptions, the group involved in producing the work identified six significant figures for the history of the Marches region, and for each of them a clay sculpture portrait was produced based on iconographic sources. The six busts thus obtained (the Heads) were positioned in six points of passage in the company and subjected to an original hydraulic mechanism for the collection and dispersion of rainwater that exposed them to an unavoidable process of corrosion. This gave rise to a clear metaphor of time going by and the consequent corrosion and dispersion of memory, with a positive value consisting of the fact that the rainwater brought back memories of the land, able to generate new possibilities. After six years the artist intervened on his work again, placing on the spots where the completely worn down heads had been, marble plaques with the names of the figures who had appeared in the first phase of the work. Entrusting the memory of the people depicted to the passage of time more clearly highlighted the contrast between the ephemeral nature of memory and that of a work of art that can instead make it current and lasting, even giving up its characteristics of monumentality and permanence. Lastly, the use of materials commonly used in the production cycle of the company's product, the kitchen hood for the construction of the special "gutters," shows how elements taken from the production cycle can become constituent parts of a work of art.

Teste, which de facto does not respond to a specific need for rejoining the personal and professional identities of Elica employees, is however interesting, because it allows us to show how such an intervention provides concepts, a space, artifacts and memories to which an employee can refer in the need for rearranging their personal identity with regard to their professional one. The story told by Francesco Arena decodes the operational nature of the work situation, nourishing creativity and lateral thinking. The work of art and the process through which it was created are an interesting example of how the construction, destruction or disappearance of a sign of identity (in this case the identity of a territory and a company) can be reconstructed, revisited, lost and acquired again through memory. In this sense, the reflection on identity leads to a challenge to the self, that can be supported thanks to art.

Technically, the phenomena through which this comparison and this search for meaning takes place can be summarized with the concepts of *sensebreaking*, *sensemaking* and *sensegiving* (linked to how we give meaning to ourselves, to others and to common actions), and those related to *job crafting*, *context shifting* and *mindfulness*.

We speak of *sensebreaking* of professional identity when we are faced with a break in the meaning the individual has constructed for themself in the workplace. Breaking the system of meanings that constitute one's work identity is a very powerful "gesture" or event; it represents a true challenge to yourself, since it constitutes the development of an awareness that what you are in the workplace does not resemble the person you are. The awareness of this gap guides the individual to a condition of *searching*, describable as the desire and need to find the meaning of self within the company, referring, for example, to one's own values and culture. Thus, if *sensebreaking* is successful, a circular process of continuous improvement begins, in which the individual calls into question his identity, in the attempt to find coherence between the personal self and the professional self. If *sensebreaking* fails, the process of identification is interrupted, as is the desire to resemble an ideal identity, leading instead to a sense of resignation.

The need for improvement that characterizes *sensebreaking* can be implemented thanks to a process of *sensemaking*, that is, the attempt by people to give new meaning to the activities performed within the perimeter of the company. Art represents a potentially positive occurrence, but also a break with the ordinary that can contribute to creating the opportunity and the context for people to act to reconstruct a system of new meanings to be attributed to their work.

The process of orienting the individual towards a new identity takes place through *sensegiving*: that may be intentionally guided by the company. All types of artistic interventions in companies – from corporate collections to collective experimentation – potentially favor *sensegiving* since they offer a system of symbols and stimulus that represent company values and identity (or their evolution) thus providing the necessary references to construct and update identity.

Art guides these processes of breaking and "recovery" and is able to do so because it can change the way we usually look at our role or at our work in a company, making us perceive the confines of our actions and responsibilities in a different way.

In particular, an artistic intervention in a company can help this process of recovery, renewal, or assignement to work identity by influencing the potential of employees to do *job crafting*, i.e. to pro-actively modify their work in relation to what are usually perceived as the limits of the duties to be performed and the relationships to be constructed (Wresniewski and Dutton, 2001).

Those changes contribute to greater psychological well-being, to more active and conscious involvement in one's work. In the process described, contemporary art can have a fundamental role because it helps modify the perception of the work environment in a dynamic process, that is continuously updated and also deeply subjective. Art, per se, cannot intervene directly on how one's work is organized, but it can create the conditions for a different perception of the limits of one's role and the motivation to change them or even simply discuss them. The people who participate in an artistic intervention strive to create a (real and ideal) environment that allows for the discovery of themselves, independent of the nature of the work performed in the company. Art uses a series of new stimuli that help employees give meaning to certain events, certain actions performed by them and by the company; it is able to stimulate *sensemaking* and force the individual to discover new and deeper ways of looking at daily activities and their relationship with the work of others.

Artistic interventions also often entail the creation of a story, a new plot that generates a *context shifting*, with the goal of providing the members of an organization a different view of the work context already known to them, challenging the status quo and stimulating questions and reflection. Again referring to *Teste*, we can easily see how having participated in this workshop and having seen the stories linked to the local territory become works of art that interact with the production materials, constitutes per se a variety of experiential elements able to imply a different way of looking at the company and at oneself within the company. An intervention of this type offers many ideas for alternative reflections on the relationship between the company and the hosting territory, inevitably ending up involving one's personal story. This change of context can lead to a reflection on one's work identity, and even in the case of a perception of distance between the identity of the self and the "self at work," the artistic intervention can offer many ideas triggering *sensemaking* and *sensegiving*, supplying stimulus on one's individual history, the history of the territory and the history of the company.

Artistic interventions contribute to the dynamic of searching for meaning in processes of identification, in part because they help generate a feeling of *mindfulness*. This concept, that can be considered a sort of "collective consciousness," takes shape in the ability of groups and individuals to become conscious of significant details, to notice errors during the process, and finally, to have the freedom to act and share meanings. Perceiving mindfulness helps to positively identify with the organization itself, that through the artistic intervention becomes, in the employee's eyes, the bearer of a critical capacity, an opportunity to develop consciousness of one's role in relation to the ends and history of the company. Moreover, mindfulness allows for activating cognitive resources both to question one's own identity, and to seize on positive stimulus in the work environment.

Therefore, in this process of discussion and construction of identity, the employee-artist-work-company relationship is fundamental to create an area of discussion and stimulus. We speak of the creation of a constructive area, in which to inspire the members of the organization, together with an area of disturbance in which there is a perception of uselessness or failure; both co-exist in a so-called "creative confusion" described in Chapter 1, a fundamental premise to understand the relationship between art and identity in companies.

2.5 The Game – a three-goal soccer game: the artistic intervention as a moment of self-representation and reconstruction of identity

Art can help a worker overcome the sense of alienation and competition that can derive from the tasks that characterize the modern industrial system. The introduction of artistic collaborations such as *The Game – una partita di calcio a tre porte* (a three-goal soccer game) launches a process of adaptation and innovation of certain company practices by workers, who for example are asked to dedicate part of their free time to the preparation and playing of a very special game of soccer. The game, in this case, becomes a form to communicate social phenomena, like the insecure conditions experienced by workers in this moment in history and the need to modify the routine of work in factories, but it also goes directly into the rules of business, proposing a new model of competition that overcomes the traditionally dialectical model, to become "trialectical" and offer a new, additional method of resolution of possible conflicts and a sense of rivalry (Smarrelli, 2014).

The Game – una partita di calcio a tre porte, a project created by Danilo Correale as the winner of the 14th edition of the Ermanno Casoli Prize, involved the organization of a soccer game with the employees of three Tuscan businesses: ColleVilca, PR Industrial, and Trigano. But it was not just a game.

First of all, because the game involved the use of three goals, an inspiration that came to Correale thanks to the thinking of the Danish situationist artist Asger Jorn, who in the 1960s theorized this unusual discipline with three teams simultaneously playing in a hexagonal field with three goals, to "formalize" his notion of trialectic. Second, due to the methodology applied by the artist, who did not limit himself to recruiting a few dozen players, but involved over eighty employees in a process of strengthening their identities. The project was detailed during long meetings outside of the workplace, using a camper van set up by the artist as a mobile office, for the organization of the soccer game.

Thanks to a serious and constructive discussion, three teams were created: *Real Cristal*, *GladiaTori* and *Esuberanti 301*. The three names tell three different stories: the first chosen by the employees of ColleVilca, the second by the PR Industrial workers and the third selected by the Trigano employees. Along with the identification of the names, Correale worked with the participants on the choice of the teams' colors, symbols, the model of the jerseys, and the scarves and banners to be used by the fans, demonstrating the value attributed to the visual component of the project. Subsequently, the groups met in training sessions to understand the nature of three-goal soccer, in which unlike "true" soccer, the winning team is the one that allows the fewest goals, and is able to construct temporary alliances with the other teams at different times.

On December 8, 2013, in Colle Val d'Elsa, the three teams took to the field to play the game – documented in the film *The Game* – in which the fans also played an active role, animating and coloring the Gino Manni city stadium.

The Game decribes the art of play and that of competition, introducing the themes identified by the artist during the course of his relationship with the workers in the companies involved in the project, through the experience of an encounter between a personal passion shared by many (the game of soccer), the questioning of a social reality (rivalry) and the uncertainty of the world of work (insecure working conditions). In *The Game*, we have the diary of a process, a collection of human stories coming from different contexts and told through an unusual lens and medium, in order to provoke curiosity and "educate." It is not just a company event for the purpose of socialization, but a true moment of self-representation of the workers in order to give them the possibility to express part of their individuality. The underlying motive for the event lies in the competition in the context of business, which is resolved in the third period, where the concept of conflict is overcome, to be substituted with a feeling of brotherhood.

Involving people in artistic projects such as this one allows employees to "see more and differently" (Barry, 2010) from the present condition (insecure working conditions, or simply one's own routine and consolidated identity). It allows for a moment of reflection and broader vision of one's life, and thus of one's work (Skolberg, Woodilla and Antal, 2012) through a moment of expression of the self. Art thus transforms apathy into action, and people become "activist poets" (Gergen, 1999, in Skolberg, Woodilla and Antal, 2012); they tell a story through art and act in its expression. *The Game* reflects the reality of things, proposes an alternative view of competition and helps company employees to recover their own personal and professional identity. The project developed by Correale allows the employees involved to look differently at their personal and work present, to seize the stimulus for discussion of some constructions of meaning around the self at work strongly linked to the concept of competition.

The Game certainly represents an opportunity to develop a stronger perception of the individual possibility to change one's work and the way it is carried out (*job crafting*). This artistic intervention entails a transformation of the perception of the work environment into something new, dynamic and characterized by the continuous intervention of the subjectivity of the members of the organization. The employees involved create an environment suitable for a new affirmation of the self, independent of the nature of the work performed. Art intercedes in this situation to stimulate a process of discussion and re-attribution of sense (*sensebreaking, giving, and making*) and allows the employees to look at their identity and everyday work with a new vision, oriented towards questioning conflict and transforming it into collaboration.

In the sections that follow we will analyze more in detail the three fundamental components of *The Game* – the soccer game, the final event in which the employees were involved and the rules that characterized the event – to more deeply understand how these artistic choices encountered the identity dynamics of the persons involved.

2.5.1 *Soccer*

The game of soccer serves only as a pretext to bring together different groups. It is the most popular game on the planet: all you need is a ball, the desire to be together and something to indicate two goals. In many countries this sport plays an important role in people's lives and involves feelings of community and solidarity, uniting different social classes, ethnic groups and cultures. But it can also be considered as a powerful tool for engagement of the masses, that can be used by politicians to obtain consent, or as a tool in international relations. Soccer is also often perceived in a sacred dimension as a true rite. Think of the audience, the gestures to ward off bad luck, the frequent arguments and acts of violence between opposing fans. Artists, who are intrigued and inspired by the enormous visibility and emotion of the game, have often drawn on it trying to highlight its multiple aspects: from the figure of the soccer player, to the event of the game, to the social phenomenon per se.

Danilo Correale's choice of soccer, with the characteristics cited above, is thus no coincidence: there is often talk of real enthusiasm in the combination between art and business (Darsø, 2004). A moment of work life suddenly becomes *artful* (Richards, 1995), rich in art, generating true creative energy. Soccer is a powerful game for identity, since it is potentially rich in symbols and emotional energy. The people who were involved in Danilo Correale's artful soccer had the opportunity to express their identity through a new platform for interpretation of human relations.

2.5.2 *The event*

On December 8, 2013, in a hexagonal field conceived of but never created by the situationist artist Asger Jorn, revived, rethought, and built by Danilo Correale with the employees of the three companies, a match was played between the three teams *Real Cristal*, *GladiaTori*, and *Esuberanti 301.* The employees were asked to form teams, decide on an original name to identify them and choose their own colors to create pennants and uniforms. Everything was set up based on criteria of subjectivity for each group, to leave the possibility of free expression of their creativity and communicate a message. Through these elements, each team was able to tell their story.

The team from the ColleVilca company took the field with the name of *Real Cristal*, with the aim of referring to its distinctive element: working on crystal. The name derives from an association with soccer (*Real* like *Real Madrid*) and crystal, while the logo, a diamond and a stick for the removal of the molten glass, stresses the transparency and purity of the shaped material, together with the audacious spirit of the members in performing their work.

The group from PR Industrial formed the *GladiaTori* team, whose name comes from a word play on the suffix "*tori*," in reference to their activity of production of generators and lifters (that both end with "*-tori*" in Italian). Represented by a bull (*toro*) whose nose ring recalls the company's symbol (the letter omega), they are fighters who draw strength from their union. Their founding values are friendship, work and sports.

Lastly, the Trigano company was represented by the *Esuberanti 301* team, that responded to the personnel redundancies (a reduction from 500 to 301 employees, with 199 redundancies) with their main characteristic: exuberance, a word with the same root as redundancies in Italian.

The Game acted as a platform to respond to some questions and pose others, always through the expression of the employees' subjectivity. It was a space for a new organization of the self, a revival of personal and professional identity. The workplace can become a place of "non-encounter" and competition, but the artistic intervention can be transformed into a moment of breaking and positive recomposition of these meanings, and suggest new ones. In fact, in *The Game* the meeting between the three teams takes place in a provisional, hexagonal field ("playing outside of the box"), with three goals for scoring, in a location completely different from that of the workplace: it is an anthem to free time that is detached from work and the opportunity to approach a completely new way of considering oneself at work, to create a renewed, richer self.

Three-team soccer stimulates the formation of strategic, elastic alliances that instead of merely feeding rivalry, as happens in a dialectical system, leads to the use of diplomacy and cunning. We can speak of the birth of a notion of 'breaking' that is now necessary, a subversion of the rules that can allow for new interactions, and thus new perspectives. And then there is the concept of 'third eye', of the need to see company processes in a different way, in this case through an initiative for reflection, recreation and personal expression.

The employees of the companies involved met in a camper van and thought of and organized every detail: the names of the teams, the uniforms, together with the stories and tales of their experience, working conditions, and above all their hopes for the future.

The identity of the company and the products emerge, told through the logos chosen for the teams, in a single whole with the personalities of the employees: not only the story of a slumbering personal identity, but also a broader involvement of the values, products, skills and distinctive traits of the work situations from which the employees come. Think of the "rule of group identification" for the decision of the uniform colors, referenced at multiple points in the film the artist produced as the final phase of the project.

As already stated, *The Game* is an example of an artistic intervention that allows for explaining how art in companies acts on identity dynamics, encouraging moments of discussion and breaking traits of current identity, moments which provide stimulus and positive events for the construction of future identity. This artistic intervention has a true storyline (a plot), that contributes to the creation of a sentiment of *mindfulness* on the part of the employees of the companies involved, in a "collective consciousness" of significant details of the work, of the possibility to make mistakes and the freedom to act and share skills. That rediscovery contributes to the opportunity to question the way the participants saw themselves in the workplace up to that point, and provide a series of details that help find new meanings (*sensebreaking* and *sensegiving*).

The space of the hexagonal field is a classic example of context shifting, in which the artist has used the means provided by the company to refashion the work practices of the employees through the creation of new experiences in an *inverted context* with respect to the one known; the game of soccer is perceived differently, as is the workplace, of which soccer becomes a metaphor. The scenario chosen by the artist and the active intervention of the workers, through continuous collaboration, gave life to the work of art. The use of a similar analogy helps load, prepare, and trigger the process of *sensemaking* and *sensegiving*, a positive identification with the organizational identity (Weber and Glynn, 2006), attempting to bring the various personalities of the employees closer to the company identity.

2.5.3 *The rules*

The rules recall those of traditional soccer, with some small, but interesting changes: the inverse assignment of points (negative points given, based on how many goals other teams do not score) and the management of the match between three teams, rather than two, with the possibility to score in two different goals.

What happens when there are three teams? It becomes impossible to control the offense with respect to the adversary; thus the rules are inverted and points are assigned negatively. The game has a new meaning: you must not be rivals, the third team is able to neutralize this ancient tension. The conflictuality typical of two-team soccer becomes the "art of defense" (Jorn).

More than victory on the field, the players aim for escape, free expression and the feeling of participating in something new and useful. The perplexity and suspension of known norms allow for artistic experimentation in an even more effective manner (Skoldberg, 2008).

The game, in fact, serves above all as a pretext for remembering one's personal identity and giving it a voice. Not just the match, but the entire preparation of the event – forming the teams, training, organizing the rules, coordinating the fans, building the field – contributed to the creation of a new community made up of workers from the three companies and also their families and friends who organized the supporters activity for the teams, ready to get to know each other, sweat together and reconsider their role in the organization in which they work. The very structure of the game helped the participants become intrigued, to discover the concept of "trialectic," to study the new rules.

The match saw the presence of loud and colorful supporters, a first phase of explanation and discussion of the rules for the public, the presentation of the teams and the game itself.

The "third period" represents the crucial part – this is the part where we see the encounter of the individual identity with the professional identity. As for the first two periods, the third is also twenty minutes, in which players could decide freely what to do on the field. Any type of activity was allowed (whether as a group or individually): setting up a picnic, protesting, dancing or singing, but even simply resting, thus creating the ideal context for carefree and creative self-representation.

One of the spectators in the stands during the game said: "At first we were skeptical, […] then the event really got going and we took it to heart." This gives a good idea of what contemporary art brings to the workplace. The relationship between the artist and the group of employees involved played a fundamental role for the creation of an area of encounter and stimulus. The camper van lent by Trigano that the artist used as a mobile office, the gym made available by the middle school where the practices took place, and finally the field itself in which the match was played, represented a constructive space in which to be inspired, but also an area of disturbance and discussion.

First there was surprise and then curiosity, that with the artist's help and storytelling, became engagement, passion, and finally affection. Thanks to *The Game*, the construction of a new identity, of a new sense of self, allowed for experiencing different moments, from discussion to the recomposition of the meanings that the individuals attribute to themselves and their work, that can then be transformed into an affective relationship with the company, and potentially, into more positive behavior from both a social and work standpoint.

2.6 Managerial implications

In this chapter we have described the dynamics of the identification process and how contemporary art can play a fundamental role in shaping them. From the story told through the experience of the FEC we see not only how art and professional and organizational identity interact, but also how an artistic intervention must be planned and organized with skill and in detail so that it can launch a coherent and enriching discussion on professional and company identity.

To summarize, the benefits that derive from developing an awareness of identification processes are:

- the creation of a strong emotional, long-term attachment with employees.
- the sharing of a common mental "map" of values and expectations of behavior, a map which forms the basis for the opportunities to engage in creative and innovative behavior.
- the opportunity to innovate organizational routines without betraying the history of the organization itself, but rather providing the opportunity to always find a point of reference to reconstruct the relationship with the company.

The intervention that uses the metaphor of contemporary art is able to generate this positive dynamic, stimulating:

- situations of "breaking" in regard to how meaning is attributed to one's work.
- opportunities to mend this "tear," offering new perspectives, new ways to see reality, to conceive of one's work, to place it within the company, and to have a new consciousness.

In order for the artistic intervention to succeed in triggering this positive identity dynamic, the experience that the companies involved had with *The Game* thanks to the FEC suggests that this intervention must be:

- *Authentic*: authenticity not only refers to the coherence that the artistic intervention must have with the company identity at that moment, but is connected to a "lasting intentionality" of the company to use contemporary art, contributing to constructing new scenarios where the artist can operate by designing and producing works of art. The artistic intervention need not necessarily be coherent with the company's identity at that time, but its effects must be considered sincerely by the company and thus at least coherently with the future direction the company wishes to take. The use of contemporary art must come from careful identification of the artist most suited for the situation and conscious planning for a specific context. Naturally, it is not possible to understand all of the implications at the moment of planning, but it is necessary for management to grasp the general scheme, before it is implemented, and understand how it fits into the professional experiences of the persons involved, whether employees or artists. In the FEC, the monitoring of this authenticity takes place through the choice of governance, that provides for the presence of an artistic director with training as an art historian and a manager who comes from the business world. Through the organizational practice of discussion and coordination between these two figures, the most suitable artistic intervention is designed.

- *Cautious*: not having the pretense of acting rapidly. The interventions with artists able to act most incisively on identity dynamics are those that are the most structured, both in terms of the time they require and the variety of techniques used, together with the intermediate artifacts produced for their realization and the involvement of individuals. Identity dynamics take time, but this opportunity to settle and reflect makes them more "natural" and highlights the nature of art as an organizational moment of breaking and reuniting. In this chapter we decided to analyze *The Game* precisely because it implicates a very vast process, both in terms of activities for the creation of the artifacts necessary for the game, and in terms of the complexity of the rules to be implemented for the performance of the game itself. The event and its preparation required intense real and metaphorical time, made of dialogue, the need to make decisions, the production of physical objects, involvement and ultimately the organization of a game. Despite working on concepts with a different approach, *Teste*, already cited in this chapter, also has the characteristic of being a structured intervention over time, in the techniques used, and in the interaction between artists and employees. These elements make the two projects discussed more suitable than others (shorter or linked to the use of a different way of relating to the company and its employees) to influence identity dynamics and the positive behavior that can derive therefrom.
- *Practical and theoretical*: to be effective, the artistic intervention must help train not only *making* but also *thinking*, something that contemporary art, which is naturally more conceptual, is able to do very effectively. The artistic experience certainly has the strength of redefining self that comes from undertaking an activity commonly classified as noble (painting, drawing, or sculpting, although by now it seems increasingly necessary to go beyond this language, given that many artists often choose to try new, heterodox tech-

niques, leaving traditional ones aside). Artistic making is liberating per se, because it is able to break our professional routine, and at the same time give a good reason to reconstruct a relationship with the company one belongs to. The deeper identitarian processes seem to take place, though, when next to making[4] there is also an activity of thinking during the artist's intervention, that is useful to give a name to the meanings that take place through making. This operation is not only linked to the act of explaining what happens during the creation of the work – what the artist, the trainer, or the curator can do – but also the fact that, if artifacts are not produced, the artist's actions are able to reproduce and repeat the fundamental concepts that the work wants to express (think of the loan of the camper van to Danilo Correale, an important gesture to reiterate an alternative concept to competition, closer to the issue of giving and generosity). For this reason, the interventions most suited to understanding and intervening on identity dynamics are once again those that are the most complex, in which a timeframe and roles exist to provide space for both making and thinking.

[4] See chapter 3 for a more detailed discussion of that process.

3 Art as a Training Tool: How to Organize a Training Process Based on Contemporary Art to Upgrade Skills and Competences

In this chapter we will introduce theoretical principles through which contemporary art can be considered the preferred tool for the implementation of training interventions in companies, explaining its relevance and illustrating the benefits, at both the individual and team level, and in terms of organization. We will also provide elements that can act as a guide to the planning of a training intervention based on contemporary art, concentrating first on the issue of aesthetic knowledge; and, and then, more in particular, on that of error management, cognitive dissonance, and "making." Finally, we will summarize the individual skills that a training intervention through contemporary art can construct. The *VITRIOL* experience, realized by the FEC with the artist Andrea Mastrovito for the Angelini pharmaceutical company, will be analyzed in order to investigate parts of the process of organizing a training intervention based on art and to discuss if and how the benefits theorized at the beginning of the chapter are applicable to this experience.

3.1 Why art is not just another metaphor for training, but has value per se

> Why would we seek out the wisdom of artists? Why would we embrace beauty? Why would we adopt the unconventional and risky conceptual and leadership approaches of artists? Because we passionately care about the future of our families, organization and country – because we care about our planet and civilization. Now is the time for each of us to reclaim our artistic skills. Now is the time for all of us to invoke beauty (Adler, 2015).

With these words, Adler rhetorically questions the appropriateness of more strongly including art in managerial practice. The response that Adler gives is both simple and vast, and was picked up on by Purg and Sutherland in a recent piece in 2017. For these authors, art is not just any metaphor used to advance our managerial thinking. We should deal with art more because it allows us to question the meaning and motives of our actions. Through art we are pushed to ask questions on the meaning of our managerial actions, asking us what really matters, what is the ultimate goal of organizing our activity in a certain way, and if that goal makes sense.

The possibility to focus on art in managerial practice is strongly felt in the world of business, in part considering the need to overcome the rifts and consequences resulting from the way work has been organized until now, in terms of stress, lack of satisfaction and the desire to participate in the company life. The introduction of art into managerial practice is also a need recognized by the academic and professional world as never before, given that in the past two years the link between art and management – and the use of art as a training tool – have been discussed by magazines such as the *Academy of Management Review*, among the most prestigious in the world. In addition to the articles that have appeared in this publication, we can add many other very recent ones, together with two decisive books on the issue (Berthoin Antal, 2015 and 2016) and the success of another magazine, *Organizational Aesthetics*, in which academics, artists and managers are invited to discuss the role that art plays, as a training tool, to create relationships and expand people's creativity and skills, increasing flexibility and the store of behavior (Schein, 2013).

All of these studies continue an already-existing tradition in theorizing the role of art as a protagonist of training in companies (Ladkin, 2008; Scharmer, 2007; Mirvis, 2005; Austin and Devin, 2003; Taylor, Fisher and Dufresne, 2002), but now they attribute a fundamental role to art as a tool for deep discussion and reflection on the quality of our actions in the workplace and in private life.

Art is thus introduced into companies through training because it makes it possible to pose important questions and to promote a renewed reference to "beauty" (Adler, 2015). This reference to beauty obviously does not have a connotation linked to visual pleasantness, but the fact that various studies have documented that companies which are able to perform better are those able to transform unfortunate events, dimensions that are apparently uncontrollable, into something "beautiful," that is, a capacity to *envision* the future, to heal "rifts" with interlocutors instead of exacerbating them, to see conflict as an opportunity for recomposition rather than loss (Collins and Hansen, 2011). The context in which this reflection on art as a training instrument takes place, is one in which, for more than ten years, various authors have used their studies to illustrate how the commodification of managerial training has destroyed the famous "good practices" making the organizational contexts places in which increasingly sterile language is used and where the meaning of citizenship and social community is increasingly limited (Adler, 2010; Ghoshal, 2005).

Art thus becomes a training tool to initiate a dialogue and deep reflection on our behavior in the workplace, and by offering the opportunity to create unexpected solutions, to solve problems and propose new solutions.

In order to reach this goal, it is important to be aware of what learning philosophy a company decides to use, and how much this philosophy can be joined with the nature of an artistic intervention, together with the characteristics of the actors, spaces and skills that art requires bringing into play.

If we think of *I Saettatori* (the Darters) by Francesco Barocco, the winner of the 12th edition of the Ermanno Casoli Prize, we can understand how complex, and above all different from other training metaphors the structure of an intervention is based on art that has the goal of renewing the dialogue between and with the employees of a company, thus beginning a process of interaction on different levels: art, company and personal. The artist's intervention is in fact structured on multiple levels (a laboratory demonstration, a permanent exhibit of engravings and the creation of site-specific works for Elica) in which Barocco presented a path aimed at knowledge of the world of ideas and references which inspire artists, sharing their daily and repetitive nature, how they fall and get back up, and the doubts that characterize artistic and creative work, making it similar in many aspects to all other trades.

The employees involved were able to learn information of a historical/artistic nature, the artist's area of reference, and thus enter a cognitive context different from their own.

This process began at the Fabriano Paper and Watermark Museum, a non-business location in which it was possible to stimulate different perceptions and intuitions than usual, and it continued in the company with multiphase artistic production that went from the creation of engravings to the creation of a permanent thematic exhibit based on acquisitions, to an almost performance activity of the employees involved in the project. In using what they had learned during the training activity, the employees acted as guides to the exhibit for their colleagues, explaining the crucial points of the history of art, from the Renaissance to today, through the works exhibited in the company's premises.

As we will see more precisely in the subsequent paragraphs, Barocco's project implies the opportunity to think differently, through cognitive, but also emotional and tactile stimulus. It allows the company's employees to temporarily live in a museum, and based on this experience, to settle in the company anew as artists, guides and then again employees. This project has the ability to guide the perception of what was done during the training activity with the artist in a future in which the experience they had can be told and shared with other colleagues, transmitting the knowledge of a different and more complete way of experiencing the organization and reconstructing that indispensable sense of social community.

To understand how a training intervention based on art can generate the rifts and recompositions described above, in the sections below we will discuss the concepts of "aesthetic knowledge" and the advantages that derive from using contemporary art as a tool for "learning" in companies.

3.2 Art, aesthetic knowledge and its advantages

To understand how it is possible to approach art and promote it in the workplace according to the perspective described above, it is important to illustrate the reasons for introducing contemporary art as a training tool and to shed light on how it can generate a process of innovative learning.

These reasons usually refer to the concept of *aesthetic knowledge* (Strati, 2002), a form of knowledge that people acquire through the activation of specific abilities relating to perceptive/sensorial faculties and their personal aesthetic sense. Aesthetic knowledge is in fact derived from three fundamental elements (Taylor, Fisher and Dufresne, 2002):

- The possibility to perceive the sense of a concept not only through classic deductive reasoning, but also through inductive reasoning; that is, not through logical and sequential thinking, but by forming an overall, general impression of a situation.
- The opportunity to perceive a personal sense of enjoyment and satisfaction due to having been exposed to a concept, a situation, or an experience, without being led to think, at least immediately, to the result that this can generate in one's personal and work life.
- The opportunity to establish a connection between a concept, an experience proposed, and one's own personal and work experience, through both an immediate impression and a reflection.

According to the concept of aesthetic knowledge linked to organizations, people take on an active role in giving value to a process first of separation and then of empathy towards the work environment. In this case, aesthetics does not represent art itself, but that process of judgment by the participant that allows art to take on meaning and become a means of learning.

Art in a company can renew our way of thinking because it develops a more inductive and freer method of learning, that compared to other methods, is more able to bring people to establish an authentic "connection" between themselves and the company.

Therefore, how can art and aesthetics lead to the creation of innovative learning processes and the generation of knowledge? The process through which this takes place can be summarized in three points and imply reflection, the activation of all of the senses and the activation of the organizational space.

In detail, we speak of *aesthetic reflexivity* (Sutherland, 2012), that is, the rethinking of one's actions through the appropriation and transformation of sensorial and emotional characteristics of one's experiences, through art.

This rethinking takes place through multisensorial knowledge, *sensible/sensuous knowing* (Strati, 1999; 2007). A workspace can be considered for all purposes a sensorial dimension, in accordance with the five senses and how they are exercised within it. The development and existence of *sensible knowledge* does not reduce knowledge to a mere direct, physical and objective way of observing reality and learning from it; on the contrary, emotions and sensations begin to play a fundamental role in the creation of concepts from the cognitive standpoint.

These reflections and this new form of knowledge can also be transformed into an *aesthetic workspace*, a space that allows for continuous interaction and the exercise of the five senses, that in turn are reflected in the potential creation of memories and work reflections full of meaning, because they are experienced by people cognitively, emotionally and physically (Sutherland, 2012).

This definition allows us to see that an artistic intervention in a company can produce an ability to consider and rethink one's actions at work, to access multisensory knowledge and modify the organizational space aesthetically, because the artistic intervention:

- Acts to stimulate the members of the organization through thoughts, feelings and desires that are triggered by participation in the work, observing and remembering it. An artistic intervention in a company allows the employees to learn not only cognitively and therefore through thinking, but also through the emotion of participating in a project that is larger than daily life, that belongs to another "domain." The creation of the work also implies physical and emotional, not only cognitive involvement.
- Remains physically in the organizational spaces of the company through the works and installations. This presence also persists in organizational and individual memory, through materials, documents, but also memory and its re-elaboration. It should be noted that even in the absence of works of art, the goal of the training intervention generates a new way of perceiving the workspace, of reflecting on it, and through it, on one's way of working.
- Broadens the range of resources to which people appeal in performing their work and in facing daily decisions, increasing the potential for innovative solutions or new proposals to perform their duties.

3.2.1 *Some examples*

An apt example of what we have presented to this point is *Sillage*, the project by the artist Ettore Favini conceived for Elica and FEC on the occasion of the EXPO Milano 2015 and presented in the Save the Children pavilion, to support the initiatives carried out on education and food safety.

The creation of this project represented a moment of reflection within Elica, not only with its employees, but also with its clients, very effectively illustrating how art has aesthetic power (in the sense described above) and how this role can also extend to relationships with all of the main stakeholders.

On the occasion of EXPO, Elica chose to contribute to the creation of the community garden experience within the Save the Children Village, proposing the artistic intervention entitled *Sillage* that led to the production of a limited edition of *Marie*, the fragrance diffuser invented by the company. The proceeds from sales were in part given to charity to support initiatives on education and food security promoted by the well-known NGO.

The title of the project is drawn from the vocabulary of perfume and indicates the trail a fragrance leaves around us, able to spread in the surrounding environment. In fact, from the standpoint of transformation and recycling – in line with the practice of reutilization that characterized the construction of the entire pavilion – the artist used the frames of some extractor hoods for home use as vases for planting: from sterile metal structures to fertile sculptures able to host and hold the growth of plants such as barley, oats, almonds, fennel and anise, from which at a later time, a specific fragrance was studied, extracted and created for *Marie*. The same plants were also chosen by Ettore Favini for the composition of the still life that, in his photographic abstraction, became the new cover for the diffuser that was reconceived and signed by the artist.

Sillage thus represents a concrete example of product innovation obtained thanks to the action of the FEC, that created communication and close collaboration between the artist and the designers of Elica involved in the genesis of *Marie*, making it possible to achieve a combination between function and artistic expression.

In addition to this aspect, we must consider the sensorial involvement of the intervention, that changed the perception of space and how to live in it, innovating the product idea in a new way, thus touching not only cognition, but also the body and emotions. This way it is possible to offer a more lasting memory of the experience, on which we can reflect through multiple points of view and drawing on memories that have different sources, from vision to smell, from hearing to touch. In that regard, we should speak of the launch event, the culminating moment of the project, held in a very prestigious location in Milan, Palazzo

Visconti, in the presence of numerous guests, including journalists, people from the art world, representatives of Save the Children and Elica's international clients. Based on the multiple inputs and changes of state proposed by *Sillage* – from the solid state of the raw material to the liquid of the essence, to the gaseous state of its diffusion – the event aimed to recreate a multiform and emotional environment in which to stimulate the five senses: the participants' smell was stimulated by the scent of the essence that enveloped the space; the *Marie* diffusers set up in various points of the spaces, together with the decorations and furnishings of Palazzo Visconti, were inputs for sight; some musical moments entrusted to the musician Marco Mencoboni activated hearing; taste was involved by the culinary creations born of the five plants cultivated in the sculpture-vases during the months of EXPO 2015; finally, there was touch, with the floral compositions that enriched the space, to be smelled and touched; inspired by the products which provided their fragrance, they ideally completed the journey.

Disguise, the work created by the Chinese artist Yang Zhenzhong, also represents a strong example of the creation of a sensuous atmosphere within the organization. This project, conceived in 2015 by the artist who won the 15th edition of the Ermanno Casoli Prize, was created during a residency of two months at the Elica plant in Shengzhou, China, where the artist worked in close contact with over fifty employees, conducting a series of workshops. *Disguise* refers to a theatrical atmosphere stressed by the presence of a series of masks that exactly reproduced the physiognomic traits of the employees involved. Produced through the 3D scanning technique, the masks were worn by the employees for a performance held in the company, while they carried out daily work tasks in a sort of liberating dance that creatively reinterpreted the repetitive movements of factory work. The video recordings of this symbolic moment were used to create a video installation on multiple channels, that together with the masks was presented in the Elica showroom in Shanghai in May of the same year. As can be seen from the description, the intent of this artistic intervention was to create a new atmosphere, a "sensitizing" work environment. The experience was enormously powerful for training purposes

The intervention by Grzegorz Drozd, *Opera* (2010), also expresses one of the ways contemporary art can change the work environment aesthetically. The project that Drozd proposed for E-STRAORDINARIO on tour[1] is based on the concept of collective action, and highlights the creative potential of the community made up of factory workers. The idea is to introduce unusual elements in the daily life of the plant, while maintaining the method and organization of industrial work. After having entered the company environment through a video self-presentation, the artist met the plant employees, with whom he created a musical performance. In the project conceived by Grzegorz Drozd, each employee committed to playing their own part to reach a shared goal, that of generating a collective work of art in which everyone is an author and protagonist.

3.2.2 *The benefits*

In light of these examples, what are the benefits for the company in organizing training interventions that imply the use of art and the approach to aesthetic knowledge? From a training standpoint, the results of these interventions can be detected on three levels that communicate with each other (Berthoin Antal, 2014):

- *At the individual level*: people acquire particular skills during the artistic intervention in the company; on the one hand, they become better able to conceptualize and abstract, while on the other they can better and more frequently "prototype," putting into practice and rapidly testing their ideas to determine their feasibility. Along with these two typical skills of opening and closing a decision-making process, art trains the ability to pose questions and exercise critical thinking.
- *At the teamwork level*: through group training interventions people acquire a new ability to occupy and experience the organizational space, as a place for interaction, critique and sharing of strictly work and non-work experiences. The result is a better ability to communicate, deal with conflicts and construct positive relationships since art, de facto, constitutes a new source of identification and dialogue.
- *At the organizational level*: training interventions based on art can produce, in the long term and based on the abilities and skills de-

[1] On tour indicates the editions of E-STRAORDINARIO presented outside of the borders of Italy.

veloped individually and in the working teams, results that regard the sphere of process and product innovation, a strong ability for strategic thinking and the opportunity to revitalize the organization's values and culture.

In the next section, we will illustrate some theoretical principles underlying the appropriate use of a training intervention through art and the production of its benefits in order to be able to draw implications for its efficient organization.

3.3 Art, training and learning

Learning through art functions on a principle of centrality of the participant, who becomes the protagonist of an artistic project and is required to reflect deeply, during and after the intervention, on how to connect what is created with the artist to their own work and personal experience. In this way art, or better, the artist, represents the intellectual knowledge that must connect itself to know-how; the practical construction of the work cannot, in fact, avoid a reflection on the contents, the message to be communicated and the impact this message is intended to have (Carè, 2016).

The vision and participation in an artistic initiative is not followed by a single type of reaction between the teacher and the pupil. Each person reassesses what has been seen/done. This reaction translates into inner growth, and thus a fostering of sensitivity that is absolutely subjective and is then shared with the artist, curator, trainer and the working team. Therefore, the stimulation that training prepares (in this case understood as vision, contemplation of the work or proposal through participation in the creation of the work itself) corresponds to the most varied mental representations – which form a new basis for learning at every level of the company, from the individual to the working group, to the entire organization.

Creating a contemporary work of art through a training project entails *discussion* (speaking), *decision* (what to create and why), and *the practical realization of the artistic product* (construction of the work), in the ultimate attempt to understand and communicate the multiple facets of meaning of a potential work of art and of the concept intended to be discussed and communicated through it: art in training processes has precisely the goal of generating meaning from experience (Purg and Sutherland, 2017). The cited mechanisms of collaboration, a practice used often by artists to create their works, leads to the process of learning: not only of technique (think of the skill of the artist who asks the employees to replicate what he has done), but above all of an overview of things from a completely different standpoint (the "third-party" view cited repeatedly in Chapter 2).

During the interventions (workshops, talks, presentations) the artist should play the role of facilitator: the employees have an active role, while the artist takes on the role of a guide. The artist creates the work together with the employees, allowing them to learn his techniques and vision. The entire training experience takes the form of a platform for interaction in which mistakes are possible (and often hoped for) and free expression is continuously encouraged. Those who want to learn play a real game (Dewey, 1996) in which they must speak, move and construct objects and mental representations, searching for and interpreting the meaning of reality. The participants in creating the work choose to change their point of view, to learn; and in doing so they bring their identity to the process, while the autonomy granted in the production phase further strengthens the meaning of the training experience.

Given this general premise, what principles should be followed in the planning of a training intervention based on art? What actors are to be considered? What is the role of the organizational space? Below we try to provide some responses to these questions.

3.3.1 *The principles: the training approach to follow*

If we were to follow only the most consolidated principles of training paradigms in planning an artistic intervention in a company, some peculiar elements of the role of art in business would be lost. If the fundamental principles to follow in adult learning certainly include the possibility for the participant to explore the concepts proposed on their own, to manage their emotions during the training intervention and to be free to make mistakes (Bell and Koslowski, 2008), then when we speak of training interventions based on art we can go even further. It is possible to include cognitive dimensions, such as that of error, but also to push this dimension even further, to the goal of creating discussion and dissonance between the conceptual categories we habitually use to analyze work and those proposed to us by art. And even further, to understand more aesthetic, inductive and sensorial dimensions. Thus the principles to follow in planning an intervention with art could be summarized as follows:

- *The acceptance of error.* The value of discovery of error through art is among the elements that characterize the training value of an artistic intervention; art is seen as a discovery, and is thus a surprise that generates curiosity, leading to learning. In that regard, we speak of *positive error framing* as a method to contextualize the possibility to positively make mistakes without generating the fear of error and going outside of the lines. From a psychological point of view, it has been demonstrated that errors can make learning possible (Fisher and Lipson, 1986). This approach to error allows the individual to learn actively, working on their own skills and facing the possibility of error without fear. All of the artistic interventions conceived of and communicated on this basis have a strong potential for learning. Consider the project entitled *L'intelligenza del caso* (The intelligence of chance) developed by Cesare Pietroiusti for training purposes and implemented by the FEC at Elica in 2009: a workshop whose goal was precisely that of highlighting the positive power of error and attributing value to chance events and thus to the possibility to make errors that always exists. Through the creation of some drawings,[2] approximately seventy employees of Elica embarked on a creative task characterized by the absolute lack of fear of error; rather, the possibility of making mistakes with respect to the original plan was considered an element that could enrich the artistic work and an element of growth. By making mistakes people learn how to fix errors and not repeat them; the opportunity to make mistakes allowed the participants to focus on the exploration of the concepts to be discussed in the training process and not to waste energy attempting to avoid mistakes; error allows for expanding one's perception of autonomy in the learning process. Contemporary art offers an excellent opportunity to organize training by making the acceptance of error and its elaboration central, making it a struc-

[2] For details on its implementation see the reference to *Duemila disegni da portare via* in Chapter 2.

tural part of the approach of many artists and the evolution of the concept of art itself.

- *Dissonance.* Art is a starting point for what Berthoin Antal (2015) defines as a *dissonant translation* within an original invention, i.e. the consideration of art itself as a source of innovation to be transposed into the company. We can speak of an implicit assumption of dissonance between very different types of things in the meeting between art and companies: the world of organizations on the one hand, with its rules and vital routines for the efficient functioning of the system, and on the other hand art - that is difficult to define exactly - that is broad and constantly evolving. The dissonance is expressed by a tension towards what is unusual and different from the company's routine. The meeting of two entities can generate innovation thanks to dissonance, and thus to existing differences (Hutter, 2013). What we could define as the irrelevance of the languages and codes used by artists, together with their behavior, represents the true resource to stimulate innovation within the context of the company. Not only the words, but also the utilization of the time, space and skills of individuals (in other words, the resources of the organization), together with the outline of the roles and hierarchical structure, can all be elements called into question, reconsidered by the artists from another viewpoint and even distorted if wanted. These are examples of contrast and low familiarity between the structure and routine of an organization and the vision of an artist. Here it is appropriate to describe *Aspiranti Aspiratori* (Aspiring Aspirers) the work created by Sissi for Elica with the FEC, in regard to the dissonance created between her way of working, her language and figure, and the modus operandi of the Elica prototypers.[3] In this case the artist, during her residency within the organization, became an "inhabitant" of the same, working together with the prototypers on a new product idea; an idea based on a total reconsideration of the concept, object and function of the product itself. This encounter led to a deep dissonance: first of all in terms of the vision of things, then of language and then of actions. From what we could define as an initial "clash" due to the collision of two

[3] For further information on the themes of the work see chapter 5.

very different worlds, artists and prototypers then found a meeting point through which to create the *Aspiranti Aspiratori* (2012).

- *"Making," not only physically, but conceptually.* Very often, an artistic action disregards the material component and explores the ability to "make with the mind," to imagine. That concept takes form through a conceptual, mental task, of induced personal imagination, able to allow for the reconsideration and recontextualization of one's work, role, and the surrounding work environment. This way of operating favors learning mechanisms through participation in an experience, that once again is not only physical but able to *touch more intimate aspects* and thus to give free play to imagination. We can again cite the intervention of Francesco Barocco for the FEC, *I Saettatori*, centered not only on "making" (the physical production of the work) but also on "thinking," and thus rethinking and understanding the issue of the artistic experience of each person in their own mind, attributing it a personal significance. As described above, the artist held practical and theoretical lessons to allow the Elica employees involved to experiment with the technique of engraving, used by the great masters of the history of art, from Albrecht Dürer to Carol Rama. The title of the work refers to a drawing by Michelangelo which depicts nine archers without either bows or arrows, transformed into tools of a force that goes beyond will and conscience. Symbolically, like the archers from the Michelangelo drawing that draw a bow without arrows and seem to throw themselves forward, the participants, together with the artist, seem to want to embark on a voyage in space and time. So note that artistic experiences for training purposes, such as that just presented, are characterized not only because they are modulated on the technical skills of the participants – in this case the creation of engravings – but also, and above all, due to the conceptual and emotional sharing of the collective artistic experience. Or, we could also cite the *Hand* workshop, conceived by the artist Francesca Grilli, in which a purely "physical" action (the reading of the participants' hands, with the help of an expert in fortune-telling) becomes the opportunity for discoveries regarding oneself and others, in an emotional dimension.

3.3.2 *The actors involved*

In a training intervention conducted through art, the work of the *trainer* or a *training expert* is essential to identify the training needs and their translation into artistic collaborations. That person plays the role of intermediary, as they independently identify which organizations could benefit from the artistic intervention and to what extent, understanding the company's most strategic needs and succeeding in connecting the artists' philosophy and the company's values. The trainer is also assigned to support the communication between these two worlds, disseminating their point of view in the contacts between them (Berthoin Antal, 2012).

In proposing the artist and project that are most suited for the employee training needs, the figure of the *curator* comes into play, who identifies the artist that in terms of philosophy, language and research can best meet the needs of the training activity. The curator manages and supervises the methods by which the artistic intervention will be carried out, actively participating with the artist and the former in planning the activity. The curator of the artistic intervention looks at art as a *system of knowledge transmission*, that is democratic and circular, recognizing it as a powerful method of training (and the essence of their professional identity).[4]

The artist acts as a teacher, being a professional figure characterized by a strong intent to share, especially with respect to the hidden message, to be revealed by way of the artistic intervention. In the process, the artist represents the energy, the dynamic force that allows the employees to overcome the inertia that impedes the experimentation of new ideas. This mental advancement is possible in the right organizational context, that must also be open to new ideas. In that path of mutual learning, artists can contribute new and original stimulus to the organization, and for their part, employees can return just as much energy drawn from the company's environment, in a true osmotic process of contamination. The artist often hopes that her public will actively participate, allowing them to explain their intent and make a message that is otherwise obscure understandable.

[4] See Chapter 2.

Curiosity, despite being mediated by a phase of astonishment and conflict, this approach encourages the individual to open up, and thus to learn in a process of co-learning that unites the work of the artist and that of the team.

The presence of an institution as a key actor in this process, as a foundation, guarantees greater solidity and rigor. A foundation, with its stable personnel and its precise mission to promote the aspects of art linked most to its social function and role as a training and teaching tool, guarantees that in carrying out the artistic interventions a codified and repeatable methodology is used, that respects the single specificities that characterize the system of art and the world of companies. This methodology must foresee a working team made up of:

- A *trainer* specialized in managerial training, who works both on putting the foundation in contact with the companies requesting the training activities, and on the process of decoding the messages that emerge from the workshops, translating them into effective organizational behavior.
- A foundation that deals with contemporary art and can benefit from the presence of artistic supervision and thus a curator who identifies the artist based on the training needs expressed by the company, supporting the artist in all phases of the project, from ideation to realization, guaranteeing recognizability and validity for the world of art.
- The artist, who carries out the project with the people involved in the workshop and guides them in producing the work specifically conceived for the spaces in which they work.

The *trainer*, the curator and the artist thus conduct the employees involved in the training project to create a choral, shared work of art, that is an expression of the values and symbols of the company culture, which becomes an example of the experience and of the interaction between art and business (Carè, 2016).

3.3.3 *The organizational space*

As regards the organizational space that is created and occupied for the creation of new knowledge through art, the concept of interspace is fundamental. The conditions for co-learning, cited previously, are not known to the actors involved, and thus it is necessary to create the right context: an interspace is a new place, or a revisitation of an existing space, that allows for experimentation through the momentary suspension of the rules that usually guide the company (Berthoin Antal and Straub, 2013). The interspace is a true place of creative experimentation, that allows people to bring added value to the organization. In it, the artist and employees work in a single place that is apparently isolated and far from the routine company activities. Each inhabited interspace, through an artistic intervention, can potentially give life to new practices and new processes applicable to other organizational areas. Despite its limited physical and temporal dimension, this space continues to exist in the mind of the organization's members, going well beyond the temporal parenthesis of the artistic experience that generated it (Sköldberg *et al.*, 2016). It is thus possible to speak of an *aesthetic workspace* (Sutherland, 2012), a place where artistic interventions are carried out in order to involve the participants in the training experience. Indeed, the presence of works of art in a space with a merely decorative function is not enough; it is necessary for contact with art (with the work itself and above all with the artist) to produce an interaction, an exchange that involves all of the actors.

In order to create an organizational interspace thanks to art, the following processes are also necessary:

- *Framing.* The work environment, in constant interaction with art, must be framed with respect to a learning goal – the reason the working team is a triangulation that involves the artist, curator and trainer.
- *Aestheticizing.* The activities carried out in this space must in some way be evocative, with recognized aesthetic qualities, so they will capture the participants' attention and spur their imagination. The vision and contemplation of this aesthetic dimension (always considering this concept in a broad sense, linked to the themes of sensoriness, dissonance and recomposition) strengthen the sense of belonging and the commitment to the organization: in the continuous interaction with this work setting, individuals enter a personal and emotional dimension of the surrounding environment.
- *De-routinizing.* The environment must remind people as little as possible of what they expect from a training intervention. Compared to a simple classroom, in which people enter and know where

to sit to follow a training course, an artistic experience for training assumes a detachment from routine also in the conception of the space that facilitates learning. An *aesthetic workspace* is unusual and thus able to generate novelty and curiosity.

3.3.4 *The individual skills that can be developed*

With the aim of promoting the use of training interventions based on contemporary art, the literature has dedicated attention to the exploration of the skills that art can create or facilitate within a business context. Below we present a summary, starting from a process dimension (how to learn to learn through art) to then come to more specific skills that have been codified to this point by existing research:

- The participants in a training intervention based on art learn to develop skills that go beyond logic and rationality, to derive knowledge from experiences (*experiential knowing*). Through art it is possible to move from mere transmission of knowledge (teacher-pupil) to an appropriation and production of the same. The encounter/clash with the work of art represents the catalyzer of the process of knowledge creation. The introduction of art in an organizational context changes the way of looking at things: production of new knowledge is born precisely from the connection between what emerges from the encounter/clash between artistic activity and everyday life (Sutherland, 2007).
- An intervention based on art fosters the development of a critical spirit because it implies the need for the participant to subjectively re-evaluate the context in which they are working, their routines and the actors with whom they interact. The critical spirit is also trained because the artistic intervention poses the important challenge of understanding how to readapt what has been learned to future work situations (Sutherland, 2012). In fact, the participants in a training experience through art get used to new views of the organizational world, storing new information (the *downloading* phase), they interface with new forms of knowledge (*seeing*), and then reflect on their work (*sensing*), until they reach a deeper understanding of who they are and how they relate to their surroundings (*presensing*) (Darsø, 2004, in an adaptation of the of Otto Scharmer's presensing model).

- During the intervention, the action of the single (artist) is imitated through a process of *prototyping* and *embodying* of the people involved (Darsø, 2004). It starts with an emulative mechanism useful for the physical construction of the work: think of the artist that gives directions in the realization phase of the artifact, or of the various situations to be created in an artistic performance that includes the employees; to finally reach the phase in which the people interiorize what they have created and attempt to reproduce it by adding something personal, in a mechanism called personification (or *embodying*). The ability to attempt to execute the work and then add one's own experience and innovative drive are easily reapplicable for the improvement of the decision-making processes in companies, where a phase of experimentation of the decision is followed by a moment of actual choice of the action to be undertaken.
- A training intervention based on art allows for transferring skills from the "creative" environment to the managerial environment (*skills transfer*). Skills, like the spirit of observation or attention to detail, are often considered possible to transfer from the work of art directly to one's work, when appropriate and functional (Taylor and Ladkin, 2009; Eisner, 2002; McCarthy, Oondaatje, Zakaras and Brooks, 2004).
- Artistic actions allow members of the organization to reveal their thoughts and feelings that otherwise are difficult to access due to conventional methods of expression (*projective technique*). Art thus becomes a tool for reflection that allows for turning an experience into an object of contemplation, facilitating what is the complex mechanism of understanding. A work of contemporary art, for example, often contains logical and/or moral contradictions, which can make sense for the spectator/user through a cycle of attention, understanding and projection (Crowther, 1993). The artifacts[5] thus create a "window to the unconscious" of people (Malchiodi, 1998) allowing them to concentrate on details of their work life that they otherwise would not have noticed.
- The use of art to describe and communicate the essence, the reason of being of a concept (*illustration of essence*), represents an even more

---

[5] See Chapter 5 for further discussion of their role.

powerful tool of communication – based on the sharing of a general evocative message, able to interpret situations and universally recognized conditions – and to give them the proper weight within the organization (Taylor and Ladkin, 2009).

- The artistic act itself (or *making*, intended as the creation of the work and participation in the process) allows for an effective stimulus of creativity (Taylor and Ladkin, 2009). The "*making*" – and thus the concrete realization of a work of art – is considered an opportunity for personal expression, of one's imagination, authenticity and spontaneity.

Having defined this set of skills that can be developed through an artistic intervention, it is also important to clarify that some scholars have illustrated the existence of a widespread assumption of only the positive impact of training interventions on the organizational population. And this is an assumption that is typically extended to training in general, of which the positive effects, rather than the possible problems, are more usually praised.

So it is useful to specify that there are also potential negative effects of training interventions based on art; outcomes that, instead of going in the direction of the renewal of skills, go towards harmful phenomena, like an incorrect representation of the themes to be addressed during training. In this sense, art could lead employees to cultivate expectations or develop a conceptualization of an organizational experience that is very different than what can happen in a company. According to the entity of this cognitive or affective detachment, the recomposition of this "rift" can be more or less effective, and thus can also generate frustration and obstacles to knowledge sharing and learning itself. Similarly, even though "questioning" and the exercise of critical thinking are skills that art develops during a training intervention, it is necessary to understand to what point the exercise of criticism is beneficial and how much it may exacerbate conflicts, making them unhelpful for a better decision-making process. In this regard, though, it is very important to consider the recommendation of Berthoin (2014): the fact that there can be negative effects on work life should not discourage the work that companies do with art, since the worlds of both management and research require an increasing number of actions to advance their knowledge and improve the degree of consciousness with which these interventions can be used.

At this stage of the research, it is still not possible to know the "breaking" point, or the characteristics and the level beyond which a training intervention based on art can generate lasting negative effects. At the moment, the aesthetic theme, the theme of recomposition and composition of rifts, and the numerous skills that have been codified as a result of the use of art in training, lead to preferring to continue along this path, while waiting to develop a better idea of what to avoid.

3.4 VITRIOL: the artistic intervention as an innovative moment of learning

VITRIOL is the title of the site-specific project that the artist Andrea Mastrovito conceived for the 16th edition of the Ermanno Casoli Prize with the participation of approximately one hundred employees of the Angelini pharmaceutical company's facility in Ancona, assisted by both a trainer and a curator.

The acronym *VITRIOL*, which represents a Latin sentence celebrated among alchemists – *Visita Interiora Terrae Rectificando Invenies Occultum* Lapidem (in English, "Visit the Innermost of the Earth and by Rectifying you will find the Hidden Stone") – inspired the artist in the design of a cycle of seven murals spread around the spaces of the company's facilities in Ancona, where all of the activities linked to its realization took place.

The organization of a preparatory workshop was very important, with the goal of prodding the participants' sensitivity towards teamwork and the discovery of the message that the company walls, even of different ages, could "whisper."

For a week the artist, together with the large working group divided into teams, produced the *VITRIOL* cycle by creating permanent incisions on the walls of seven places chosen in the Angelini factory, extrapolating a series of emblematic figures that came to life through the colors present in the various layers of the wall, revealing in the stratification of the walls the passage of time and thus leading to the emergence of a true "archeology of space."

The first intervention of the multiphase cycle was created on the outside wall of the company. Stressing the relationship between medicine and the plant world, a watering can (whose tank recalls the solid reproduced by Albrecht Dürer in the celebrated engraving *Melencolia I* of

1514) gives life to a forest of ampules and alembics, that flower vertically like trees. The mural becomes a metaphor for creation: from inert and imperfect material (the multifaceted solid) life is born (the plants), summarizing the relationship between research and spontaneity, between culture and nature.

We then move to the internal spaces of the coffee room with the second mural, that represents the activities of the pharmaceutical company in a dimension balanced between science and mythology: a machine for finishing products seems to come to life, evoking both the entwined rod of Aesculapius – the symbol of medicine – and the Caduceus of Mercury. The machine operator's helmet has small wings (a feature of Mercury) ideally representing a point of intersection between the "daily" nature of production of medicines and an alchemic process – that is almost magical and divine – that flows into containers with the form of Dürer's solid.

On the wall of the *Sala Tachipirina* (the room named for Angelini's paracetamol product), the engraving is a scene from the myth of Jupiter and Danae. The golden rain (the form in which, in mythology, Jupiter appeared to impregnate the young princess) is in reality an endless series of tablets floating in the air collected by two youths in the solids that recur in all of the works of the cycle, again representing the new encounter between the imperfection of the geometric figure and the "exactness" of medical science. The rain of tablets seems to rebel against falling and gravity: while on the one hand it is collected in the containers, on the other it seems to emanate from the solids themselves, poetically evoking two key moments of Angelini's activity: packing and distribution.

The fourth mural, in the *Sala Mensa* (cafeteria room), depicts a youth riding a creature formed by alembics, test tubes, scales and other elements that represent medicine (that is similar to unicorn, due to a protuberance on the head). It is accompanied by the search for knowledge, represented by the philosopher's stone that dominates above – once again a reference to the stone in Dürer's *Melencolia I.* Medicine thus becomes a tool to reach a type of variable knowledge because it is the result of an always new investigation between science and inner life.

We then go up a stairway dominated by the image of Adonis (a divinity venerated by the ancient Greeks, who was of unrivalled beauty), who represents an ideal of physical perfection. Yet the depiction shows him "maimed," lacking significant portions of his body in the shape of two hexagons and a pentagon. These geometric figures were chosen on purpose because they recall the structure of benzydamine, an anti-inflammatory active principle discovered by Angelini in the 1970s. Once again, medicine becomes an indispensible element of man's life, an integral part of his physical and spiritual well-being.

The wall of the Museum Room, on the other hand, lacks any human figures, and the mural again centers on the depiction of the solid from Dürer's *Melencolia I*. In this case, the element is free of any (physical or conceptual) gravity, and floats lightly in the air, as if it were a kite, held up by the flame of an alchemical furnace. The end of the solid/kite corresponds to the structure of trazodone, a psychoactive substance with anti-depressant properties, also discovered in Angelini's laboratories. Medicine confirms its role as a tool that accompanies man in the search for knowledge.

Lastly, the entrance into the offices represents the conclusion of this very meaningful path. Here we find the title of the entire project: *VITRIOL*, the acronym of the motto that offers the key for interpreting the entire cycle of interventions and invites the viewer to investigate their interior self, but also provides a constant push for scientific and medical research in an attempt to ideally find that hidden stone, the philosopher's stone, and with it, to reach a form of knowledge able to improve our lives. The powder obtained by scraping the walls to bring the previous layers to life was collected in ancient pharmacy vases and glass ampules, displayed below the letters, to tell the story of the company that is characterized by various materials (especially powders that constitute both the excipient and the active principle of the drugs), colors and meanings.

The idea underlying this work is thus complex: an artistic intervention in tune with the pharmaceutical product, presented by the artist as a true *alchemy* between professions, a syntony between the work itself and the work performed by the employees. The intervention created by Andrea Mastrovito for Angelini is based on the spiritual principle of matter: it is not necessary to use new materials to construct the work; the materials themself claim a message that the artist has the duty to reveal.

Neither colors, nor installations of any kind, only tools for scraping away the layers of the wall, uncovering past colors, hidden materials, the history of the wall, and thus of the company and its people. Six teams alternated during a work week. For each group, the working environment became a worksite, a "shop" in which the artist and employees created something unique together. It all happened through an element that already existed and was encouraged to tell its story: the wall.

The creations of Andrea Mastrovito and the employees, expertly produced on the walls of the company's facilities, thus represent some of the themes characterizing the artist's philosophy, but also the history of Angelini and of medicine.

The existence of multiple relationships, such as "medicine-plant world," but also "science-mythology," illustrates how apparently opposite disciplines can be considered mutual through art. In addition, the presentation of certain contrasts such as the imperfection of the shapes of the work together with the perfection of the molecule discovered by Angelini, or the continuous relationship between tradition and innovation represented by the work of the riding youth (who looks straight to the future, and thus to innovation) created as a set of ancient objects from the trade (to underline the importance of memory of the tradition), are distinguishing traits of *VITRIOL* and Angelini. The continuous use of metaphors as the reference to creation through a combination of medical instruments and the spontaneity of the plant world, as well as the example of the riding youth, transpose into images the intention of Angelini to always look forward to the new. Lastly, there is Adonis, who due to some missing body parts that create holes with geometric forms, symbolizes the indissoluble link between medicine and human life.

As we will see later, *VITRIOL* emblematically represents the method through which the FEC intends to bring contemporary art to companies, both due to the sensitivity that is required in interpreting the contexts, and due to the ability to transform the audience into an active part of the creation of the work, and above all due to the novel opportunity created for interaction with the company environment. In this case, to understand the needs of the company and to create a correspondence between the work of the artist and that of the company, the role of the trainer was fundamental. Piero Tucci, the founder of M&D, the training company that collaborated with FEC for *VITRIOL*, stated:

> The trainer is important in this process because contemporary art requires a context of "safe" training, to be discussed and practiced effectively. The training expert has the task of creating this sense of psychological security, first of all through a process of accreditation of the training method with contemporary art, and subsequently through a process of knowledge of the company and the artist [...]. Our role is to lead the company and the participants through a process, to explain to them how it takes place, to highlight the possible

> connections between what happens during training through contemporary art and what they will then take with them to the workplace [...]. The beauty of working with contemporary art lies in the fact that there exists a component of unpredictability regarding how the training intervention will end, the quality of the artifacts, and the quality of learning. Our role as trainers is to however create a process of training that is "certain," where there is clarity on the general steps and where there is the opportunity for a deep reflection on how what is done through art has value in and of itself and for one's work life.

The goal of *VITRIOL* was not to carry out a simple team building intervention, given that the company needed to create a more lasting experience, able to produce a memory and a tangible result in time, directly linked to people's work. M&D and FEC wanted the intervention to be designed specifically for the Angelini company, for its historical moment and its development needs, that entailed the need to enhance individual contributions for the success of teamwork. In a somewhat unusual way, instead of a simple "celebration" of the value of collaboration, the company decided to carry out a training event that stressed how the effort of each individual was essential for group performance. In the words of the production manager at the time:

> Sometimes training mostly succeeds in fostering a culture, but changing behavior is difficult; we know this well because we have always invested in training. However, sometimes methods are needed by which people are strongly influenced by what they are doing [...]. Unlike a sport, the *VITRIOL* project lasted longer, it meant that everyone was part of the project, a project that was so complex people realized how the work took shape thanks to the indispensible contribution of each individual [...]. To this we must add that maturation of the awareness that creative work is not so distant from the exercise of the individual effort expended in any other work [...]. The impression that remains after having participated in such an activity is so strong that it marks you deeply and the connection with one's daily work is immediate.

VITRIOL is a complex training intervention, due to the number of people involved, the time and physical energy they dedicated to the activity, its specific nature with respect to the company's history and spaces, and its aspiration to be "unforgettable" since it permanently changes the most stable element in a social space, the walls that delimit and identify it as a workspace.

But *VITRIOL* is also a complex intervention because it is able to trace a continuum between the history and discoveries of Angelini, the philosophy of the artist, and the FEC method that aims to reflect on a specific goal with artists and businesses, so that there is a clear sense of responsibility among the actors involved and so that this circumscribed goal can always be resolved in a creative, not predictable way, according to paradigms which traditional methods could not reference.

Looking more carefully at the structure of the intervention, we can reflect on some issues already analyzed previously from a theoretical standpoint, such as the recognition of the value of errors, dissonance as a starting point for learning, and physical and conceptual "making." Through *VITRIOL* it is also possible to understand how an artistic intervention can modify the organizational space and generate new skills.

3.4.1 *Error*

From the beginning, the aim was for all of the employees involved in the project to challenge themselves, without fear of being judged on their artistic abilities. Each was assigned a sketch which indicated the parts of the work to be created and the portion of the wall on which to work, always under the supervision of the artist and his assistants. The artist, curator, and trainer – as the Angelini employees say – never expressed a negative judgment on their work; you had to admit you didn't know what to do and ask for help, otherwise the creation of the entire work would suffer. Thanks to this approach it became possible, in the employees' perception, to go beyond the rhetoric of considering error as something positive, to make it real: discussing one's error or the inability to use a certain tool or reach a certain result was naturally shared, in order to allow for the completion of the work in the relevant timeframe, that had greater value for the participants than their egos or desire to appear. The Angelini employees were always supported by the artist and his team; holding discussions with them was part of the project, and made its execution an experiment close to the ideal of daily work that the company wanted to achieve. This experience with regard to error, the reasonable trust placed in someone who is more experienced, the act of exploiting one's skills and pointing out one's inabilities to contribute to a company and not just individual goal, were goals that *VITRIOL* wanted to achieve. In the words of one Angelini employee:

> We are used to training, but this intervention was not taken by anyone in the usual way […]; everyone was interested in the final drawing, and since everyone contributed to making it, we were all curious, we all supported and encouraged each other. Truly, every one of us was a part of the process, and as we worked we couldn't guess how this experience would end. Even though it was training, nobody explained a concept, such as the concept of "working together," for instance; but I realized that by myself I would never have been able to complete my task. I needed the physical and psychological support of the others. But nobody explained it, we lived through it. A group was created which was assigned part of the work site. Many of us knew each other, many others didn't. The dimensions of the project, that shifted our attention to other more technical aspects, did not immediately lead us to think of the question of the group, but after an hour it was evident and absolutely necessary to form a team. Some said: "I can't do it, you do it" […], then there were some who worked more on the holes to make, and others more on the lines […]. From a work standpoint it's not easy to say that you can't do it, but when you do so you find help. As for me, I was certain I wouldn't be able to do it, I was afraid of making mistakes; but I realized I shouldn't think this way. This is something that I carry with me in everyday life, above all because it is possible to repair an error, and also because it may not be an error at all.

3.4.2 *Dissonance and recomposition*

In the case of *VITRIOL*, there was never a real conflict with the artist's vision; rather, curiosity and surprise immediately arose upon learning that the activity suggested by the artist consisted of manual, very physical activity, something that would require an intimate effort of creation, and thus could make the company a more personal and "close" place. Obviously, many of the participants recognized elements of differentiation between their way of working at Angelini and the artist's modus operandi. For example, some participants in the project stressed the complete absence of hierarchy: the working teams were always mixed, reducing to a minimum what in an organization is normally the large or small distance between its members. Thanks to overcoming this hierarchical barrier, some participants experienced moments of interaction with their colleagues, as transpires from these words: "Rather than sending e-mails, people spoke with each other. […] I saw colleagues who previously didn't get along so well talk to each other and work side by side!" This absence of hierarchy, this "randomness" in the composition of the teams and absence of competitive spirit allowed for exalting the vision of each individual's role as a contribution to a project and a higher goal; as if the organization of the work process, so able to avoid personalisms, had made a non-rhetorical perspective on teamwork possible, as the ability to organize the process and the desire to contribute to it. From an interview with one of the Angelini employees:

> We performed a job in the complete absence of competition, and for us, this was a factor of difference with respect to how we usually work [...], while attention to detail, and careful work is typical of Angelini. This attention to detail cannot be reached in a job performed individually. The work itself, at times, seemed even too simple, given its repetitiveness (using a cutter or other tools to scrape the wall and remove the plaster), but it provided an interesting interpretation of teamwork: work that is simple, but well-organized, with precise tasks, great attention to detail and a very ambitious goal, that of creating a work of art. A work done by a large team, with little details and little mistakes made by each of us, still led to something beautiful. When big numbers are involved, the individual contribution tends to get lost, but this time there were no specific catalysts; there was a small contribution from each of us.

3.4.3 *Physical and conceptual "making"*

Angelini employees not only played an active part in the process of conceiving the work, but they also participated in the physical act of its creation. In fact, a work of art is always a metaphor for birth, the materialization of something new that didn't exist before, and that is observed, meditated, assimilated and stimulates thoughts and reflections on its form and meaning. The work allowed for a mutual learning experience: the employees saw the company through the eyes of the artist, they modified it physically and experienced it differently thanks to the realization and experience of the work. At the same time, the artist learned and revisited his ideas through the organization's vision, values and daily practices. The active and continuous participation, the interaction, having "personally gotten their hands dirty" allowed for Angelini employees to truly learn. The physical trace – which is the permanent character of the work – represents an additional element of efficacy of the *VITRIOL* training experience. An artistic intervention reaches this level when it leaves a mark: both when it is simply a work still visible in the company (the walls, in this case), or when it is an experience and its memory exists in the minds of the participants. On the one hand, we thus observe what we have defined as the "practical making" – the physical engraving of the wall, the scraping and drawing of Mastrovito's outlines on the company's walls – while on the other, we note the interaction among the people and the construction of new relationships in the space of the artistic intervention: listening, helping and involving became imperatives in the making phase of *VITRIOL*, constituting an experience that is not only physical, but above all conceptual: "Andrea brought out the beauty [...] not because the work has to be considered aesthetically beautiful, but because we made it physically, and we didn't think we were able to do it." And, "when something is beautiful like this, then everyone likes it and everyone takes something from it." And also: "That is mine. I made that!" Or: "There is a part of me on that wall." These are statements associated with *VITRIOL*. The employees showed enormous enthusiasm and a real sense of pride for the work performed directly by them, as well as that of their colleagues. As we can see from these brief quotes, it's not simply having "built" the work, but most of all having left something of themselves in it as employees of that company, something that allows for memory and opportunity for reflection over time.

3.4.4 *Creation of interspaces*

As mentioned in the previous pages, learning in adults is more effective if it takes place through actual immersion in concrete situations correlated with those of daily life. Contemporary artists often use contexts well known to their public, and in the case of a company training intervention, to the employees they collaborate with. It may be the work environment itself (Angelini for *VITRIOL*), or an environment that is external but well-known (think of the soccer field described in Chapter 2 for *The Game*). These are familiar contexts for the people involved, that are modified in view of the efficacy of a training intervention that is engaging for the participating adults. In the case of *VITRIOL*, the interspace is in fact represented by the same factory in which the seven works by Andrea Mastrovito were conceived and created. One of the peculiar characteristics of these artistic interventions is the permanent value of the work: not only in physical terms (given the type of intervention that is very visible on the engraved walls), but principally in conceptual terms (in the memory of the people who executed it). The company space is contextualized as a space for learning and renewed to host a new interaction, between the artist, the employees and the company.

When we attempt to determine if *VITRIOL* has activated a process of generation of new knowledge and of transformation of behavior (through the development of new skills or the updating of existing ones), we need to examine the following points:

- *The awareness of the aesthetic value of the work and the organizational locations (Aesthetic awareness). VITRIOL* represents an example of the training potential based also on the concept of *beauty* (consider this concept also to be open to many aesthetic categories, as described in the introduction to this chapter). This is a central issue in the works of Andrea Mastrovito: he describes a concept of beauty located in something that already exists, that could be defined as beauty "regained" from the redemption of daily places and materials, thus skillfully brought to light through a multisensorial experience. The concept itself is now an integral part of every modern company since it is useful to interpret organizational life by way of its simple applicability to very different contexts. Again, from an interview with an Angelini employee:

  > I like doing things manually, and I'm good at it, but even people who aren't good at it helped the others as they could, bringing tools, indicating points, [...] we were considered the tools of a work of art that we all made together, inside and for the company. For me personally, the best intervention among those we carried out is the one that closed the sequence, at the entrance to the offices, consisting of pieces of wall and powder coming from the other works, because it was made with what remained from the other interventions; it was created from destruction. What we did was "ruin" the wall to extract something beautiful.

- *The transfer of skills from the artistic intervention to daily work (skills transfer).* The "creative" or "artistic" skills that are experimented with in the execution of a work of art may then be transferred to work:

  > I discovered that I could combine the sense of art with the scientific knowledge that characterizes my work. [...] For me art is imagination and fantasy, it pushes you to experiment. [...] Now I try to make use of this artistic element in every project I participate in.

The execution of the project can also lead to transferring "organizational" and "managerial" skills to regular work, if they were part of the totality of the artistic intervention:
After this experience, I listened more to those who didn't feel capable of doing things, I found that I was more open to dialogue, to the possibility of sharing. During the artistic intervention this came very naturally to me, and I said, "if it comes so naturally when I don't think I'm working, why shouldn't I make an effort to do it when I'm at work as well?"

- *The clear "vision" of a concept (illustration of essence).* An artistic intervention, compared to other training metaphors, is able to immediately and inductively communicate the sense of certain concepts. In the case of *VITRIOL*, the concepts of collaboration, listening and valuing the individual as part of a broader goal, emerged as recurrent in the interviews:

  My work consists of personal relationships and their management, with various parts of the world. [...] I tried to bring the same group vision that we obtained with *VITRIOL* to external relationships as well. [...] We are all colleagues, aren't we?

3.5 Managerial implications for the design of a training intervention based on art

In this chapter we have explored the reasons for using art as a medium and protagonist of training in companies. The resulting benefits became evident both in terms of individual skills that art allows for developing in companies, and in terms of consequences that these individual skills have on the working team and the company.

What are the specific dimensions for this type of intervention to be concentrated on when designing training interventions with contemporary art?

- *Recomposition, composition.* Art has the power to mend the "rifts" of organizational life, giving people a broader perspective, a possibility to locate the history or themes of one's company in a broader scenario. This scenario belongs to a different world – that of art – but is linked to the organizational sphere through all of the skills it allows for developing and that are part of both the artistic and the business worlds. It is important for this intention of recomposition to be expressed well when designing a training intervention of this type, so that art is not lumped in with just any other training metaphor, but its unique value is recognized. Recomposing, giving order to something that no longer has it, is not the only general intention that can be pursued: there is also composition, giving perspective to an organizational theme that has been neglected or that has produced negative consequences, and that needs to be addressed in a different way. Whatever the starting point, whether it is more critical (and thus requires a phase of recomposition) or less critical (and thus is to be composed or developed), it is essential to make the final goal explicit for all of the actors involved and coherent with the potential of art (for example, we adopt art because it is an efficient way to recompose what we think in regard to the style of leadership adequate for our organization; we adopt it because we want to compose, structure our thinking better about what collaboration means within our organization).

- *Aesthetics.* When we think of a training intervention based on art, we cannot but think how suited it is to transfer knowledge and a method of aesthetical learning, in the sense described in this chapter. Thus, it is not possible to think of the intervention and the results it produces (even only in terms of organizational memory) only as an exercise of cognition. To be adequately valued and in respect for the artist's philosophy, it must have a strong inductive and sensorial component, an articulation in time and space that allows for the exercise of intuition, the senses, and not only of traditionally structured logical thinking. The moment of education can take place, during or after the intervention, in a guided or autonomous way, depending on the training goal being pursued.
- *Dialogue with the most current training trends.* However as much as the autonomy and uniqueness of a training intervention has taken hold through art with respect to other metaphors, it is important for those who decide to use that type of training in companies to be aware of the recent debate around the more traditional training themes. For example, the theme of error management, that has always been part of the debate on training interventions based on art, is also a subject of autonomous and current research when we speak of adult learning. The debate on this question has evolved in the

direction of identifying for which training goals it is more or less important to leave people free to err, guide them a bit, or correct them when they err, making the acceptance of error a contingent, more than absolute question. This increases awareness during the design of the intervention and facilitates the dialogue between art and management from the standpoint of constant updating.

- *The artifact and the artistic space.* We will discuss the space and the object as protagonists when we address the relationship between art and business innovation more fully in Chapter 5. However, the objects that are created, but also the way a company's employees occupy a space through art, are fundamental elements of the training. It is thus important for the actors involved (in particular the trainer and the curator as intermediaries) to have the opportunity to bring people's attention to the new way of experiencing the physical space that art has created, how much it has made that space one of collaboration constructed according to parameters different than usual, and also a place to carry out actions that imply the use of one's own body and way of reasoning that is unusual and thus memorable. The same is true for the objects that are produced during the artistic intervention: whether they are displayed or not, for those who created them they remain the objects that incorporate the memory of that experience. It is obvious that display and use in the company make these objects "celebrated," that is, it officially recognizes their role as bearers of an organizational, not just personal memory. To the contrary, to not display them, or to remove them, implies a sort of desire by the company not to establish an opportunity for a living memory and collective interpretation, and thus at least not to legitimize them in a lasting manner in the company. Yet the employees will in any event have a memory and an interpretation, although it will be exclusively personal.

4 Contemporary Art in Process and Product Innovation: From the Concept of "Artifacts" to the Renewal of Company Thinking

The goal of this chapter is to discuss how contemporary art can act within companies as an occasion for rethinking work processes and at times products. In particular, we will focus on the potential of art to support: the elaboration of strategic, future-oriented thinking; the exchange of knowledge; and the more informal and freer perception of workspaces and organizational logics. These reflections are discussed in depth through the *Aspiranti Aspiratori* project by Sissi, an interesting example of how rethinking an ideational and productive process of a company, through the lens of the artist, can lead the organization to adopt a new perspective, to experiment with new ideas and introduce a new way of experiencing organizational spaces and products. From the same viewpoint, we will also discuss the work by Ettore Favini, *Sillage*. Through interviews with both artists, the chapter will present some salient passages of the philosophy of their work, to understand how an encounter can take place between the two worlds: that of the ideational and productive process typical of a company, and that of the artistic process. The chapter concludes with the managerial implications of the artistic intervention in terms of design, and its repercussions on life within the company.

4.1 Art, knowledge exchange and innovation

> Without the artist, we would have done something like every other project. [...] We've been here for many years, we know the routines. We know how the collective mind works. We needed someone to open the box, even throw the box away (Antal, 2013).

Having come to the fourth chapter of this book, perhaps the question of why we need art and artists in businesses has not received a definitive answer. In the following pages we will present some ideas for reflection, to add to the previous ones, to discuss how art and artists have the potential to represent a source of innovation for processes, spaces, products (more or less directly) and company practices. Returning to the quote from Antal, this chapter aims to add an element to the discussion on why it is very likely that the presence of art and artists in companies can disrupt the dominant and routine thinking, triggering processes of innovation and change.

The existence of a link between the way of operating of the not strictly managerial world and innovation in this same area has been the subject of study for a long time. As we mentioned briefly in the previous chapters, the practices and modus operandi of design and designers have often been analyzed to understand how processes of knowledge exchange in preparation for product innovation take place (Hargadon and Sutton, 1997), to understand how to structure the dynamics of understanding and articulation of processes of change (Stigliani and Ravasi, 2012) and the renewal of strategy (Ravasi and Lojacono, 2005). In these studies, design and its practices are not addressed due to their impact on the aesthetics, price, or performance of a product, but to understand how design can lead the company to a broader reflection on the renewal of its strategic orientation.

This fundamental research has shed light on the importance for companies not only of learning from professional communities other than those considered close to their core business, but also the great significance of this contact for both process and product innovation, and for a broader rethinking of strategic processes and organizational change.

In this debate, in which design is the protagonist, it should be stressed that art has not yet entered the process of business innovation in such a decisive way.

This can be explained, on the one hand, in light of the desire of the world of art – for historical reasons – to maintain a certain autonomy with respect to the process of industrial production, and on the other to a longer-term collaboration of design and principles of design management in the life of companies (including those companies in which it does not represent a strategic or core process). As of now, various studies exist that consolidate the legitimacy of art as an opportunity through which to renew processes and products. For example, think of the practice of organizing spaces such as the "studio" or the "atelier" inside a company, understood in art as a place for work, research, and reflection relating to the themes of artistic activities, and brought into companies as a place in which, following the typical ideational and decision-making processes of artistic practice, it is possible to better face the phases of problem solving and product innovation (Barry and Meisiek, 2015; Meisiek and Barry, 2016).

The transposition of the studio into a company implies a sort of direct importation from one world to the other; it is an example of how artistic practice can be imitated in order to stimulate processes of change and innovation. Such immediate interventions are similar, in terms of dynamics and final effect, to the interventions that artists make directly on products through the creation of "limited series." In these cases the artist creates a new version of the product that they transform based on their philosophy. Referring to some artistic interventions organized for Elica by the FEC, the example of *Pescecappa x Pescetrullo* by Gaetano Pesce, created for the Milan Furniture Fair in 2009, is emblematic. The artist proposed a new image of the kitchen hood starting from its predecessor: the fireplace hood. *Pescecappa* is in fact a prototype of an extractor hood, the first of fifteen unique pieces, numbered and signed by the author, conceived for the kitchen of *Pescetrullo*, the uncommon and innovative residence created by the architect and designer in the Apulia countryside. Experimenting with unusual materials, the artist proposes a new very personal image of the extractor hood, seen as "an element of diversity in the kitchen space, a point of color that is a bit disorderly and full of light, a presence that brings a smile when looking at it." The hood by Gaetano Pesce thus represents a direct intervention on the product that becomes an object of sale, although to a limited extent, according to the logic of the serial work of art rather than the commercial product.

In this chapter, in the tradition of the studies cited previously, we will attempt to look not only at these direct implications and "practices" (in the sense of implementation that is not extremely complex), but also and above all the indirect way that art can influence the company's processes and products.

One of the first examples that can be cited within this more indirect way of linking art and production is the *Dal progetto all'oggetto* (From the design to the object) workshop, created by Ettore Favini, Christian Frosi and Nico Vascellari in 2008, for the Elica employees, designers, prototypers, marketing staff and laborers, joined by the inclination and personal motivation to adopt the perspective of "producing art in the factory," to combine the conceptual aspect with the merely technical phase of work. The project was born with the goal of reflecting on that complex process that transforms the status of an object elevating it to a work of art. The study sought to highlight how the creative moment of ideation is the fulcrum of every productive process, emphasizing the value that the project can give the work, whatever its nature.

In this sense, another good example is the work by Andrea Nacciarriti, *Less than air* (2010), created for Elica with the FEC on the occasion of the 2010 Milan Furniture Fair. To create it, the artist interacted with the technical personnel of the Elica Propulsion Laboratory, the industrial group's research and certification laboratory, a space for experimentation and innovation for everything that regards the company's core business: air treatment. Starting from the assumption that in the prototyping and engineering of the hood the aim is to "hide the air" – as Nacciarriti puts it – the artist tried to do the opposite, to "reveal it," through four works in which this element, that is so hard to perceive, became materially present. *Less than air* is a project consisting of opposition and integration with respect to the characteristics and functions of the company product, enriched by references to works already existing in the world of art, but that are not immediately traceable to the product. All of these elements imply an opportunity for the company, to rethink not only the product, but also its aesthetics, its functioning, and the way we were used to thinking of it up to that point.

To understand even better the innovative impact of art on organizational processes, products and spaces, below we highlight some principles linked to the theory of materiality, institutionalism and knowledge management, together with the discussion of some artistic interventions organized for Elica by FEC, and in particular, focusing on *Sillage* by Ettore Favini, 2015, and *Aspiranti Aspiratori* by Sissi, 2012.

4.2 Art and its potential for innovation: materiality and artifacts

To understand the relevance of art and artistic interventions to stimulate change and innovation in work processes, and indirectly in products, we refer to those theoretical currents that have investigated the relationship between materiality and organizational practices (by way of example: Leonardi, 2012). Materiality is intended as all of the physical objects or digital materials that are encountered in a particular organizational situation and acquire meaning with respect to the activities being carried out. This current of studies is very important when we want to discuss the processes of change and innovation, since it has illustrated not only how language, interpretations and discourse are essential, but also how the objects that are present and utilized during the work have a role in influencing the ability to express thoughts, recognize concepts, formulate new ones and suggest ways of acting that are not yet present in the company.

In the coming paragraphs we will consider, among the elements of materiality, organizational artifacts intended as physical objects. People always seek a material representation of ideas and concepts, and the materiality that characterizes the physical representation of a concept accompanies the individual in a series of actions: first of all, the acceptance and admission of the existence of an artifact and of some sort of intrinsic value in it, then its comprehension, and then a rendering of the most stable concept in the imagination; and lastly, what could be defined for all purposes as an identification with its meaning, to the point of transferring one's own ideas and interpretations to it. People see and perceive an object in the organizational environment, they ask what purpose it has, and they develop their thinking accordingly.

To provide an example of the importance of artifacts for the process of developing organizational change and strategic reformulation, the study by Stigliani and Ravasi (2012) is crucial to understand how objects support not only individual cognitive processes, but also collective, team processes, and allow for expressing strategic, future-oriented thinking in a company. In the design company analyzed by the authors of the study, the individuals organize their thoughts, share them and interact with each other through multiple objects: whiteboards, drawings, notes, slides, imagines, small articles that can be related to the decision-making process, and the very rooms they work in. The objects are not in the background of the individual and group cognitive process, but are described as protagonists for an effective process of recognition of new concepts and ideas, to classify and verbalize them, join them in relationships and share them, in order to design the product and the enterprise's strategic future.

The role that art can have in light of this relevance of artifacts for the formulation of innovative ideas, in terms of strategic and product positioning, can have a different scope and potentially add to that described above. When the artist works in the company, they introduce into the environment a series of objects, works of art (or the physical parts of which it is composed), the materials they work with, the preparatory drawings, the prototypes, and the tests they conduct, down to the documentation material (that is particularly relevant when the project has a strongly conceptual and performative nature). For the members of the organization, these objects can have a strong propulsive power towards the "recognition" of new concepts and new ideas and their consequent novel reorganization, since they come from the philosophy of an artist, that is, from a world distant from the company, but at the same time are objects that the artist creates thinking of how their identity and work fit into the company's context.

To this we must also add that the work of art created during an artistic intervention, as well as its intermediate artifacts, can remain in the company for a long time or can also be hosted in public institutions. Moreover, the experience to which these objects are linked (when structured effectively, as discussed in the previous chapters) is always memorable. The finished work, and the objects through which it is documented during its intermediate steps, thus remain available as artifacts after the artistic intervention as well, with the potential to participate in new ideational processes. As said previously, this is also true for objects more traditionally linked to the business or identity of the company: think of the function of the preservation of prototypes, designs and products, with the goal of generating product innovation (Hargadon and Sutton, 1997, just to provide an example). Without wanting to substitute this excellent company practice of preserving the intermediate and finished products linked to the ideational and productive process, it is also important to recognize that the art object possesses all of those "aesthetic" characteristics (in the sense described in Chapter 3) that make it extremely significant for both individual and collective memory or emotivity, and that its preservation and exposure therefore have a potential to catalyze even greater ideational and knowledge exchange processes than those of the artifacts traditionally linked to business.

Consider, for example, the *Sillage* project already described, an artistic intervention directly linked to the diffuser of *Marie* fragrances produced by Elica, that in terms of material production, consists of various objects and moments, all respectively documented. As Ettore Favini explained:

> Consistent with my artistic interest for the issue of continuous transformation of the object, the first step of the work was the idea of planting and cultivating plants in the frames of the Elica hoods, that once grown, became material to produce the fragrances for the *Marie* diffusers that I had covered with a film decorated with still life themes. I worked entirely around this theme of the object that changes, and all of the objects that resulted function as a "bridge" between one stage of the work and another.

Multiple artifacts were created in Favini's project, all linked to the hood and diffuser products. We can easily understand their potential to provoke discussions, new interpretations of the product and new ideas, with a potential at least equal to that of a collection of prototypes and projects. The potential presence of these artifacts in the company (or the testimony of their existence), linked to each other thanks to the underlying artistic idea they share and its cogent logic, thus generates greater potential value for product innovation.

4.3 Art and artifacts, continued: boundary objects, knowledge exchange as a precondition for innovation

To further reflect on the potential of art in the generation and sharing of new concepts, it is important to refer to a specific category of artifacts, *boundary objects* (Carlile, 2002; Bechky, 2003). Boundary objects are defined as such because they are able to live in different professional worlds and satisfy their information needs when they engage in problem solving or an ideational process. It could be said, perhaps simplistically, that these objects speak the language of various professional communities in companies, and can be effectively used in interactions between them to favor explanations and exchange knowledge.

In this context, the boundary object acts as a bridge, an object constructed "at the border" able to help overcome the barriers present within the organization. An accepted and shared artifact in different working communities is able to facilitate collaborative work, promoting continuous negotiation between the parties and thus supplying an alternative interpretation of the entire organization (Henderson, 1991). Its vision in the organizational context and the presence of a mechanism of authority that represents its purpose (Star and Griesemer, 1989) represent basic preconditions for its presence to produce organizational advantages. In this sense, boundary objects help construct an infrastructure (Bowker and Star, 1999: *boundary infrastructure*) and a process (Carlile, 2002: *boundary process*) that individuals can use to manage knowledge with respect to the confines of the organization.

It is very complex to assimilate a work of art in a company and the artifacts linked to it with the idea of a boundary object. As can be recognized from the definition presented above, an artifact cannot be a boundary object per se, but it can be one if it represents a comprehensible tool of communication and knowledge exchange between professionals who belong to different fields. It is thus more direct to assimilate boundary objects with objects that are usually present in company life, such as prototypes or models, since they have very often been the result of a collective effort or reify the knowledge of various company functions and processes. On this subject, there have been various studies that have illustrated the company museum, which principally gather company products, as a place in which artifacts are kept able not only to generate a process of common identification for the members of the organization, but also to create a platform for knowledge sharing and communication.

The work of art and the artifacts linked to it could be considered boundary objects when they are immersed in the organizational context, where a setting and opportunity for their recognition by the members of the organization are intentionally created for them. The material objects that belong to the artistic process, in theory, would not contain sufficient information because at least a part of the company's professional community can consider them explicative, able to communicate something relevant to other professional communities. However, when the intervention and the work of art are introduced in the company with continuity and broad involvement of people, it is possible for the material objects linked to the artistic intervention and the work itself to become the opportunity and medium through which various different professional communities find the occasion to communicate, interact and exchange knowledge.

This process of mutual learning is defined as a *boundary crossing*, since it implies that professional communities learn how to go beyond part of their specialization to learn and enter into dialogue with other communities. In particular, the concept of boundary crossing through artifacts includes the following phases:

- *Identification.* With the identification of a common artifact, the members of the organization rethink their work identity and reassess their role and relationship with other functions and professions in the company in light of the artifact (see also Chapter 2).
- *Coordination.* The artifacts can support professional communities in establishing a channel of communication more immediately and in finding common ground to translate their specific languages.
- *Reflection.* Thanks to artifacts, professional communities can more easily develop the awareness of the existence of differences between them through a *perspective taking* methodology, i.e. the adoption of a new vision. Artifacts help look at the organization and its profession from another perspective, contributing to the ability to reflect on a vision that is negotiated and common to multiple professional communities.
- *Transformation.* After having accepted and integrated the presence of the artifact in the organization, the organizational practices can change as a function of the artifact, or "intermediate" practices can arise. Moreover, the spaces in which common problems can be shared are recognized. This way, it is potentially possible to see the creation of a new cultural form, and thus a new language, of new purposes.

In this case as well, *Sillage* can be of help to give an example of *boundary crossing* at least between the artistic and design communities in Elica. The creation of the cover for the *Marie* diffuser generated a relationship of extreme interest, due to the discussion and mutual learning generated, between artists and the world of design around the concept of authorality of the product and the reproducibility of the same. The covering for *Marie*, made from a special film that stuck to it by floatation, was not able to produce the same results for all of the diffusers in terms of the aesthetic characteristics of the product. While for the artist this represented value added, since it somehow made each piece unique, it had a different value for the designers, linked more to the need for replicability of the object, including in limited editions. That difference in understanding the identity of the article in question, together with the need for interaction between the professional communities to create it, generated the opportunity to go beyond the typical borders of the professional communities, to reach an idea negotiated and accepted by the parties (and thus mutually learned) of what an innovative and sellable product is.

4.4 From artifacts to organizational spaces

Contemporary art, by its very nature, sometimes transforms the spaces in which it is hosted. This happens predictably when the artist's approach concentrates in particular on the reflection of the relationship between work and display space. This dynamic is even more true if we think that artistic interventions in companies can be conceived specifically to influence the aesthetics and meaning of company spaces; or if we think that companies can keep or intentionally direct the results of an artistic intervention. Or, we can try to think of the fact that an artistic intervention, even if it does not directly intervene in the configuration of the company space, durably changes its perception, because in that space people have had the opportunity to undergo a complex experience, able to activate not only the traditional mechanisms of thinking, but all of the senses. This is why, in the two previous chapters as well, we spoke of the possibility for art to generate *interspaces*.

It is obvious that the generation of interspaces is stronger the more it is possible to connect the artistic intervention to objects, to a materiality of the same space, modifying it or populating it permanently with new artifacts. The creation of these interspaces, separated from the usual way of working, in which art can create its own domain and its personal way of connecting to company life, can at this point seem to be an almost automatic practice to import the logics of art into a company. An idea that is more complex, but also more interesting to understand what other stimulus art can provide to the company, comes from the study of informal communities of experts originating from different sectors and their dynamics of interaction (Furnari, 2014). This study introduces the concept of *interstitial spaces*, defined as "contexts limited in time and space, that are informal, in which professionals from other sectors meet and interact on common activities to which they dedicate a limited amount of time." Thus not all occasions for informal interaction are interstitial spaces, because they require that people come from different backgrounds and interact for a limited time, for informal reasons and not official requests from the company. The interest for these spaces, that are both physical and abstract at the same time, derives from their great potential to generate new organizational practices, new ways of working.

The birth of new interventions should be favored, in interstitial spaces, by the informal nature of the encounters, able to create a favorable context for greater propensity for risk and experimentation. Another essential component of these contexts aimed at favoring innovation is that they are characterized by the presence of emotional energy and mutual attention: people, meeting up informally to perform a task of common interest in a limited time, are encouraged to mutually learn and have the emotional tension necessary to learn and perform the activities rapidly. In addition to these dimensions, those spaces work if they can make use of the presence of a catalyzer, whose role is to support interaction between the various professionals and the construction of meaning.

In this case as well, given the level of development and the not yet decisive spread of artistic interventions in companies, it is complex to create a clear parallel between artistic interventions and the creation of interstitial spaces. In companies, art is not yet so pervasive and the presence of artists not yet so regular as to create an occasion for informal encounters around art with professionals coming from the different company areas. It is true, though, that artistic interventions, if they are more widespread and entered into the company's values, would have the potential to generate these occasions and thus create opportunities for innovation. Artistic interventions thus generate artifacts able to stimulate a construction of renewed meaning for the company, given their aesthetic scope and potential to favor communication not only between the world of art and the world of the company, but between the various company functions. Moreover, in artistic interventions, the artist, trainer and curator can be understood as catalysts of the interaction between the different professionals and as guides in the elaboration and ideation of new concepts. In addition, as explained in Chapter 3, an intervention of this type certainly has the characteristics of emotional tension and mutual and focused attention, presenting a new challenge to the employees, in which it is not complex to identify oneself, though. As already expressed in the previous sections, the artistic intervention also leaves objects that, belonging to the world of art, generate a perception of their durability and memory in time that is even greater than that of the artifacts linked more traditionally to the ideational and productive process of the company. In order for artistic interventions to translate into spaces for innovation according to the model just described, it is important for the artists, artworks, and artifacts to be regularly present at the company, to be part of an organizational culture, without distorting the unique nature of the artists' philosophy and the processes, and thus their potential for innovation and spontaneous aggregation of people.

4.5 Aspiranti Aspiratori: the artistic intervention as an occasion for process and product innovation

As mentioned in Chapter 2, the FEC collaborated with Sissi on a project aimed at reconsidering the concept of air purification (2012) that acted as the basis for a new product to be offered by Elica. Consistent with the artist's goals, that were very different than those of design and production, Sissi was not asked to intervene directly on the product, but to freely rethink the concept of air purification through her tools of investigation. This passage is very important to understand the unique way in which the artist can generate innovation in the conception of the product, which happens above all through the introduction of a new ideational and decision-making process, and new concepts, but above all new objects and new spaces that live in an "intermediate" new world: that of art in companies. As the artist explains:

> I didn't want there to be confusion, since the creation of a product is not among my activities: I don't create products that can be mass reproduced and sold, that respond to logics of function imposed by design. [...] This is why I considered it important to stress my presence as an artist and the fact that, after having entered the company, I wanted to interact with it. I wanted to be clear about the difference between my presence in the company and the generic presence of a creative person. As an artist I developed a process in various phases and applied it to the company. [...] At the end of my intervention, I did not want to deliver a finished product, to potentially be reinterpreted, but I wanted to give a series of concepts that Elica could develop and adopt as its own: a series of finished contents, like the chain of DNA that can be opened and closed inserting variations on the theme. In this way, I felt that my intervention was more invasive, more decisive, and could gain the strength to transform a situation just as could happen in an alchemic reaction.

4.5.1 *The role of artifacts and the potential of boundary objects for the generation of new ideas*

Sissi decided to use totally different materials and techniques to create three air purifiers of those ten *Aspiring Aspirators* conceived by her, whose genesis is documented in a book, in a short animated film, in a multitude of drawings and intermediate objects that the artist created, and by the space of the atelier she constructed and lived in during her residence at the company.

The creation of new purifier designs, the construction of new prototypes and the re-occupation of the company space often violated the habits that the organizational population of prototypers was used to. As one of the prototypers said:

> Sissi used the drawings of our projects to do her freehand charcoal sketches, she made strange organic shapes above the geometric ones. For us the project drawing is everything, it is the basis of the work; to see that it was the basis of her work as well, but in a completely different way, was new and surprising for us.

This issue of reuse of designs, familiar tools for the members of the organization, exists not only for the "drawing" object, but also for some materials. Sissi used very different materials than those commonly present in the hood production and prototyping process, but also others found on site which she used in an unusual manner, giving them forms never thought of before at the company.

Through this complex and extended material production, the artist initiated a conceptual form of creation from which the people in the organization were to start for the construction of new interpretations and new ideas. The artist created artifacts full of meaning for her world and that of the company, and documented this process to take all of the phases into account. As the artist said:

> I had been asked to reflect on a new product and new thinking, and I found it fundamental, being part of my habitual way of working and thinking, to break down its parts, renaming them. [...] I wanted to show the phases of the creative process I was following, in which the artist, upon entering a new environment, takes possession of it, makes it hers, makes it become her home, her atelier, stimulates it, pours in her contents and all of her experience and

> thus begins to blend with it, to generate osmotic contamination and react with everything that surrounds it. [...] I did not create a product, but a way of thinking. I suggested a system in which ideas develop and can change inside of us.

The artist wanted to enter this process, change it and look at it from another viewpoint: Sissi produced new objects, modified existing ones, changed things' names, and recontextualized them based on her sensitivity and vision of the organization, providing her meaning to the company. This deep and visceral dialogue established during the period of residence could potentially go on infinitely thanks to the material documenting the work and the permanent exposure in the company premises of the three *Aspiranti Aspiratori* created.

As previously stated, it is complex to posit a parallel between the material production of the artist in a company and the boundary object, even in a case like this one where the long period of residence of the artist, together with the complexity of her production and the continuous interaction with the company, certainly made it possible to show how the production of the work of art can turn its attention to the company's production system and design process, and vice versa.

However, Sissi's work encourages and reflects on the opportunity that the artist's production, when it becomes a true boundary object, represents the occasion through which the communities in the company interact with each other, even once the artistic intervention is over, i.e. even in its absence.

It's interesting to note that the artist, questioned about her project, was able to analyze the definition of boundary objects, identifying as the boundary object not so much the intermediate artifacts or the three final *Aspiranti Aspiratori*, but the book published for the occasion:

> The *Aspiranti Aspiratori* represent more than pretexts. Perhaps more than anything, the book I produced can be classified as a boundary object. For me, writing is very important: I don't just write notes, I write narratives. I feel a strong need to transmit what I do, which probably comes from that archaic approach that from our childhood passes down stories and fables from which we derive our experiences, what we believe and how we identify ourselves. The story is thus an element that could not be lacking in the process of construction of the *Aspiranti Aspiratori*. [...] During the various phases of my work, I tried to conjecture the individuality to which they could be linked. To succeed, I sometimes put myself in the position of the individual who looked at

> the object, while other times I was on the side of the object that looked at the individual, with the goal of generating a reflection on the type of individuality.

It is interesting to note that for the artist the boundary object has the function of documenting the artistic intervention and explaining it through storytelling.

While the parallel with the *boundary object*, in the case of Sissi's work, has an interesting potential to be further explored, it is just as important to analyze how an artistic intervention of this type was able to generate so many passages of the boundary crossing, essential to share knowledge and to create the conditions for innovation. Retracing the steps of the boundary crossing, below we will illustrate how these different moments can be found in the process that led to the birth of *Aspiranti Aspiratori*:

- *Identification*. The encounter between the Elica prototypers and Sissi produced an attempt on their part to understand the artist's motivations, a curiosity to understand the reasons why she used certain materials and shapes, and to understand where the artist wanted to go with the presentation of her ideas on the product (air purifier). The encounter and the assistance in the artist's practical work provided by the prototypers implied a process of discussion and identification with their own work ("what am I, what is the artist, what are my practices, what are hers, what are my objects and what are hers"). The same thing happened for the artist with her atelier, where meetings took place that were open, casual, or structured as talks and workshops, in which practices and materials were discussed. Sissi says: "The employees played an active role: they could participate, intervene, help with their skills and initiate what can be considered an assembly line."
- *Coordination*. The objects (designs, prototypes) served to create a first channel of communication between the artist and the prototypers, to develop a provisional but common language, and thus to coordinate the respective activities in a certain sense.
- *Reflection*. In reference to *Aspiranti Aspiratori*, observing the product (air purifier) through the eyes of the artist and practically contributing to the creative work in her studio represent important moments to develop awareness of the fundamental differences that exist in the way of thinking and working of the groups involved (artist, pro-

totypers); this leads to people's capacity to see their daily work activities more and better. The Elica employees described these months of collaboration with the artist as an occasion for interaction with a world that was their own, but completely revisited. For her part, Sissi always maintained a dual perspective on her work: one oriented towards the world of art and the other to the world of the product.
- *Transformation*. The organizational space in which the artist was able to work on her idea, as already stated, was created ad hoc, inside the prototype laboratory, and renamed by Sissi herself as "Cubator," a singular name that immediately exemplifies its function. Although the artist's reasons and aim were not immediately clear to the people who already occupied that space, the "Cubator" contributed to breaking the routine by bringing something new to daily operations.

Thanks to Sissi's intervention at Elica, the artist's ideas regarding the presentation of *Aspiranti Aspiratori* inspired the creation in 2014 of a mirrored hood that in a certain sense recalls the *Reflector*. The artist thus left to the organization what she herself defines as a new "method of making" inspired by her very personal way of working, while the company contributed to the personal growth of the artist linked to the experience inside an organization. "I was greatly enriched, I learned to collaborate and work in a team; I visualized an unconscious method that I had inside me, but had not yet made explicit."

4.5.2 *The role of spaces*

As we have seen, the realization of *Aspiranti Aspiratori* included the creation of a dedicated space within the company's prototype area, the "Cubator." This represented much more than a simple atelier, since it aimed to be an artifact, a material reality in which the organizational population and the artist exchanged stimulus and communicated effectively. As the artist recounts:

> The decision to have an atelier within the company made my presence more acceptable and understandable, in addition to defining my role. The presence of a physical space allowed me to have an official, serious spot, and to be close to the prototypers. We were like classmates: they could enter my atelier and

> explore my world looking at it closely, and at the same time I could make use of their collaboration. We supported each other mutually, like true collaborators. I absolutely did not want them to see me as an intruder who, by sneaking into their studio, would only take what she needed for her work. Throughout the whole process I followed, what I wanted most was to give my work symbolic value, including through the act of renaming things. "Cubator," for example, was an important name that aimed to explain the meaning and value of my atelier: not a simple studio, but a place in which the artist reproduces herself and reworks the messages she receives from the outside.

The "Cubator" acts as an interspace, or a new place or revisitation of an existing place aimed at allowing for experimentation through the momentary suspension of usual norms. From each interspace new practices and processes can potentially be born that are applicable to other areas of organization. Despite its limited physical and temporal dimension, it continues to exist in the mind of the members of the organization, going well beyond the temporal parenthesis of the artistic intervention that generated it (Sköldberg *et al.*, 2016). In fact, in the case of *Aspiranti Aspiratori*, although Sissi is no longer present at the company, the prototypers have preserved the memory, that is still available in the documentation of the work produced (the three *Aspiranti Aspiratori*) and in the fact that Sissi's work was displayed in various public and private museum spaces, giving it recognition and a public dimension.

Many of the artifacts belonging to the various projects that different artists, in addition to Sissi, produced for Elica thanks to the FEC, are kept in the organization's space. The Foundation itself occupies these spaces in which the artists can intervene, thus upgrading the scope of creativity and innovation of the artistic interventions themselves. At Elica, artists can generate new spaces effectively also considering the fact that the company already recognizes the Foundation's place and legitimacy in the organization.

As regards the link with *interstitial spaces*, as already discussed in the theoretical introduction, in order for the objects produced by the artistic intervention to create the potential for the formation of these contexts of aggregation oriented towards innovation, it is necessary for the artistic interventions to become continuous to the point of making the encounters informal, but it is also necessary to recognize that the artists, curators and professionals of the art world can have a role as catalyzers of business, and not only artistic innovation. Sissi's "Cubator," considered in the complexity of the entire project, certainly planted the seed for the start of the material production of an artistic intervention able to at least potentially stimulate a spontaneous aggregation focused on innovation. Sissi was "in residence" for a long time and her philosophy lived in the company, remaining an artistic practice but merging with the rhythm of production.

Everything that *Aspiranti Aspiratori* produced – works of art, studies, drawings, publications, exhibits, etc. – remains "unique" and authorial as is typical of artistic production, but at same time its inclusion in the company, and the perfect integration of its processes, protracted for a long period of time, makes this project a candidate to become a new occasion for the generation of *interstitial spaces.*

4.6 The advantages of adopting the logic of artifacts and spaces

Having considered the theoretical approaches to artifacts and spaces, the advantages that the organization can find from introducing and managing artistic interventions from these perspectives always regard the motivational sphere of the individual. However, a part of the advantages refer to the growth and evolution required of the people management style must have, so that what we have analyzed so far is not only applied, but can reach even greater heights in its realization:

- *Empowerment in the process of generation of new ideas.* With a greater availability of moments in which art enters company spaces and a greater emphasis on the preservation and availability of the materials produced during the artistic interventions and their documentation, people can feel more autonomous and responsible in the ideational process, linked to the stimulus provided by the artistic interventions. The objects of art and their testimony could in fact, according to what has been said so far, be more numerous, distributed and accessible for the employees. Given this accessibility, the members of the organization, stimulated by art, could thus become the natural autonomous sponsors of new moments of knowledge exchange, generators of interpretations and renewals of processes and products.
- *Motivation linked to the rethinking of the layout and occasions for interaction.* This greater emphasis on the material production of artistic

interventions has the potential to change the layout of workplaces. Managerial literature has seen more "democratic" layouts (such as open spaces and revolving desks) ebb and flow, in terms of their positive or negative impact on motivation and employee performance. Working on artifacts, material production and documentation of artistic interventions has a new potential given that displaying these "objects," giving them a space, does not imply a direct intervention on people's daily work tools, and thus is not perceived with an immediate, more "utilitarian" intent of impact on the efficiency of work itself. Thanks to the reflections in this chapter, to the definition of "aesthetic" space that art can generate, we can add that of an "informal" space generated by art that has the potential to increase the motivation to produce new ideas thanks to the creation of a non-vertical way of accessing artifacts useful to stimulate the process of innovation.

- *Opportunity to spread a sense of responsibility and develop a diffused model of leadership.* When artistic interventions are managed based on the ideas presented in this chapter, one of the fundamental advantages for the company is that they represent the opportunity to train a model of diffused leadership and ensure that people who manage people have the opportunity to exercise a sense of responsibility in regard to the intervention and the results that it can produce. In fact, an artistic intervention requires strong sponsorship by senior management, but above all by individuals belonging to different levels of the organization, who can feel free and independent in proposing an investment of this type, whether they have to manage personnel training, or need to manage the ideational and innovation process. By producing artifacts, intervening in spaces and fully entering the knowledge management system in the company, an artistic intervention makes the initiative of the manager who promotes it visible, shareable between functions and professions, and continuous in time (given the ability of art to persist in organizational memory). Art gives the manager the opportunity that comes from "authorality," in the sense that the sponsor of the artistic interventions becomes the author of this important and recognizable intervention.

4.7 Managerial implications

We will now define the fundamental managerial challenges that a company should address to design and implement artistic interventions able to generate implications for the "realm" of artifacts, knowledge and innovation:

- *Boundary objects.* The same importance that materiality and cognition have in artistic interventions has been analyzed in terms of implications for management in Chapters 2 and 3. The conclusion of this chapter, we wanted to stress the managerial challenge of making the materials and artifacts produced though artistic interventions in companies of materials and of "boundary objects," artifacts close to boundary objects, with which various professional communities can identify, and that together with other artifacts, they can use in their communication, ideation, and prototyping processes. In order for this to happen, the investment by the organization should take place on different fronts: the first is that of designing an artistic intervention that, despite being unique and consistent with the artist's philosophy, is somehow able to include in its characteristics the features of the product, and the values or identity of the company, so as to stimulate new interpretations. This challenge is very complex because it implies preserving the authenticity of the artistic intervention, its possible distance from company routine, not jeopardizing the aesthetic nature, but at the same time finding areas of proximity and interaction with the company and the professional communities present in it. In addition to this balancing, the challenge lies in the choice of a policy of preservation and display of the objects, including intermediate objects, the works produced in the artistic interventions, and the documentation material, as in any company knowledge management project. This way, the material production of the artistic intervention can truly be perceived as being available to the members of the organization and becomes the location for an exchange of knowledge, a possibility to go beyond the boundaries represented by each individual's specialization, to develop new practices of integration of knowledge, new concepts and new ideas.
- *From formal to informal, to formal again.* Artistic interventions can have great potential for innovation of processes if they are transformed from sporadic activities in time and space for which the com-

pany management must reconstruct a context and sense each time, into activities that are present in the company more regularly. Such regularity reduces of the distances between the managerial world and that of art (positive for the processes of identification and for originality with respect to organizational routine). At the same time, this type of regularity generates greater informality of the use of art in companies, both in ideational and decision-making processes, giving greater legitimacy to artistic professions, as representing areas of competence able to catalyze innovation. The managerial challenge, in addition to making artistic interventions more pervasive, is thus to find a process through which concepts and ideas, generated by members and catalyzed by artists and curators, then become part of the company's character, and can enter into the official channels of preservation of company knowledge and its use.

- *Top management leadership*. Given the significance of the implications described above in terms of organization of artistic interventions, their pervasiveness and management for innovation purposes, it is essential for them to be able to accompany a leadership style by top management that we could define as "distributed." This means that the senior management may not only be the ones who decide on the introduction of the artistic interventions, but could also support the legitimation of the resources invested in the interactions with the artists (including prior to the actual project), contribute to the construction of a collective interpretation of the stimuli and artifacts that emerge from the artistic intervention, including through speeches and public interventions, ensuring that the ideas developed during the intervention find official channels of communication to be formalized. In order for this to happen, it is important to create a model of leadership in which the senior management can delegate the management of the various artistic projects to a lower level of organization, without giving up its function as the sponsor and without depriving the managers at lower organizational levels of the possibility of autonomy in sponsoring the design of an artistic intervention themselves (Antal, Debucquet and Frémeaux, 2017). This mix of delegation and direct presence in the project by the top management should guarantee the opportunity to work with artifacts and the informality of artistic interventions so as to make their impact more innovative and effective.

5 Competitive Advantage When Speaking of Art in Companies

In this chapter we will discuss the nature of the contribution of art to business performance, shedding light, on the one hand, on the legitimate need to measure the benefits that derive from an investment in art, and on the other, on the complexity with which this action of quantification should be developed. In the arguments proposed, through the analysis of various projects organized by the FEC, we will illustrate the need to consider the centrality of the person and an approach more oriented towards the relationship with all of the company's stakeholders, when there is a desire to understand the advantage that comes from investing in art. We will also summarize the main conclusions of two studies conducted in Italy with the goal of concretely measuring these benefits. Lastly, for the managerial implications, we will illustrate the fundamental steps to structure a project to measure the benefits produced by art for companies.

5.1 Art in companies and its contribution to competitive advantage: the dilemma of measurability

As happens for many other activities that a company carries out, for artistic interventions as well the debate on the measurability of the benefits that can be produced is very heated. Research and collective opinion have made the discussion about both the actual possibility of carrying out such a measurement, and the real need for it.

As regards the possibility to carry out such a calculation, it is easy to understand that, as for all intangible investments, a numerical quantification of the impact that artistic interventions can have on individual and company performance is very complex. This is a debate that can coincide with the difficulty to quantify the return of training, to determine the quality of the organizational climate and to measure leadership styles in companies. For these activities it is impossible to produce a single indicator, a number that is representative, since the phenomenon is very broad and has implications that touch the individual, the way they perceives their work, and their relationship with co-workers and the company itself. It is important to stress that, despite this difficulty, organizational sciences have focused on the development of models to quantify the impact of investments increasingly linked to people's skills and innovation. This has been made possible especially by conducting "measurements" through a multiplicity of approaches, that are both quantitative and qualitative, using methodologies and tools made available by scientific research and not by intuition or managerial practice.

On the other hand, as regards the advisability of carrying out this quantification and whether it is correct to do so, we should reflect on all of the contributions that managerial literature has provided with respect to the improper use that at times is made of performance indicators in companies and all of the distortions that can be found each time we try to measure – apparently objectively – people's performance or behavior.

Numerical indicators seem to be essential in the rhetoric of "persuasion" that is used in companies to obtain the budget and sponsorship for a project, but it is also true that awareness is increasingly spreading that intangible projects require an approach to measurement that is more complex, and that the use made of those estimates must be considered carefully in order to guide future decisions.

Aware of these debates, we focused on the indirect advantages that investments in art produce for companies, in particular on mechanisms through which art can support a company's performance in terms of innovation, rather than on final indicators of results. In the analysis we conducted, together with the mechanisms, we also shed light on the factors on which company management should reflect and insist, in order to achieve those advantages.

Consistent with this approach, more oriented towards understanding how art can influence the final business result, the *method* that is illustrated in this book is exclusively oriented towards thinking of the use of art as a possibility to change the nature of relationships with all of the company's stakeholders and not as an isolated investment from which to demand an immediate effect on economic-financial performance. Art can make a company more innovative by increasing the ability to establish active collaboration, influence and rapidly respond to and welcome stakeholders who, in different capacities (due to their power, the opportunity to offer a partnership, or the rights they hold), can offer ideas that are to be preserved, managed and capitalized. In this sense, investment in art is not only philanthropic and ethical, but above all has a business purpose; it regards the competitiveness and sustainability of the company because art works on the openness and involvement of that system of actors that can support the process of continuous renewal and improvement.

In this regard, it is important to cite the project *The Wishful Map* by the artist Pietro Ruffo (2015/16), divided into four editions produced for: Angelini Acraf Spa, *Il Sole 24 Ore* Business School, Banca di Credito Cooperativo di Bellegra, and Euler Hermes Italia in the Allianz insurance group. Each of the four workshops studied and analyzed on a global scale the core business of the respective organizations, working abstractly to transform the data and main elements that emerged during the training days into shapes and colors. This process allowed all of the participants to create concept maps in which new elements are added to classic geographic references, and the company's data and values are translated into symbols and returned in the form of works of art. Like other interventions organized by the FEC for companies and institutions, Ruffo's project has the peculiarity of having been produced in multiple editions and proposed to different clients, specifically three companies and a class of students at a business school. The opportunity to "repeat" the project, adapting it each time to the stories and needs of the different interlocutors, demonstrates that with the assistance of art it is possible to engage in a dialogue with different stakeholders even with an artist who repeats a project, always adjusted to the relevant context, obtaining effective and original results each time. The necessary condition for this to happen is respect for the peculiar characteristics and the history of the groups involved.

All of this helps understand that contemporary art can be considered a passkey that opens the doors of any institution or business to thinking and reflection, even before action. This is a necessary condition to trigger a process that leads to innovating, or to a new way of seeing and approaching a particular issue.

For example, take *The Wishful Map #4* (2016) created for Euler Hermes Italia. In this intervention, to invite the participants to reflect on the concept of risk, a notion that distinguishes the company's business and identity, Pietro Ruffo started from a very particular projection of the world, created for the first time in 1745 by the French astronomer Joseph-Nicholas Delisle. The projection of the world was divided into twenty-four segments and each participant was asked to work on a portion of the world and choose a country to analyze based on the five main factors for studying risk assessment: economic risk, financial risk, commercial risk, political risk and business environmental risk. On their portion of the world, each participant thus indicated their analysis translated into colors, and at the bottom of each segment the symbolic characters indicating the currency used in the analyzed country were drawn. In *The Wishful Map #1* and *#3* (2015, 2016), the artist had worked, respectively, with a pharmaceutical company and a cooperative bank, each time personalizing the concept of map and the theme on which to reflect to create it (from the shapes of the company logo to the money to fund a potential local business). Lastly, in *The Wishful Map #2 - Pocket Museum* (2015) the concept of map acted as an object through which the students in the Master in Economics and Management of Art and Cultural Heritage at the *Il Sole 24 Ore* Business School, reflected on the political and cultural strategies of management of a museum.

In the *Condominium* project by Margherita Moscardini, created for the pharmaceutical company MSD Italia and repeated for a class of students (2012/13) it is also possible to find a structure similar to that just described. In this case, the artist's research is centered on the relationships existing between image, architecture and landscape understood as context: through her work, the artist investigated the connection between a place and the social reality that permeates it, reflecting on the continuous transformations to which the space is subject. In these interventions, considering the utopian models adopted in business environments, Moscardini started from the Crespi d'Adda Village to ask the participants (managers, functionaries and students alike), as well as herself, what would a residential model be like today that meets the needs of the employees of a large company, and what elements and characteristics distinguish it. This case also represents a project aimed at a broad community of stakeholders, whose general structure is repeatable, proposing through art a theme relevant for society, for the life of the company, and also for the single individual.

As in the examples already cited, the FEC aims to propose an original project each time, fully respecting the artist's philosophy and the value dimension of each interlocutor, that can be repeatable in some way, so that it becomes a means of communication common to different stakeholders. This method of relationship not only allows the FEC to have a code of dialogue that is consistent with the stakeholders, but allows the different interlocutors to feel like a part of a network in which contemporary art acts as a bond. The bond is well defined from the standpoint of its identity and its work, since the FEC, as already defined in the initial chapters, prefers giving space to artists and projects which investigate the major political and social themes that strongly impact people's daily lives, but in a very close relationship between micro and macro history.

In the coming sections, we will explore a view of art understood as an investment able to develop performance in companies, by promoting the centrality of the person to put them in a condition to produce innovation.

Subsequently, we will analyze the theme of "quantification" and the measurability of the contribution of art to business performance through the analysis of two studies conducted at the Catholic University of Milan, to then examine other examples of projects carried out by the FEC. In closing, we will suggest an investigation "canvas" that managers can follow in order to better understand the benefits of artistic interventions.

5.2 Before competitive advantage: the centrality of people and the community of stakeholders

In the spring of 2017, the *Journal of Business Ethics* published a *symposium* on the issue of *Art, Ethics and the Promotion of Human Dignity*, hosting articles on the theme of art and its contribution to the possibility to construct and increase a sense of dignity of organizational life, in the broader discussion linked to ethics and well-being in the performance of work.

Together with the other recent international publications cited in this book, this symposium also demonstrates the crucial nature of the introduction of art into businesses and how art can be the bearer of a deeper ethical meaning that helps recognize this state of dignity in individuals, where dignity can be summarized with the concept of recognition and appreciation of one's value. Art is identified by the authors of the symposium as one of the most effective ways to reach dignity, because in art people can find the reflection and realization of their selves and their autonomy (Bostrom, 2009).

This opportunity that art opens to the recognition of value and the possibilities for individuals is the basis of the processes analyzed to this point: from the opportunity for a renewal of the identity of a company's employees to the occasion to learn effectively, to that of feeling able to modify and produce artifacts that inhabit the space, with the goal of putting into practice new ideas and novel decision-making processes.

At this point it becomes almost automatic to associate that approach with dignity through art, i.e. the official and substantive recognition of the value of people and the relationships between the business and its employees. However, it is essential to also consider it a way of relating to all stakeholders, so that the network of relationships of a business or institution that invests in art can truly turn out to be an occasion for full spectrum innovation. A network of relationships based on the recognition of the value of all of the stakeholders can in fact be experienced as a network based on psychological security and the possibility of the actors who inhabit it to express themselves.

To identify these stakeholders for an organization is not simple, given the vastness of the definitions present in the literature on this theme. Miles (2017), through the analysis of approximately six hundred definitions of the theory of stakeholders, has developed a classification into four types (not alternatives, but that overlap), in which stakeholders can be classified as follows:

- The individuals and groups that can have the ability to influence the performance of organizational activities and that have a strategy to exercise this influence. This category of stakeholder has the power to support or hinder the achievement of a business's goals.
- The individuals and groups that can claim a right, or a title to the activities of the business, but that do not have the power to force it to respect this right, since it has ethical and social roots rather than legal and economic ones.
- The individuals and groups that can collaborate with the business in activities in which value is created for both partners. The potential of this collaboration goes beyond the ability of the actors to influence the company's activities and their possibility to claim rights in that regard.

- The individuals and groups whose activities are strongly influenced by the company but that do not have the opportunity to modify the course of action, giving rise to an asymmetric relationship.

This classification shows that stakeholders can be classified based on the coercive power they exercise on the company, the resources they share, and the interest they can sustain in regard to the organization itself. Here, however, we do not want to define the exact categories of stakeholders for different companies, since each company or institution must identify its own. What we want to do is affirm that contemporary art can act as a medium through which it is possible to construct a relationship based on dignity with the company's different stakeholders. This is a fundamental step to address, before any measurement or quantification of the impact of art on business results, since it is a correct and effective step in and of itself, and as a consequence, for the company as well.

For example, think of how Danilo Correale structured the project *The Game - una partita di calcio a tre porte* and how this allowed the companies involved and their employees to find a new occasion to appreciate their value and that of their reflections, even in a moment of delicate transformation at the companies. This intervention demonstrates that the participating companies established a relationship with the employees based on the recognition of their identities and contributions. But it is not only companies that have had this occasion for a relationship with one of their stakeholders: the artist also had the opportunity to implement her philosophy, entering into a relationship with a non-profit foundation and with commercial enterprises, enriching the range of subjects with which to collaborate and through which to reflect on the practices linked to her work. In turn, the FEC developed yet another opportunity to interface with the artistic community, the training company that supported the project, the local community of the employees involved and the companies to which they belong. This entire composite network of stakeholders gathered around a complex and sophisticated contemporary art project, laying the foundation for the identification of the actors involved as groups that work based on a principle of recognition of the contributions of others, without ulterior motives.

To cite an additional example of an artistic intervention organized by the FEC, we can refer to *Filming the process #1* and *#2* by Marinella Senatore (2011, 2012), an artist whose research is based above all on the concept of participation, and for exactly this reason, she often involves entire communities in the creative process, making the public a co-author of her works. *Filming the process #1*, conceived for Biotronik Italia Spa, aims to incentivize cohesion and cooperation among participants through the use of film practices, the mode of expression chosen for its choral structure. The artist counted on the ability to collaborate and develop a working group, where the areas of intervention of the single members and the possibility for contamination between the individual languages and skills are managed in favor of a collective thought process and a shared goal. This intervention represents a good example of how contemporary art can be the platform around which to construct the relationships with one's stakeholders and to work indirectly on future success. As the HR Director of Biotronik Italia Spa said, referring to this experience:

> In contemporary art, as in work in companies, the exchange of knowledge, constant study and research are fundamental to obtain positive results. Moreover, the idea of introducing art into training projects seemed perfect for us due also to the ethical aspect that it brings to the operation: just as Biotronik aims to improve human quality of life, developing and producing technological excellence to combat cardiovascular diseases, art, with its methods and contents, gives importance and centrality to people.

Having defined this fundamental intermediate step, dedicated to the centrality of art for the dignity of people and groups of stakeholders, in the next section we will illustrate the data of two studies on the question of quantification of the advantages of art for business life.

5.3 Competitive advantage: can it be quantified?

Between 2015 and 2016, the Catholic University of Milan, with the support of AXA Art and Banca Intesa Sanpaolo, conducted a research project on the corporate collections present in Italy with the goal of mapping them and presenting some inferences regarding which aspects of governance can lead to greater benefits for both the collection and the company that manages it. The study involved a sample of 160 corporate collections that responded to the questionnaire administered by the University's research team. The FEC, together with other entities cited in this chapter, participated in the investigation and the focus groups to validate the questionnaire.

Although a collection represents only one form of investment in art, certain research data is cited to illustrate an initial approach to the definition and quantification of the benefits that art can bring to business life. The most interesting aspect of the research is to see what indicators were considered to understand the impact of the presence and management of the collection, and how these indicators were measured. Below we list the indicators which illustrate that, even in quantification, it is necessary to adopt a multi-stakeholder perspective that considers the benefits of art for businesses, due to the ability to meet the needs of stakeholders and for the world of art.

As indicators of the benefits of art in companies, the following were considered:

- The perceived business performance, in terms of capacity for innovation, to satisfy clients, and to reach economic and financial goals, measured with a Likert scale taken from the literature.
- The quality of the organizational environment, in this case considered as the environment for learning and innovation, measured through the Likert scale.
- The quality of the company's image and reputation, also measured with a Likert scale.

As regards the artistic quality of the collection, the actions to preserve, store and value the art, were evaluated, for example regarding:

- The presence of an advisory committee for the evaluation of new acquisitions.
- The presence of an updated archive and catalogue.
- The number of loans and purchases made in the last three years.
- The range of activities in which the collection is used, from communication and event organization to more sophisticated activities of artistic residence and training projects for the employees of the company and of other companies.

As can be seen, despite addressing the area of quantification, the study focused on a variety of dimensions, seeking to identify which collections and thus which companies and foundations had a positive performance on at least some of these indicators.

Out of the sample of 160 corporates, approximately 30% form a group of collections that can be defined as "virtuous," when we consider their ability to view art and the life of the company in an integrated manner. These collections, more decisively than the rest of the sample, always grasped the contribution that art has made to business performance (the collections evaluated the contribution of art to: performance, with an average score of 3.2 out of 4, compared to the average score of 2 out of 4 for the other collection groups); the company's reputation (these collections evaluated the contribution of art to the company's reputation with an average score of 3.1 out of 4, compared to the average of 2 out of 4 of the other collection groups); and the environment for learning and innovation (average score of 2.7 out of 4, compared to the average of 2 out of 4 of the other collection groups). Moreover, this 30% also showed the best results as regards the artistic vitality of the collection, having an advisory committee more often (45% of the organizations in this group have an advisory committee, compared to the complete absence of such a committee in the other collection groups), showing that the collection grows (70% of the organizations declared at least one recent acquisition, with respect to the absence of acquisitions in the other organizations), and having a broader range of activities, not only linked to exhibits but also including residences. The study also shed light on which configuration of corporate collections is correlated with these results, and it was found that the organizations with the best performance have teams dedicated to the collection, formed by experts in the art sector and personnel within the company, who manage and make use of the collections by always maintaining a high level of socialization with the rest of the company's population. In these environments, a strong link remains with the company management (where the interest for art comes from) and there is at least a minimal inclination to adopt managerial practices regarding the budget and measurement of results.

This data highlights a possibility to "measure" the advantages deriving from the presence of art in companies and also to connect it to certain organizational configurations. It is important to specify that this measurement was made possible by implementing a research strategy that includes data coming from surveys, collecting objective data regarding the characteristics and dynamics of the collection, and that the connection with the configuration derives from a quantitative analysis of an exploratory nature by which it is possible to affirm a correlation, but not a causal link. This specification is necessary to understand that establishing the certainty of a causal link between an intangible investment and business performance is an activity that requires constancy and multiple approaches.

To corroborate this idea, there is a second study conducted at the Catholic University (Ligasacchi, 2017), where again quantitative and qualitative sources are implemented together to establish the contribution of art to competitive advantage. In the study, some balance sheet indicators (EBITDA/sales, ROS, ROA, and Debt/Equity Ratio) were analyzed for 124 companies having corporate collections, over the period from 2013 to 2015. All of the indicators were compared to the average in the sector so as to determine if these companies, in the three years considered, had better, worse, or equal performance compared to the average in the sector. The analysis of the data, however, allowed for discovering much more.

In general terms, the indicators found that, in the three-year period examined, more than 50% of the companies that invested in art obtain results that were positive per se, and also obtained better results than the average in their sectors. But the most interesting thing was the processing of these results in the qualitative interviews, illustrating two fundamental and complementary points: on the one hand, the need to have more indicators linked to the specific business (not only those directly regarding economic-financial performance); and on the other, the importance of not using a numerical quantification at all costs, but of focusing on the implementation of a more complete and open managerial approach that strongly orients the organization towards innovation and lateral thinking. As defined by two of those interviewed, who are experts responsible for corporate collections in multinational companies, speaking of the measurability and quantification of the advantage that comes from investment in art:

> In my view, it would be useful to have on the one hand indicators that assess the health of the collection, and on the other, indicators for at least four or five managerial areas with detailed data [...] for example, there should be specific indicators to quantify the benefits for employees, for the quality of the work environment, and perhaps to associate it with individual performance. [...]

> There could be very many indicators, each business should identify its areas and codify its indicators and then establish the relationships between them.

This shows not only that numerous indicators are necessary, but that they would also represent an opportunity for a more general evaluation of the managerial approach followed, considering the investment in art as a fundamental tool to orient the organization towards innovation:

> The companies that dedicate attention, financial resources, and personnel to investment in art are companies of a certain type. I believe that investment in art represents more an indicator of the ability of some entrepreneurs and managers to think "out of the box," and to look further and not only be concentrated on business in a traditional manner.

It is certainly important to think in terms of return on investment, but it is just as necessary to evaluate investment in art as a whole in order to conduct the measurement in the best way possible. Moreover, each company should personalize its indicators respecting its own history and priorities. Lastly, the investment in art should be evaluated in the context of a broader investment that the company makes on the quality of the work environment, the quality of its image, the relationship with local interlocutors and with all of the relevant segments of the population.

An example of this approach can be discussed by commenting on *Mini Italia Kobra*, a performance conceived by Marcello Maloberti for E-STRAORDINARIO for Kids (2014) and produced together with fifty children of Elica employees. E-STRAORDINARIO for Kids represents, in general, the introduction of art into human resources management practices, and in particular, into the company welfare system, since it implies the provision of a service to the employees that touches the organization of their family life and their inclusion in the relevant community. In particular, *Mini Italia Kobra* involved a visit to the "Bruno Molajoli" city picture gallery of Fabriano, where the maximum expression of Italy's cultural heritage was highlighted, followed by a practical workshop in which the participating children made special "backpacks" produced with cardboard boxes decorated with collages of mixed images, typical of the Italian collective imagination. At the end of the workshop, the performance was held in the historic center of the city: a procession that enlivened the streets and squares in which the children, accompanied by the Fabriano music band, walked with the backpacks/archives they had created, carrying a flag more than twenty meters long, decorated with the national colors and a white and red checked texture, typical of Italian tablecloths. The activity represented a moment of reflection on Italian cultural heritage, regarding both its "high" history and its popular traditions, a powerful bond and element of identity that cuts across all generations.

This type of expansion of the use of art to other practices beyond training, such as, in this case, to the construction of the identity and values of a place and the life-work balance of the employees of an organization, is one of the first signs that indicate art as the platform with which a company broadens how it manages people, processes and stakeholders. It is clear that a real quantification of the benefits becomes even more challenging, since it should succeed in considering all of these multiple dimensions and values that are difficult to measure. In light of that complexity, in the next section we propose a model through which it is possible to plausibly investigate the benefits of art.

5.4 Implications for a multi-method approach to understand the benefits of contemporary art in companies

Given the considerations presented above, we illustrate below some points that can constitute the phases and guidelines to conduct a research project on the benefits of investments in art for companies, recalling that the choice of research method depends on the goal to be pursued.

5.4.1 *Preliminary analysis (generally through interviews and document analysis)*

The preliminary analysis usually involves the senior management and a group of directors and employees from the areas considered key to understand the impact of art in companies. The interviews with the top management and ownership have the goal of understanding if and how investment in art fits into a broader strategy of the organization and which areas it touches in particular. According to the approach taken in this book, although each company or institution should carry out this type of a reflection in a very personalized manner, there are some indispensable areas – such as those of training, knowledge management and innovation, and organizational identity and values – that should always be included and investigated in the analysis. The interviews should also be useful to preliminary define, for each strategic area, result indicators that will then be validated and discussed in the subsequent phases.

5.4.2 *Data collection through quantitative tools*

Quantitative analysis can certainly be carried out: the data sources, collection strategy and structure of the investigation depend on its goal. By way of example, we will briefly cite three activities that can be carried out, recalling that these are summary descriptions, and that for each, it is necessary to reflect on the requirements that each tool requires and the structure of the investigation:

- If we want to monitor the impact (or some relationships) between investment in art, the organizational environment and identity, it would be advisable to include in the usual surveys on the environment a series of specific questions to be collected over a number of years (also trying to define a moment "zero" for the collection that acts as a dividing point in the analysis). The survey is also useful to investigate the nature of the relationship with the company's stakeholders - the local community, in particular - to which part of the survey would be administered.
- If the focus is on training and individual and group learning, and there is a need to establish causal relationships with the artistic intervention, it would be advisable to organize some experiments with different training "classrooms."
- If the focus is on understanding the financial return of an investment in art, it is also possible to use secondary data from the company's financial statements and HRM database, recalling the importance of connecting these dimensions, taking into account the multiple factors that can influence business performance and the need for a longitudinal design. The secondary data can also come from the use and analysis of sources outside of the company, as can happen for the investigation of the evolution of the company's image.

5.4.3 *Collection of evidence through qualitative tools*

An exploratory investigation could be very useful to understand how art can influence process innovation, as the literature on this subject is still limited. In addition to the theme of innovation, that is more direct for the company, we propose the possibility to use a qualitative approach to investigate the aesthetic experience of employees, artists and other stakeholders, according to the principles illustrated in Chapter 3. To investigate the aesthetic experience, we usually use direct and indirect questions regarding what is perceived, or we ask for comments on significant events, giving the possibility to draw and photograph one's own feelings (Jones, 1996). More in detail, it is necessary to select the available tools, focusing attention on recognizing the aesthetic experience, that is, the transposition from the experience to its representation, from aesthetics to intellect, and from the members of the organization to the researcher.

From a general point of view, the implications linked to the choice of the method of measuring the benefits of investments in art are important, because reflecting on the measurability of this investment can give the company the opportunity to rethink its strategy, attempting to formulate new indicators (or to look more carefully at those available). Moreover, it could be the opportunity to more critically address the theme of the measurability of performance of any investment, especially if intangible, and understand the need to add in-depth qualitative analysis to quantification. Therefore, addressing this theme could be a true drive of innovation for the company, for the way it conceives its goals and for its relationships with stakeholders.

Contemporary art in companies generates a challenge for managers and a provocation for their leadership style. It may also generate a rift between employees and the company to then be mended. It is able to put the entire organizational model to the test. It succeeds in doing all of this with a perspective that looks to the future and that sets the goal of renovation and regeneration for the company. But this is conditional upon a method being developed and applied with constancy, as described to this point.

6 Artistic Interventions and the Covid-19 Pandemic

6.1 Introduction to this new "pandemic" chapter

We published the Italian version of this book in 2018, two years before the COVID-19 pandemic hit the world and before our private and working lives had to change even more radically than before. Already in 2018, organizations had been living in challenging times, times considered as fractured and deserving to be recomposed. Three years ago, management scholars were already focusing their attention on the need to find alternative ways to work and to experience our lives in the workplace, having collected evidence of the ineffectiveness and harmfulness of traditional management styles (Carlucci and Schiuma, 2018).

Now, it can be said that the situation has become even more complicated for everyone, and for people at work in particular. The pandemic has brought massive challenges to companies and changes have had to be implemented in order to reorganize processes, and very often, to rethink the strategic positioning and the very existence of a firm (McKinsey Report, 2021). In this context, one of the major challenges has been that of managing the physical absence of people in the workplace, or the fact that some of them were present physically, while others were working from another location through their laptops. This absence, or half-presence, has changed the way we consider our identity as professionals, what the boundaries are between our personal and private life, what the role of the technology is for our life and what we consider positive performance or fairness, in a workplace where we do not go and we do not interact with others. And this is to mention only a few of the issues and open concerns the pandemic has brought to working life (Gerdeman, 2021).

The question about what artistic interventions could do or not do in this scenario is particularly meaningful. In the 2018 edition of this book, we tried, as authors with very diverse backgrounds (from Management and Hard Sciences, to Art History and Curatorship) to analyze the case of the FEC, to understand how its way of approaching artistic interventions could contribute to the discussion on living the workplace. In that edition, we aimed to convey different messages both about a method, the way the foundation had decided to organize and produce artistic interventions, and about the many issues that those artistic interventions could raise in the workplace.

Regarding this method, we underlined for instance how the FEC aimed to participate in a broader way in the life and approach of the artists involved, by asking them to spend time in the companies through micro-residencies, by amply supporting their work, beyond the interventions in the company setting. An effort was made to involve museums and local institutions in the exhibition and production of their artworks generated by their interventions, together with the production of catalogues and artist books. Mainly, we wanted to highlight how the intention of the artistic interventions that were organized was to be integrated into the companies' life and processes, participating in discussions about company's identity, organizational learning and potentiality for innovation.

At the time of the Italian edition, to elaborate on the topics of discussion that, in our view, the artistic interventions produced by the FEC raised, we analyzed them in the light of the existing literature on arts and business (Schiuma, 2011), artistic interventions and learning (e.g. Berthoin Antal, 2013), and arts and organizational aesthetics (Strati, 1999). This back and forth between the analysis of the interventions through interviews with the artists, the involved companies and the FEC itself, brought us to develop four areas of discussion: i) artistic interventions and organizational identity; ii) artistic interventions and learning in the workplace; iii) artistic intervention and innovation; and iv) the impacts of artistic interventions.

While preparing this 2021 edition of the book, we are again in a different situation from 2018. However, by comparing the literature on arts and business and on arts-based methods published in the last three years, the challenges that scholars have pointed out are not very different. In our view, these challenges have been going in the direction of re-stressing the absolute importance of: prioritizing the abolishment of the boundaries among professions and knowledge domains within organizations, and between organizations and the field of art; considering the need for a more ethical, slow and collective view of the abilities artistic interventions can develop, respecting employees' feelings and more broadly their aesthetic experience of the workplace; and defending a broader view of the notion of impact and performance, for the contribution of arts to business and for business performance itself (Formica, 2020).

The FEC has not stopped working during the pandemic, producing one artistic intervention (*Gentile come un ritratto*, Matteo Fato, 2020) and preparing and organizing a second one (*Pelusa (Fluff)*, Jorge Satorre, 2021), re-affirming its commitment to the arts, in a situation where physical contact and the relationship among employees and artists is limited by necessary social distancing and by the partial presence of people in the workplace.

Considering such an unexpected situation, the possibility to translate this book offered the opportunity to add this new chapter that could analyze the latest "pandemic" artistic interventions in the light of more recent literature on the topic. While analyzing the latest interventions, we have taken this opportunity to connect them to the other artistic interventions developed between 2018 and 2021 that were not covered in the Italian edition of this book. The "pandemic" interventions certainly have their own character and peculiarities, however, they can be related to other meaningful activities conducted in the past, and not yet analyzed, due to their approach and meaning.

In this new chapter, we will analyze FEC's artistic interventions, by making reference to three topics in the current literature on the relationship between arts and the workplace: 1) the boundaries between art and business, as separated/integrated disciplines and systems within the organization; 2) the role of a more ethical, wise and aesthetic view of employees and their behaviors at the workplace; and 3) the importance of considering the impact of artistic interventions in a wider and not only instrumental way.

In order to write this new chapter, the authors discussed their point of view on the different artistic interventions and on the available literature. In addition, the artists Matteo Fato, Jorge Satorre, Elena Mazzi, Patrick Tuttofuoco and Bianco-Valente were interviewed to better clarify the traits of their artistic approach and how it could be interpreted in the light of the literature of reference, and, especially for the first two, about how their artistic interventions and their artistic intent could be understood in light of the pandemic. During the interview, it was particularly important to ask the artists about their relationship with the employees during the artistic interventions, in order to recall salient episodes.

As this book itself is a way of integrating knowledge domains, while discussing the latest artistic interventions in light of management and education literature about arts-based methods, the appendix has been enriched with pictures of the cited interventions and their technical descriptions.

6.2 Arts and business again? Artistic interventions as a platform for the integration of different disciplines

At the beginning of his book, in order to make the case about the importance of integrating humanities and scientific knowledge (in particular business knowledge) in the workplace and in the wider society, Formica says: "If the defining quality of humanities is the expression of the human condition by mood and feeling, calling into place all the senses, evoking both order and disorder, then the need for business to exercise the epigenetic rules of human nature to bias innovation, learning and choice has never been greater" (2020: 8). According to this perspective, arts and humanities, when considered as integrated with business thinking, and not as separated disciplines, could lead to a more rounded consideration of individuals, encompassing not only their rationality, but also their intuition, feelings and non-linear thinking.

Artistic interventions in the workplace have been widely referred to in these terms. When integrated in organizational life, they have shown their power to stimulate a different way of considering and tackling issues and of experiencing the organizational environment. This power includes a more comprehensive view of the human experience and contribution to the workplace (e.g. Berthoin Antal and Straus, 2013). This appeal by Formica to the importance of the integration between humanities, arts and business in the workplace recalls what two important reviews on the topic of artistic interventions highlighted in 2018. The first review to be mentioned is a quantitative one by Ferreira (2018), collecting 137 articles on the topic of artistic interventions published in refereed scientific journals from 1973 through 2015. We cite it here because the possibility to run a bibliometric analysis on a such a number of articles, analyzing the main authors, journals and network of co-citation, emphasizes the idea that artistic interventions might constitute a structured academic field; a field where this interdisciplinary approach, involving humanities- and business-centered knowledge, has been developed in academia. When considering the mirroring of this integration process in the workplace, Carlucci and Schiuma (2018), in their qualitative review on the power of arts for business, have stressed the fact that 21st century management can no longer rely on logical, consequential and rational thinking to face the challenge of an increasingly complex world. A new form of management should include the consideration of employees' emotions, feelings and energy, by managing organizations' emotive, ethical and experiential characteristics and integrating them into business processes. In this light, artistic interventions can bring all these dimensions to the workplace, challenging the view of the physical organizational spaces and equipment and triggering a new way of looking at problems and issues.

Thus, it could be possible to say that the new emergency has pushed the need for this integration even further and has provoked further thinking in the field of artistic interventions. The works by the artists Matteo Fato (2020) and Jorge Satorre (2021) show a way through which the approach of the artists could introduce in the company setting this integration between art and management and this broader consideration of employees' participation in business life, through their whole person, and not only in a rational way.

The work by Matteo Fato, *Gentile come un ritratto*, was carried out at the Elica plant in Castelfidardo in 2020, when in Italy social distancing and restrictions for accessing private and public places were still very strong and forced Italian companies to manage their workforce partially through physical presence, where possible, and partially online (when safety restrictions so required). In this artistic intervention, Fato decided to realize a collective painting, by giving up his authorship to start a collective operation, where about 150 employees were invited to leave their mark on a single canvas. Fato's intervention did not include only the involvement of employees in the collective painting. As an integral part of his own stand as a painter, Fato installed his studio on the shop floor of the company, recreating an atelier with an easel, which he conceived as a sculpture, a part of his artistic work, aimed at interacting with the production space of the plant. In addition, in order to challenge his own usual practice of painting solo and in silence, Fato decided to encounter each employee involved, one by one, in full respect for social distancing rules, to discuss his work with them and what was about to happen, before the employees left their mark on the canvas. The installation of the painters' equipment on the shop floor, the willingness to establish a conversation about the artistic intervention, the pandemic, and the company, right before the artistic act of painting, are all ways through which art creates an "interspace"' as we have already highlighted in Chapter 3 (Berthoin Antal and Strauß, 2013). This interspace allows for a momentary and effective suspension of the boundaries between art and working business life, pushing employees to perceive their usual space in a different way. Having lived through the restrictions of the pandemic, after experiencing social distancing and online working, we can all imagine the power of being back in the company spaces, individually, and seeing them changed with a "studio" installed within them, and an artist willing to talk with us about painting. As Matteo Fato explained, when commenting on the installation of the "studio":

> To me the installation of my painting space is extremely important; to me to prepare the space is like to start generating the artwork. These spaces are thought to host the artwork in the best way. I proceeded in this way also in this artistic intervention, where I re-created a painting studio; and to me, recreating the creative space is already an artwork with which to interact. The place and the people you paint with change the painting and the perceptions that I and others have of the painting itself.

This quote, in the authors' view, communicates how, especially during the pandemic, intervening on the company spaces could push for a more emotions-based consideration of the employees' life, and could bring them to consider the artistic gesture as something that can be co-located spatially and metaphorically with the business processes.

Jorge Satorre has also organized his artistic intervention by working on company spaces and artifacts and by listening to the stories of the company employees. The history of this artistic intervention is peculiar, since it has been organized and partially produced so far during alternating phases of restrictions for the pandemic, and it will be completed this year, in 2021. Jorge Satorre, with *Pelusa (Fluff)* (2021), wanted to work on different aspects of the company spaces and objects, and with the storytelling of the employees. It has to be noted that his artistic intervention has been carried in the Elica Mexico plant of Querétaro, with FEC having the opportunity to visit sometimes, discussing with a curator on the site, Francesco Pedraglio, and conducting the curatorial and operational work also remotely from Fabriano, in Italy. The Mexico plant was chosen to metaphorically integrate into the artistic interventions program of the FEC the western part of Elica company, which has not yet had the chance to be included in this kind of activities. While visiting the plant multiple times, Satorre was struck by different aspects, which he then believed could be relevant with respect to his own poetry. His starting point is different from that of Matteo Fato, since Satorre's approach is rooted in the investigation of the dichotomy between artisanal and artistic production and in addressing the paradox of instrumentality and freedom, and of subjectivity and standardization in the duality of craftsmanship and art. In addition, he was interested in the Italian "*Microstorie*" movement (Einaudi, 1981-1991), a historiographic, political and aesthetic practice "whose interest is to not sacrifice the individual to mainstream generalization (...) since small hints or individual cases could be revelatory of more general phenomena" (Lanaro, 2011:7).

Drawing on his poetry, the artist was attracted by a room, renamed by the employees "the dark room," a company storage area where the exhausted molds for the cooker hoods were kept, once they could not be used anymore. In addition, he was surprised to observe how the system of bottom-up suggestions, driven by Lean management principles (Spear and Bowen, 1999), encouraged employees to provide the management with ideas for continuous improvement and to transform those ideas into quick graphical representations. Satorre thus decided to produce 19 engravings from his drawings of the molds and then to organize a workshop to listen to the employees' ideas and support them in transforming their ideas into engravings as well. *Pelusa (Fluff)* has also working on the company equipment and spaces, this time trying to unveil rooms and materials that were meant to be forgotten, transforming them into engravings, which once exhibited, will again change the conception of the space on the part of the employees. In addition, this artistic intervention has been working on the idea of valuing the bottom-up participation of the employees, though not in an instrumental way, but by transforming employees' micro-stories into a form of art. An aspect that must not be overlooked is the great complexity of this intervention, carried out while facing the extreme difficulties of the pandemic, with the artist and the employees being able to meet, talk, touch and move materials and equipment, while accepting to be on the shop floor for a longer time than they expected, and by alternating presence and absence (of the employees and of the artist). In this situation of unpredictability, there has been an illustration of the resiliency of the collaboration between art and the company's operations, and of the material and metaphorical integration among many spheres (art, historiography, rooms, molds and participation processes).

The pandemic has prevented strong and close contacts between artists and employees in the company setting. However, the analysis of the FEC pandemic interventions illustrates that, by respecting the complexity of the approach of the artist and by allowing for an exchange between arts and management at different levels (including organizational spaces, equipment and processes), there can still be a path to cross-fertilization and occasions for a wider consideration of employees' development.

6.3 The individuality of people at work: a more "humanized," emotions-, and aesthetic-based approach

Prioritizing the integration of art and business thinking through direct interventions on company spaces, objects and processes is tied to an organization considering a fuller participation of the employees in the company's history and development, by addressing their emotions, their personal energetic drives and their language. According to this perspective, especially the stream of research focused on understanding the abilities that artistic interventions can elicit and develop in the employees, literature has shifted its attention towards a more "humanized" and sensible approach to these individual capabilities. For instance, Henriksen and Mishra (2020) have discussed the concept of "wise creativity," as an ability that can be enforced especially by artistic interventions in the workplace, where the "wise" part of this ability refers to the fact that employees need to be trained to consider others' interests, the public good in their actions, and not only the bottom line for themselves and the company. In recent years, while the attention to a more instrumental view of artistic interventions (what abilities they develop in our employees) has not stopped, this attention has turned to consider this goal of developing employees' capabilities in a way that solicits their responsibility, a wider perspective on their participation in the economic and social system, and a broader approach to what they feel and think when implementing a certain ability.

In this regard, though not carried out during the pandemic, the work *Mass age, message, mess age* that Elena Mazzi did with FEC in 2018 after the publication of the Italian edition of this book, is exemplary and can provide suggestions on how to amplify these traits of the artistic interventions, related to the integration of arts and business and to the broader consideration of individual abilities, under the challenges of a pandemic. The approach of Elena Mazzi could itself be closely related to the pandemic, since she is interested in investigating how collectivities (whether urban, organizational or spontaneous) organize their reactions and survival to certain, even extreme events (the artist has reflected in particular on the earthquake that destroyed certain areas in the Abruzzi region of Italy in 2009). In her 2018 work with FEC, she involved 20 Elica employees in multiple activities to reflect on the topic of communication occurring in a setting with background disturbance, which appeared to represent a problematic communication issue at Elica at that time. The artist started her project by becoming familiar with the glossary of the company, studying the books stored in the company library that were all management books. From these study activities, she wanted to understand and extract words that could be discussed in the artistic intervention. This effort by the artist represents by itself an attempt to violate the conception that arts and business are separate disciplines. It illustrates that the artist is interested in the business vocabulary, considering it as a premise of her own artistic work and as something that art can rework and re-process for a discussion and a further investigation by the employees. Indeed, starting from this work of the artist, employees were encouraged to create their own glossary and then, through the assemblage of company materials, produce their own communication devices. The intervention did not stop with these activities. The devices were reworked by the artist and transformed into sculptures exhibited in the hall of the company, with the words of the newly-created glossary hang on the wall. In addition, each employee was given an artist book, hand-sewed by the artist herself, with each book containing words discussed during the activities, and with a graphical intervention left by the artist for each employee. These further gestures by the artist aimed to create a new object for the company and to dedicate to each employee a personalized object intended both to create this integration between the language of art and of management, and to remind each employee of the importance of their individual interpretation of the lexicon of the company and of their own new glossary. This careful and individualized approach reminds us of the "wise'" approach to the fact that employees are "developing" abilities. If employees were supposed to understand more and question their communication skills, the artistic intervention was developed so that each of them felt their own individuality was considered, for a broader consideration of what communication is in a challenging environment such as the workplace, where many glossaries are intertwined and deserved to be discussed. As in the words of the artist:

> I started the process with a personal search in the company library, to study their management books and to find words to be re-discussed and re-communicated (…) and I provoked the discussion to understand whether those words were the usual ones, whether they were conflicting, or problematic and I started the communication in a disturbed setting (…) then employees could see the sculptures I realized with their devices and the lexicon we created, the words were hung there for their own personal interpretation. I did not suggest any "solution" or summary, our work was there for their consideration and reflection about how they talk and communicated in the workplace. At the end of the process, I insisted on the fact that an artist book should be realized, so that each employee could have an artifact to remember her own experience and reflection on communication.

In addition to this call for a wider and wiser consideration of the kind of abilities employees might develop when exposed to artistic interventions, the pandemic time has also called for a stronger consideration of the body, of the senses, and thus of the aesthetic experience of the individuals in the workplace. In her self-ethnography about educators' response to the COVID-19 pandemic, Chemi (2020b) has illustrated how the use of engagement in arts-based methods, poetry and live performance might change because of the impossibility of human contact. In this storytelling of her own reaction, Chemi has stressed how much the pandemic solicited her attention to the body, and how becoming immersed in bodily needs and feeling could support a different understanding of the current situation. Furthermore, the author has emphasized the importance of adopting metaphorical language and contents, relying on the use of reference to "matter (photos, bodies), discourses (dramatized fiction) and technologies (computers)" (2020b: 7). The point of view and the reflections of the educators adopting arts-based methodology during the pandemic are particularly meaningful to understand how artistic interventions could respond to such an emergency. Maybe surprisingly, their aesthetic character (meaning the reliance of these interventions on the sensorial-perceptive faculties and aesthetic judgment of employees) seems to still be at the center of the discussion, though in a setting of social distancing and impossibility to stay together physically for long time. It seems that, when absent, the body and feelings recall their roles even more than when we can look at and feel each other every day. Thus, the concepts discussed in Chapter 3 of this book about the aesthetic experience employees might engage in through artistic interventions are worth considering, but in an even more relevant way; since the consideration of the body, senses and feelings seem even more liberating now than when our physical and sensorial interactions could not be a daily experience at work.

In order to exemplify this point, we recall both a pre-pandemic artistic intervention by the artist Francesca Grilli with the FEC (*Hand*, 2019) and the pandemic intervention by Matteo Fato (2020), since both of them are important to reflect on the power of evoking the bodily presence of the participants in the artistic interventions, when the body is somehow neglected or forgotten. The artistic intervention *Hand* has been already cited and described in Chapter 3, while here we would like to recall the most recent one, where the artist worked with a group of arts management students, coming together in class after a long spring break where they were not in contact intensively and where they did not attend the university spaces. Just to briefly recall its features in this new chapter, *Hand* is a workshop devoted to the reading of the body, focused on the interpretation of the lines of the hand. The intervention focuses on the study of the hand itself, on its shape, color, softness, feel and elasticity. In the final stage, participants read each other's hands. The different stories are collected in a soundtrack that, together with the handprint, makes up of a collection of sounds and images created by the artist and the participants.

For the 2019 edition of *Hand*, it is interesting to reflect on the quotes from the experiences of some of the participants. One participant said:

> Before this experience I have used to stay with these people (the other participants) every day for three months. However, now it seems like we have shared

> so little, we have never even touched our hands before today! Today it impressed me that one of my colleagues took my hand without any hesitation; it was completely natural to him, he was not embarrassed at all, while another one remained the whole time with his arms crossed, incapable of opening himself to the activity.

The activity with their bodies powerfully revealed to this participant that she had had only superficial interactions before with her classmates, interactions where they had completely neglected their bodies. Furthermore, she seems more sensitive to understanding who is open and available, and to appreciating this opportunity. Another participant said:

> This reference to the hands to me is an attempt to understand how we were born and how we are transforming ourselves and this has been particular intriguing to me (…) somehow has tried to look at me from a completely different perspective and I realized things about myself I have never thought about before.

Again, the reference to the body is so unexpected to the participant as to provide a new perspective on herself.

Matteo Fato, with *Gentile come un ritratto*, did not organize such a strong bodily intervention, this not being within his poetry. However, his modification of the company space and his individualized and intense attention to each participant recall the traits of the aesthetic experience. Also, through this intervention, individuals are physically called back to the workplace, which used to be either prohibited to them or was known to be prohibited to workers in Italy. The artist asked each employee to make an important manual gesture, leaving their pictorial sign on the canvas, hosted in an artist studio, which in turn was hosted on the shop floor of their own company. This is how the artist recalled the feelings of the employees involved in this experience: "the most sensitive moment to me was right before the employees had to paint their sign on the canvas (…) everyone wanted to have a moment before doing it. A moment of peace and silence, a silence that had to be listened to, in an environment full of noise, it created a space between them and me." With the pandemic, again, the physical presence both at the workplace and in the artist studio, together with the engagement of the physical gesture of painting, created a sense of suspense, of surprise, as premises for the action, and hopefully, for a discovery.

6.4 The concept of impact of artistic interventions – the call for a wider audience

The issue of the impact of artistic interventions in the workplace and of their measurability has been analyzed from different theoretical perspectives, ranging from management and organization studies, to studies in higher education. In Chapter 5 we also have analyzed the debates at that time, especially emphasizing the need for the organization to conceive the impact and the results of artistic interventions with a broad focus. This focus would be best represented by an approach that considers diverse stakeholders, beyond those interested in the company's bottom line, and even beyond the stakeholders of the company itself, for instance in order to embrace the stakeholders of the art system and to consider the usual stakeholders (namely employees, public institutions, local communities) in a less deterministic way. Accordingly, the adoption of qualitative methodologies, more oriented to catching processes and results while they emerge, was recommended together with the more usual quantitative ones, in order to study the impact of artistic interventions.

In recent times, in her discussion of the notion of impact of artistic interventions and arts-based method, Chemi (2020a) claimed the need for studies on impacts that do not focus on employees' behaviors and attitudes as variables to be controlled. This research recommends bearing in mind, especially now, that artistic interventions can be serendipitous in nature, not linear, and stimulate critical thinking, rather than just behavioral change in a determined direction.

In this line of discussion, Paolino and Berthoin Antal (2020) have illustrated the potentiality of studying artistic interventions and reflecting on their impact, by integrating literature on corporate social responsibility and organizational history and innovation, since such an integrated approach could help to consider how the presence of art in an organization may affect how members of the organization perceive the nature of the business, the authenticity of its identity and its relation to society.

Even before the pandemic times, the FEC and the artists collaborating with it had adopted a broader approach to conceive the impact of their work, broader either because of the numbers of stakeholders directly and indirectly considered, or because of the breadth of their approach towards two particular communities, the artists themselves and the employees. The breadth and the depth through which the communities interested by the artistic interventions are affected represent a first step towards a problematic, critical view on impact and its measurement. First of all, this is because complexity, in any managerial setting, calls for multiple points of view and multiple methods to be addressed; this multiplicity makes determinism in interpreting the effect of artistic interventions less likely.

To support this discussion, before moving on to the pandemic interventions, we recall a particular work the artist Patrick Tuttofuoco did to commemorate the 20th anniversary of the creation of the Ermanno Casoli prize. In *The Relay* (2019), the artist created a site-specific work revolving around one of the pillars of Tuttofuoco's approach: the relationships that characterize and bring together communities, starting with family communities to arrive at wider groups, that hold meaning for individuals in a territory. *The Relay* was exhibited in a particular place, which was not the building where the FEC was located. It was hosted in the Museo Premio Ermanno Casoli 1998-2007, a municipal museum in the village of Serra San Quirico (around 3,000 inhabitants, in the province of Ancona). In the words of the artist: "my approach revolves around the concept of dialogue and exchange among communities (...) Serra San Quirico is a small place, that you have to "earn" metaphorically and physically, since it is not easy to get there. My work here has to say something about the award and I wanted to tell a story about what an award is in the arts: it is a chance to generate energies and knowledge to be exchanged. It is far from the individuality of the artist; it is a way to connect the artist with other communities." *The Relay* was not meant to be an artistic intervention; it was a commission. However, the kind of artist, his poetry, and the fact that the artistic interventions FEC had organized so far were the elements to be celebrated through the prize not in a conventional location, could inspire us to think about the many communities that could be affected by it (e.g. the FEC, the museum, the village of Serra San Quirico, the city of Fabriano, and the employees that had participated in the celebrated artistic intervention up to then). This kind of perspectives can be mirrored in the artistic intervention Patrick Tuttofuoco realized for FEC in *Family Feeling* (2016), an intervention with the children of Elica's employees, where the children experimented with different approaches to the portraits of their family, always with the aim of re-creating the bond among the family and working communities. Again within these interventions with the families of the employees, the artists Bianco and Valente realized the intervention *The Place Where I Live (2019),* where the children and their families were invited on a journey to discover the role that places play within us, beginning with tourist and geographical maps as well as photos that the children collected during the summer with their families, on request from the artists. During the workshop, the images were mixed up in order to form a single chaotic mass representing a sort of collective memory from which everyone was able to draw inspiration, create a drawing or build a story. The maps were randomly cut and assembled in order to make new ones, a testament to the individual stories of each participant. This intervention was very consistent with the approach of the artist duo, rooted in public art, and investigating the power that places have to shape communities, to inspire new reflections, thoughts and actions. It would be very hard to engage in the quantification of the bottom line of this kind of intervention: were the employees more productive afterwards? More satisfied? More motivated because their children were happier? What about the geographies they recall, would they go back there? How? When? Was the city of Fabriano affected by the workshop?

These are only a few of the questions we can ask when thinking about the impact of such interventions. We would like to finish this series of examples with the intervention Jorge Satorre has been carrying out in Mexico and by considering the critical thinking it can elicit when reflecting about its effects. The intervention involves the exploration and modification of the company's spaces and objects; it includes micro-residencies during which the artists and the employees stay together and the artist can understand their daily operations and discuss their abilities to transform their concepts into quick graphical representations; material artworks are realized, employees are listened to and a workshop is carried out, and an artist book will be published. Where do we start to measure the impact on the Mexico branch, on the company headquarters, on the national and international art system, on local and global communities, and on the lean system? This complexity, while preventing determinism and instrumentalism, could lead to warmer, closer attention to the non-linear, serendipitous and bodily impact that artistic interventions might generate, even in those who read about them, we hope.

6.5 Final remarks, limitations, pushing towards new challenges

With this chapter we wanted to expand the 2018 edition of this book on the approach the FEC has developed over the years with an analysis of the latest artistic interventions produced by the FEC and a special focus on the ones carried out during the time of the pandemic (2020-2021). In the last two years, our life has been built and rebuilt many times, and sometimes, it may be that we lost faith in the fact the digitalization and physical interaction could live together, improving, not worsening the way we have live and worked. While re-analyzing the artistic interventions of the FEC, talking with the artists again, recalling memories, and exchanging opinions and concepts among authors, a feeling of renewed trust that arts and management have to be together in the workplace was rekindled. Social distancing and alternation between presence and absence could slow what the artists and employees could do together, or delay the production of a workshop or of an installation, but slowing down the rhythm makes sense, after we have had our existences controlled by external contingencies. Artistic interventions are still possible and they bring a beneficial complexity, raising in a critical way the issue of having in one workplace diverse disciplines, rationality and bodily reasoning, technical benefits and the impossibility to collect precise and measurable information about the multifaceted impact of artistic interventions.

This analysis is rooted in interviews with the artists and some participants, and in the exchange among the authors, one of whom was always present during the artistic interventions analyzed, being able to transmit feeling, quotes and events from direct experience. It was not possible for one of the authors to come into direct contact with the employees immediately after the pandemic interventions. If another edition of the book can be written, attention is going to be dedicated in particular to the feelings, thoughts and experiences of those employees who lived through these interventions in such uncertain times. Their ex-post thinking and feeling about what happened with the artists will be further materials to understand the power and danger of artistic interventions. When thinking about these possible negative sides, it is important to mention that when employees the experience a separation from their workplace, going back through the artistic interventions could generate a feeling of estrangement from the artwork, the artistic process and its outcome. We have had to stay home to work, and the artistic process may not be the most suitable way to comeback for everyone, especially if they are not led properly (Berthoin Antal et al., 2019). In addition, although the FEC's approach is to involve as many people as possible, generally speaking, in these times it is necessary to more vividly address the problem of not involving everyone, leaving someone out, when governments, societies, schools and local communities might have already done so.

Having experimented with the works by Matteo Fato and Jorge Satorre, the new roads ahead revolve around building up this consideration of the individuality and "wholeness" of the employees and stakeholders involved. The pandemic has forced artists and intermediary organizations to work in an empty workspace, to populate them with one employee at time, to consider these employees individually and for a longer time, to understand that they can stop their artistic practice and their dialogue with the workforce, and that they can resume them later, when it will be possible, when they are going to be even something different. An artistic intervention seems to emerge that is more individualized, slower, more attentive, made of stop-and-go, non-linear in its development, and digital only in its prototyping, but not in its execution. This development of artistic interventions is however grounded in their growth before the pandemic and it projects them towards a future of further complexity. Our hope is that organizations and artists will continue to experiment so that the world of research can look for regularities and discontinuities and provide plausible interpretations to its audience.

Appendix*
Innovating Business with Art
The Fondazione Ermanno Casoli Method

* All of the projects were curated by Marcello Smarrelli.

Jorge Satorre
Pelusa (Fluff)
19th edition Ermanno Casoli Prize, 2021

The winner of the 19th edition of the Ermanno Casoli Prize – the first to be held in the ElicaMex facility in Querétaro – is the Mexican artist Jorge Satorre (Mexico City, 1979).
The artist entered the world of Elica with the *Pelusa (Fluff)* project, a complex research project that started from drawing, developed through engraving and sculpture, and then came to the realization of an artist book.
Interested in the peculiarities of industrial production in relation to artistic production, Satorre wanted to reflect on the nature of the imprint that the worker leaves on the product they contribute to creating. Contrary to the idea of a work of art founded on criteria of uniqueness and subjectivity, industrial products are in fact standardized and follow strict directives that respond to the needs of function and design. Thus the artist decided to focus on the contrast between personal expression and rules, between instinct and quality control, subjective proposal and standard of functioning. During various periods of residency at the company, through the use of the practice of live drawing, the artist reproduced a series of molds and matrices used to create kitchen hoods, objects which have become unusable due to wear and tear and the changed needs of the market. Fascinated by this archive of precious but now useless objects, Satorre used pieces of scrap metal sheets, resulting from the production of the hoods, to transform the drawings into a series of 19 engravings.
During a parallel workshop in which a large number of workers participated, the artist attempted to focus on the idea of drawing as a personal act of expression, but at the same time one that is highly functional. With the intention of "teaching" some of the techniques used by him for the drawings of the matrices, the artist worked with the employees of ElicaMex to materially translate ideas of possible improvements to objects and spaces of the factory, as required by the WCM program, but also personal and abstract ideas made objective by the formal translation onto paper.
The final work, completely integrated inside the factory and accessible to all of the workers, consists of a series of three large-format sculptures, realized in metal, that serve as display stands for Satorre's engravings and the drawings produced by the workers during the workshop.
The artist book, that is an integral part of the project, presents the 19 engravings together with 19 brief texts that contain technical data, personal observations, and peculiarities obtained through the conversations that the artist had with the engineers responsible for the matrices. The result is a *sui generis* archive, a collection that is abstract and personal, technical and emotional, of the objects represented in the artist's prints.

***Pelusa (Fluff)*, 2021. Installation view**

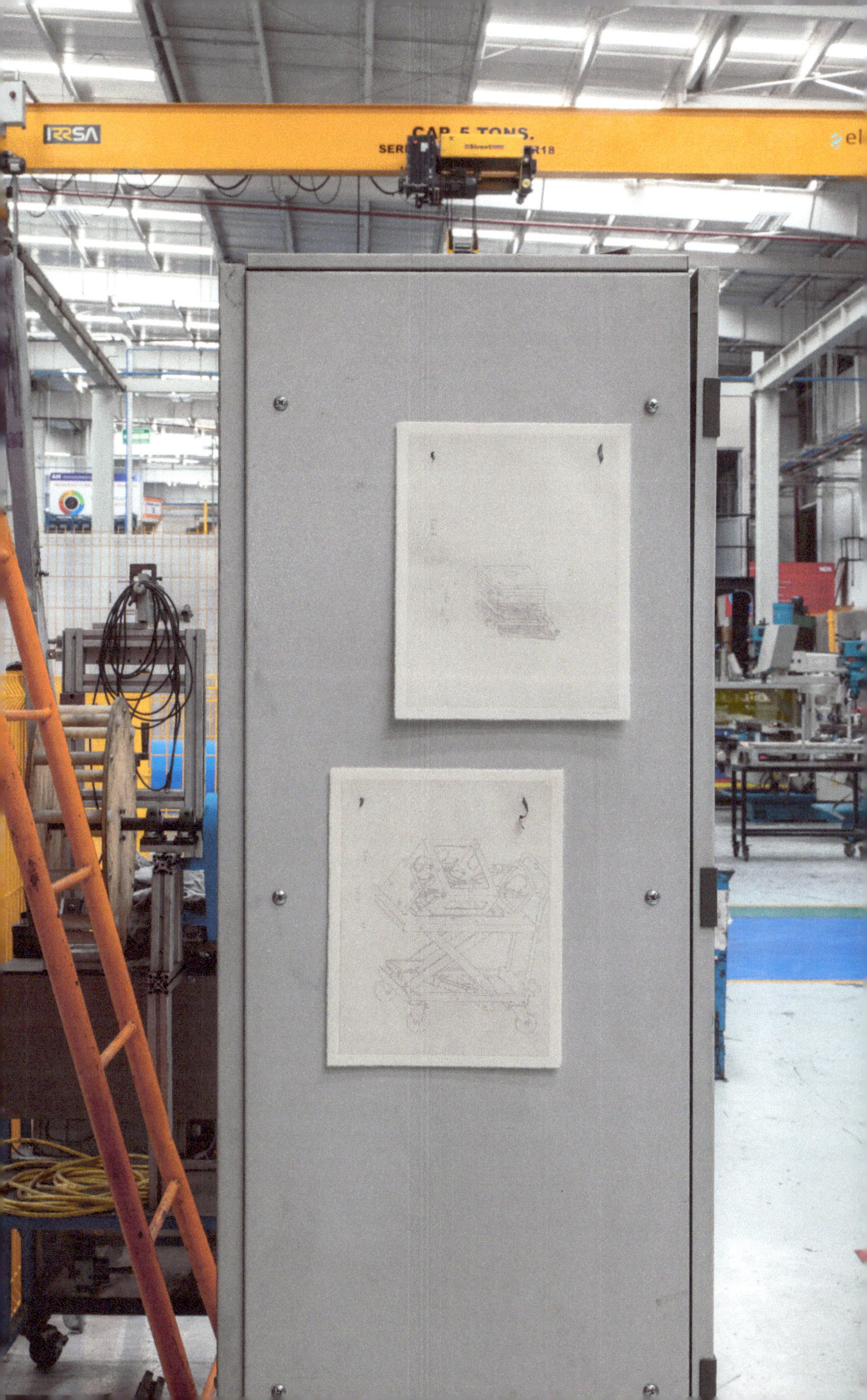
IRRSA

Matteo Fato

Gentile come un ritratto
18th edition Ermanno Casoli Prize, 2020
In the context of the Elica 50th

Matteo Fato (Pescara, 1979) was the protagonist of the 18th edition of the Ermanno Casoli Prize with the project *Gentile come un ritratto*. The title refers to the presumed self-portrait that the painter Gentile da Fabriano (Fabriano 1370 ca., Rome 1427) included among the figures that appear in his celebrated polyptych, the *Adoration of the Magi* (1423), now at the Uffizi museum.
The project represented a challenge on multiple levels: start with a masterpiece from the past, linked to the genius and excellence of the territory of the Marches region, to conceive of a collective work that starting from the past, Gentile's self-portrait, arrives in the present witnessed by the contemporary portrait of the Elica company. Thus an ideal connection was created, that with a temporal short-circuit, united the Renaissance studio of the historic painter with the company that, starting from Fabriano and thanks to the passion of its founder Ermanno Casoli, has distinguished itself in the world in the area of industry and design.
In a particularly difficult moment such as that of the pandemic, in which the relational dimension of work has also been sorely tried, the project proposed by Fato stands out for the sensitivity and efficacy with which it addressed this important aspect.
The artist chose to open his authorship to a collective operation, translating the pictorial gesture, the distinctive element of his work that "happens" in the silence and solitude of his studio, into a "doing together," creating an intimate and profound sense of closeness with others.
This made it possible to realize a work that in its plurality and abstraction is able to represent all of those who contributed to creating it.
The entire process was born in a temporary painting atelier conducted by Matteo Fato, that lasted a week and was set up in the company spaces of the Elica facilities in Fabriano and Castelfidardo (FIME Elica Motors Division), in which 159 employees participated. Each employee was asked to leave their own sign on a single canvas. During the workshop, the participants had the possibility to interact personally with the artist, one at a time, reflecting together on the nature of the portrait, a form of expression that represents not only the individuality of the subject, but also the cultural characteristics of the epoch.
This collective action produced other canvases, drawn from the scraps used for the cleaning of the brushes at each change of coat and color, in turn mounted and framed within their respective transport cases.
All of the devices produced became part of a large installation assembled in the office of the Managing Director entitled *Gentili come un ritratto*. The change made to the original title of the entire project was considered indispensable by the artist to "pay homage to the gentle eyes and hands who gave us their history," a shared history, and thus even more precious, that has become a portrait and together the landscape of our strange time.

***Gentili come un ritratto*, 2020. Installation view**

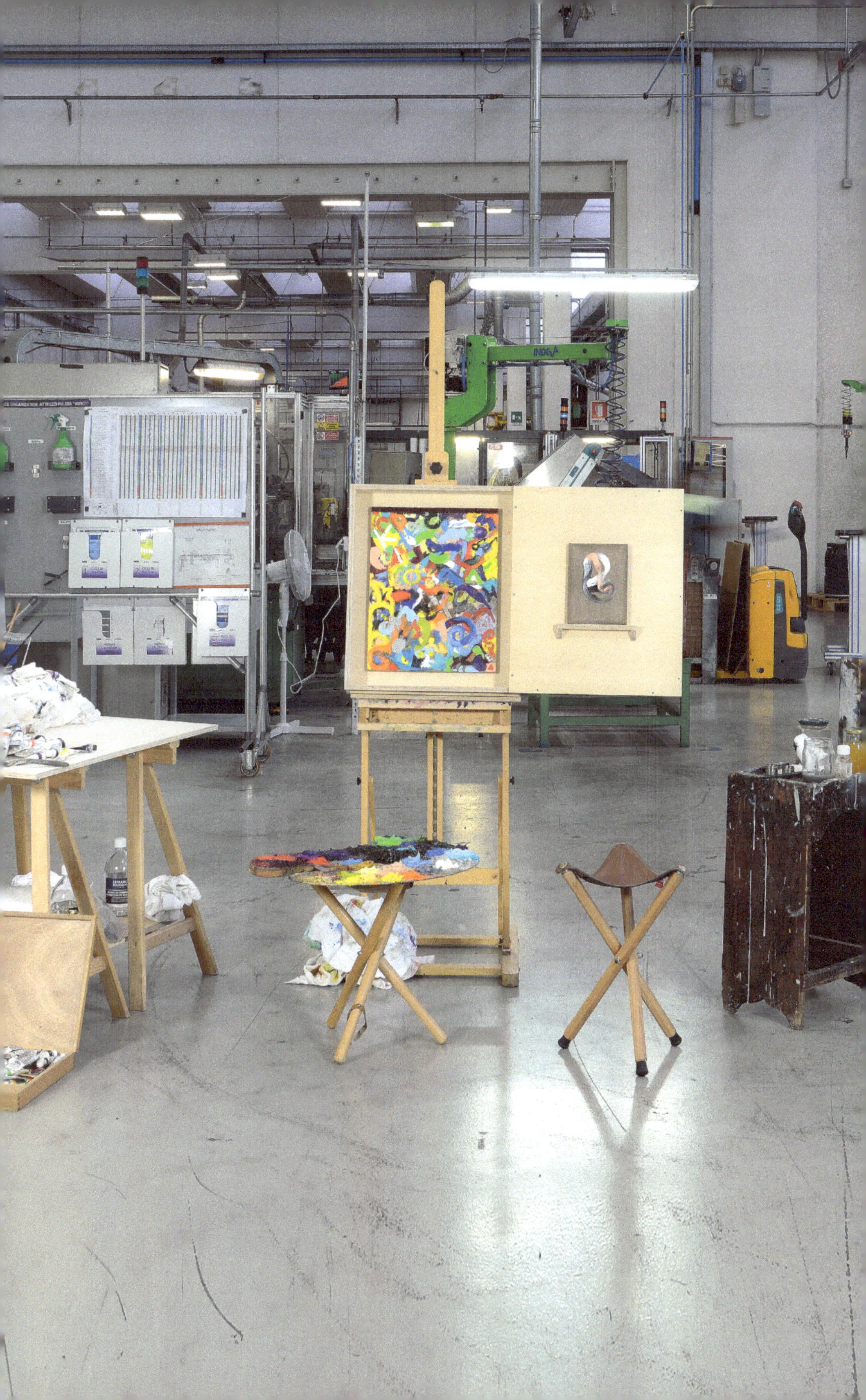

Patrick Tuttofuoco
The Relay
Special edition for 20 years of the Ermanno Casoli Prize, 2019

The Relay is the title of the large luminous installation created by the artist Patrick Tuttofuoco (Milan, 1974) to celebrate the twentieth anniversary of the establishment of the Ermanno Casoli Prize.

It is a site-specific work, realized for the monumental spaces of the Monastery of Santa Lucia in Serra San Quirico, now a cultural center and location of the Museo Premio Ermanno Casoli 1998 – 2007, that deals with the subjects that have always been central to the artist's research: relations, family relationships, generational exchange, the mechanisms and rituals that characterize communities, the bonds that unite. The title refers explicitly to an Olympic discipline, the relay, the only specialty in athletics that is a team, not individual sport, in which the members must run passing a baton with a particularly evocative name in Italian: the *testimone*.

Hands skim each other, touch each other, the baton is passed between them, and they are the true protagonists of this work. In addition to being a fundamental part of our anatomy, hands allows us to work, to socialize, to show our sentiments, and reveal much of our personality.

In this work by Tuttofuoco, the simple gesture of holding an object in one's hand and passing it to another person is expanded and every phase is reproduced, giving a spatial, three-dimensional dimension to the notion of time. The act of receiving something from someone and transmitting it to a third party also becomes a metaphor for exchange, gift, and ultimately the very prize that the work celebrates, but also the succession of generations, and ultimately, life itself.

The Relay was donated by the Ermanno Casoli Foundation to the Ermanno Casoli Prize 1998-2007 Museum on the occasion of its inauguration in 2019, enriching the collection of approximately forty works acquired and donated to the Town of Serra San Quirico during the first ten editions of the Prize that was created by Gianna Pieralisi, the wife of Ermanno Casoli, and his children Cristina and Francesco Casoli. The work thus also acts as a powerful *trait d'union* between the first and second phases of the Prize, born in 2007 with the establishment of the Ermanno Casoli Foundation, that underwent a transformation from a simple acquisition of works to a training and relational activity that engages the employees of the companies in the realization of a work of art.

***The Relay*, 2019.Installation view**

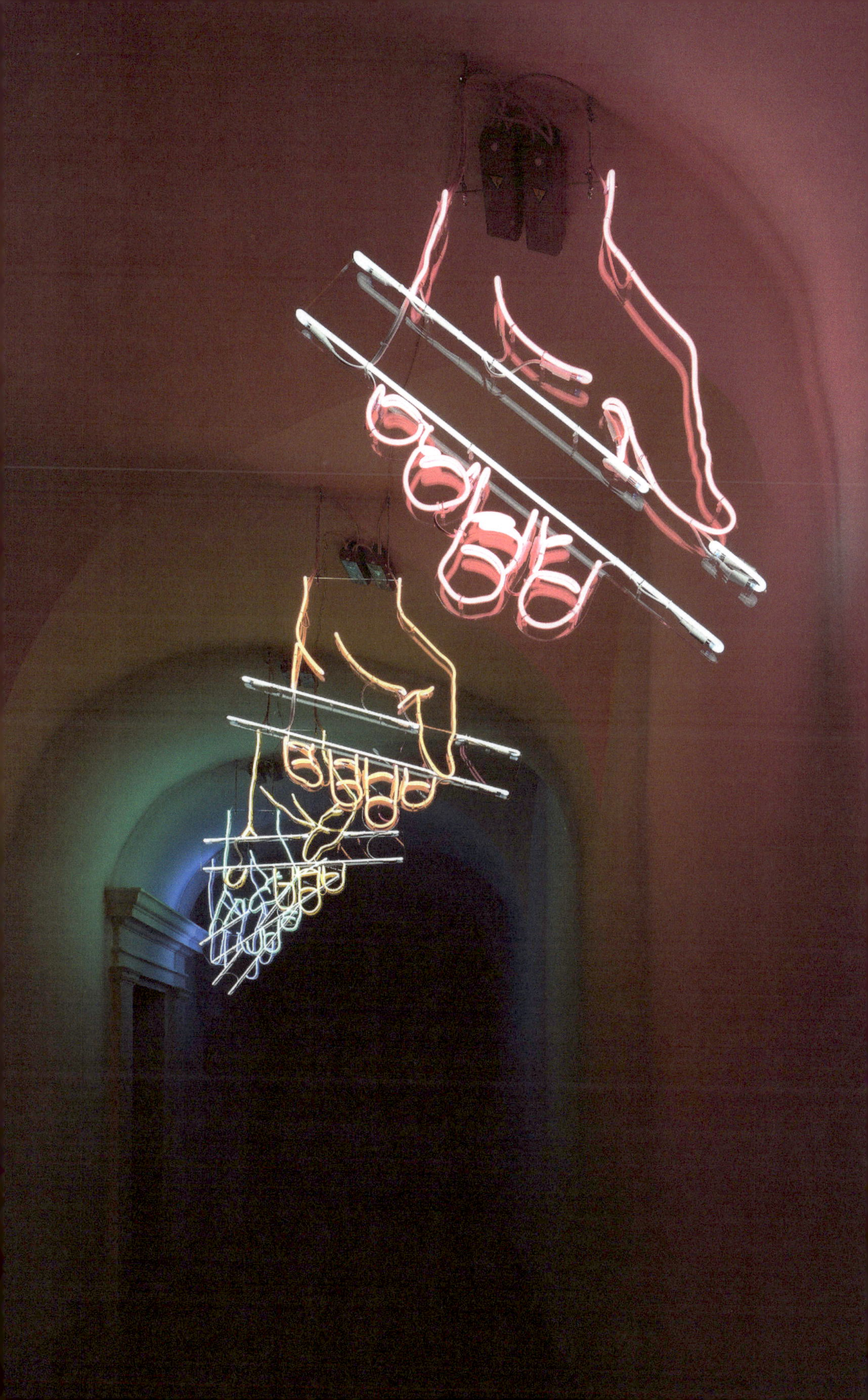

Elena Mazzi
Mass age, message, mess age (Elica 2018)
17th edition Ermanno Casoli Prize, 2018

Mass age, message, mess age (*Elica 2018*) is the title of the project realized by the artist Elena Mazzi (Reggio Emilia, 1984), the winner of the 17th edition of the Ermanno Casoli Prize, that saw the active participation of twenty employees of the Elica company. Part of a work in progress begun in 2015 with the goal of investigating and shedding light on the dynamics underlying communication strategies, the activity involved a talk open to the public and a workshop reserved to Elica employees, in the context of E-STRAORDINARIO, that took place in Fabriano at the company's headquarters.

The artist's process of research began with the study of the word "revolution" in its broadest meaning of radical change of social structures, that can be applied in different historical periods and numerous fields of knowledge, that cannot but start with an analysis of communication between individuals of the same community. Consistent with the goals of this research, Elena Mazzi, assisted by the trainer specialized in company training Diego Agostini, invited the 20 participants in the workshop to directly experience the conditions of interruption and distraction, and of accidents, which a message can suffer when it must pass from the sender to the recipient. Everyone worked together on identifying words drawn from daily managerial language, from their personal experiences of team building and relationships in the work environment, in order to create a glossary to use for the performance inspired by the children's game of telephone. Divided into small groups, the participants created devices for verbal communication through the creative and functional assembly of materials used in the factory to realize products, that were subsequently used in the realization of the performance.

Objects and words converged into an installation entitled *Mass age, message, mess age* (*Elica 2018*): a sculpture composed of two elements fused with the method of lost wax aluminum casting, a synthesis of ten devices to communicate products during the workshop and a mural that shows the words selected and "played" during the performance.

***Mass age, message, mess age (Elica 2018)*, 2018. Installation view**

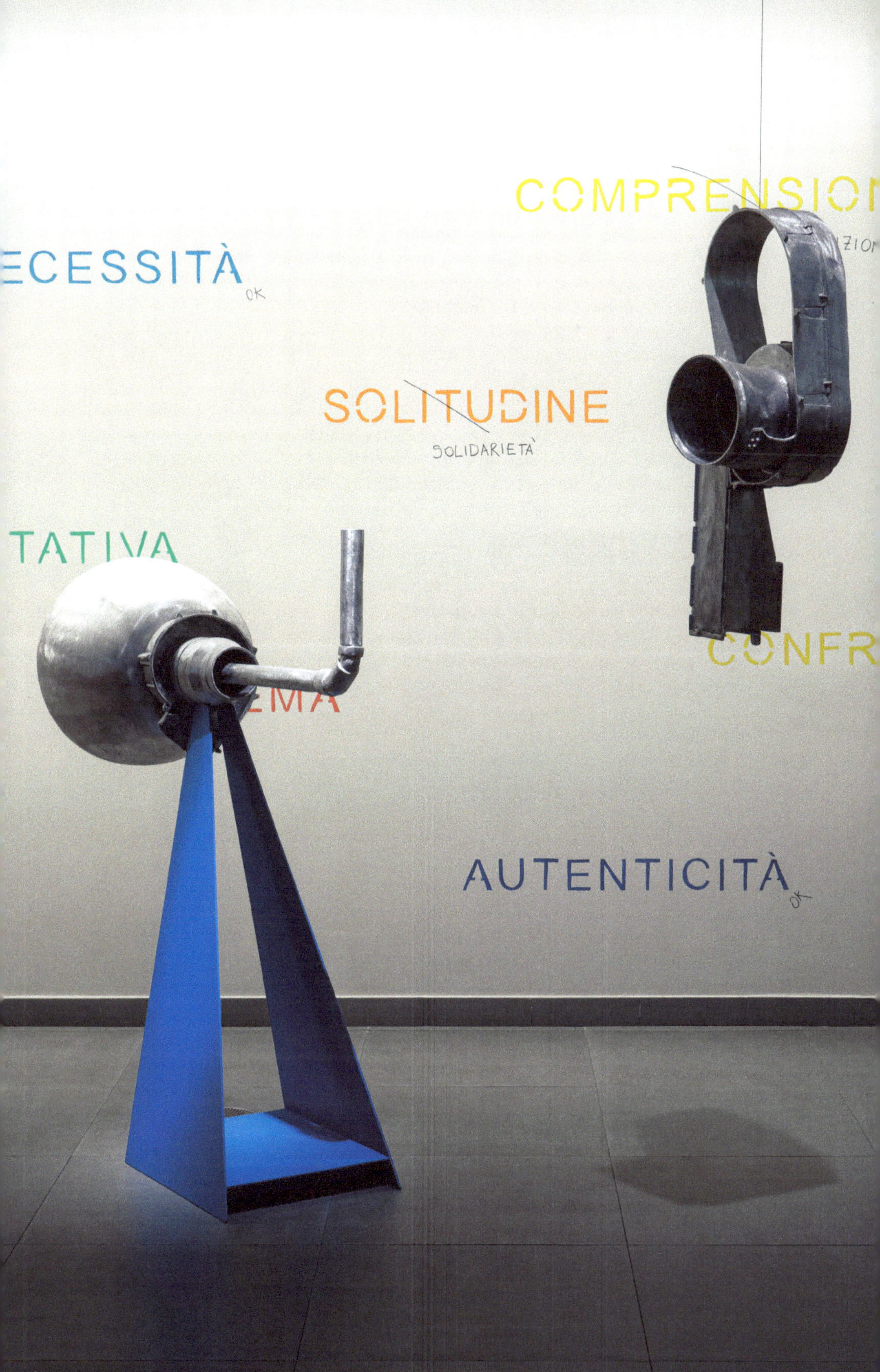
COMPRENSION
ECESSITÀ
OK
SOLITUDINE
SOLIDARIETÀ
TATIVA
CONFR
AUTENTICITÀ
OK

Francesca Grilli
Hand #1, #2, #3,#4
E-STRAORDINARIO 2015, 2017, 2019

Hand is the title of the workshop conceived and created by the artist Francesca Grilli (Bologna, 1978) on four occasions: the first for a group of thirty-four participants, consisting of students and entrepreneurs from the Marches region, at the San Francesco Museum Center in Montefiore dell'Aso, in the province of Ascoli Piceno (2015); the second at the Mudec – Museum of Cultures of Milan, with twenty-six attendants of the Master's course in Economics and Management of Art and Cultural Heritage at the Business School of the *Il Sole 24 Ore* newspaper (2017); the third at the Academy of Fine Arts of Urbino (2017) with the participation of thirty-five students of the Visual Arts course; the fourth at the Università Cattolica del Sacro Cuore in Milan (2019) with twenty-five students of the Master in Arts Management, completely in English The first two appointments saw the involvement of the trainer Piero Tucci, senior partner of the M&D training company.

The workshop was structured around the activity of body reading, with a particular focus on the interpretation of hand lines, thus the title *Hand.* Our hands speak of us: they are one of the body parts used the most to communicate, they seal new acquaintances and pacts, they are perfect work tools. The activity entailed an initial pictorial phase in which the participants, through color, learned to take handprints to have a complete view of all of the lines present. In the second part, a study was conducted on the hand itself: shape, color, softness, sensation to touch and elasticity. The intent of the artist, assisted by an expert in fortune-telling, was to bring the participants to understand how a person's character can be represented by the body, stimulating a more instinctive and free interpretation. In the final phase of the workshop, through the basic elements of fortune-telling learned during the working day, the participants exchanged interpretations of their hands. The different stories were collected in a soundtrack that, accompanied by the handprint, constituted the final outcome of the workshop: a sound installation produced by the artist and the participants, in line with the interest of Francesca Grilli for aspects of our lives that are apparently impossible to investigate, but that are always ready to come to the surface, at times in a more intimate dimension and at times in a collective setting.

***Hand #2*, 2017. Handprint of a participant**

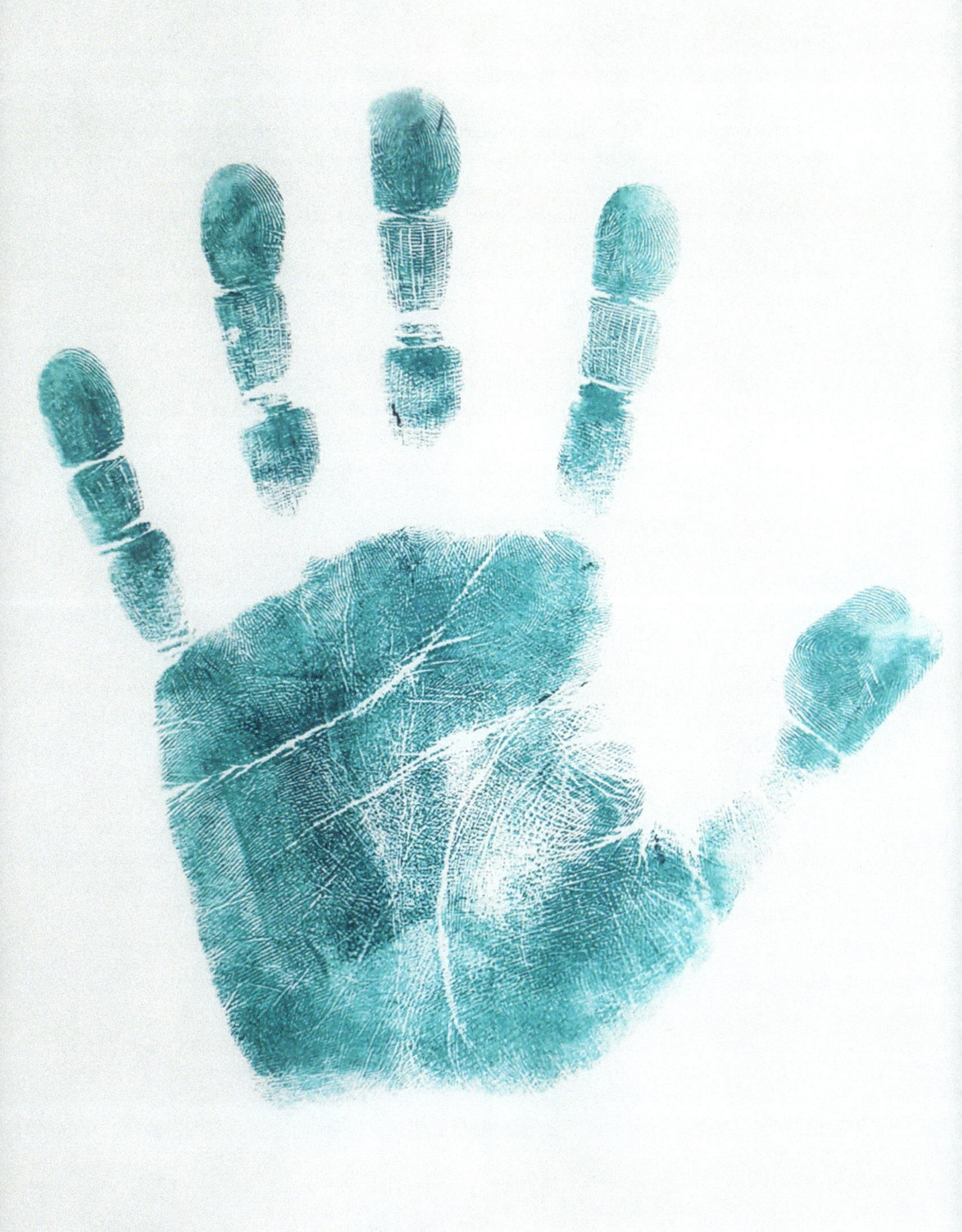

Andrea Mastrovito
VITRIOL
16th edition of the Ermanno Casoli Prize 2016

The 16th edition of the Ermanno Casoli Prize was created for the Angelini pharmaceutical company with a training project by Piero Tucci, senior partner of the M&D company. For the occasion, the winner of the Prize, Andrea Mastrovito (Bergamo, 1978), created a path between art and training entitled *VITRIOL*: this term/acronym, which represents a sentence known among alchemists, "*Visita Interiora Terrae Rectificando Invenies Occultum Lapidem*" – inspired the artist in the design of a cycle of seven murals spread around the company's premises.

The seven works touched different points of Angelini's headquarters in Ancona, creating a path between internal and external spaces, visible to all of the employees and people who visit the company; from the Cafeteria Room to the coffee machine areas, from the little "auditorium" (called the *Sala Tachipirina*) to the outside walls near the entrance. The interventions were placed at strategic points, guaranteeing full access for personnel and visitors.

Each image – engraved on the wall and made through "removing," following a technique used by the artist in other works – was executed by Mastrovito together with a group of one hundred Angelini employees. Dense with references to alchemic processes and medicine, the seven interventions thus arose from a shared process, producing a great collective work able to represent the company, its values and the people who work there.

There are geometric solids in all of the works. They represent not only a reference to the artistic tradition (think of the celebrating engraving *Melencolia I* by Albrecht Dürer), but also the world of alchemy, and by extension, that of medicine, thus recreating a historical connection between these two worlds that were once very close.

The seven works conceived in the *VITRIOL* project stand out for their monumental dimensions, thanks to the graffiti technique used to make them, and have become a permanent part of the company's community, and a point of pride for the employees that contributed to making them.

***VITRIOL*, 2016. A moment during the realization of the work**

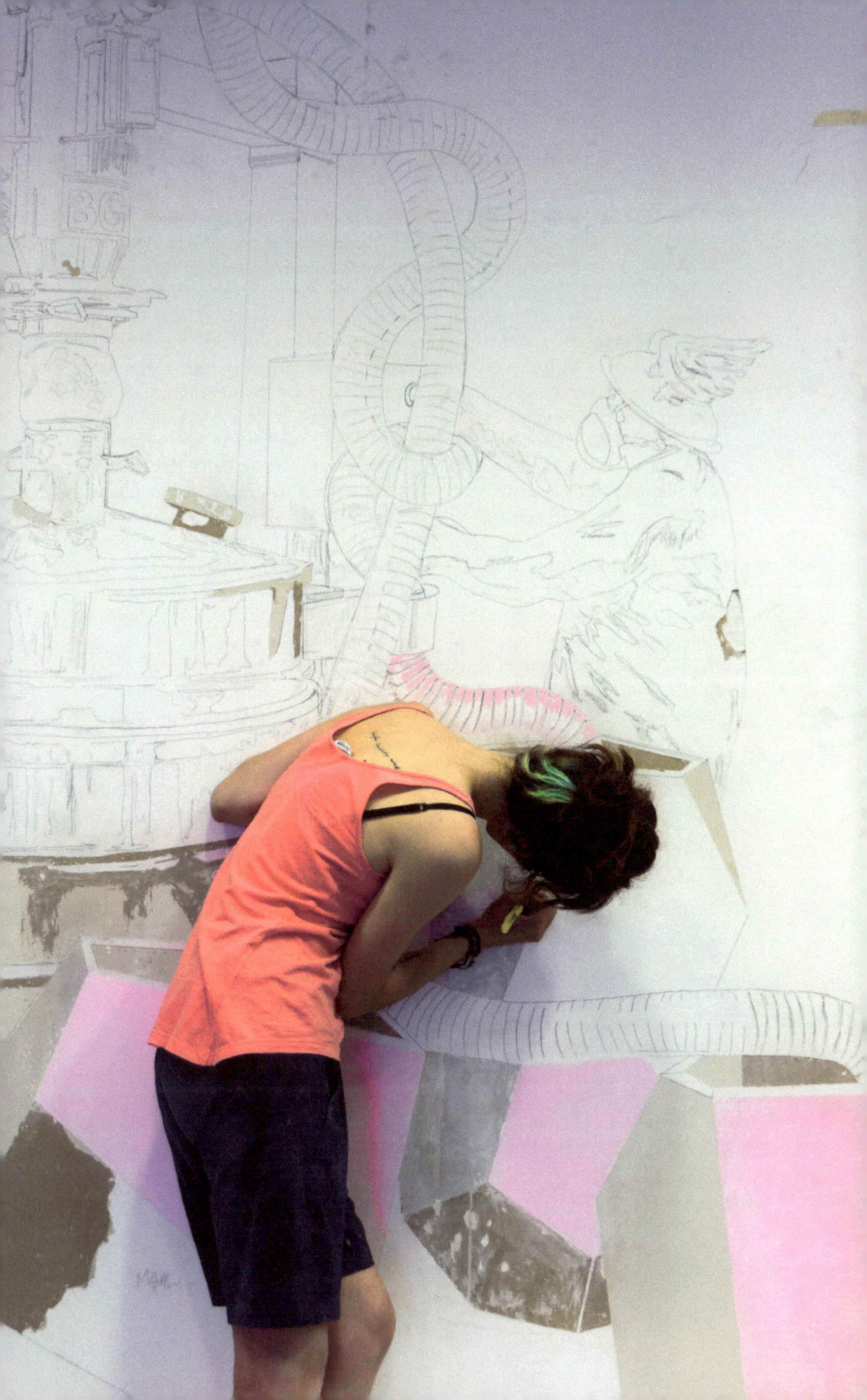

Pietro Ruffo
The Wishful Map #1, #2, #3, #4
E-STRAORDINARIO 2015, 2016

The Wishful Map is the title of a series of workshops conceived by Pietro Ruffo (Rome, 1978). The project was proposed in various contexts: at the Lanificio Luciani in Rome, with the participation of sixty employees, including executive and middle managers; at the Angelini Acraf spa company (2015); at the Mudec – Museum of Cultures of Milan, for approximately forty course attendants at the Business School of *Il Sole 24 Ore* (2015); at the San Francesco convent in Bellegra in the province of Rome, for thirty-five clerks and managers at the Banca di Credito Cooperativo of Bellegra (2016); and at the La Borghesiana sports center of Rome, for forty employees of Euler Hermes Italia, that is part of the Allianz insurance group (2016). All of the training activities were planned by the trainer Piero Tucci, a senior partner of the M&D training company.

The Wishful Map had the goal of producing a series of concept maps able to represent the identity and values of the participating companies through a shared work of art. The technique used to create the works was the same that Pietro Ruffo has proposed for years, the distinctive feature of his approach: recreating geographic maps with elements in relief, generally of different colors, able to highlight values and aspects that characterize the different groups of participants. This produced collective works with a strong visual impact, in which each employee's contribution was decisive. The great capacity to organize the work, a characteristic of Pietro Ruffo's artistic practice, made the contribution of the participants simple, engaging and fun, allowing them to express the complexity of the relevant community or group.

The globes created during the workshops were subsequently placed in various public spaces of the companies involved in the project.

***The Wishful Map #4*, 2016. Detail of the work**

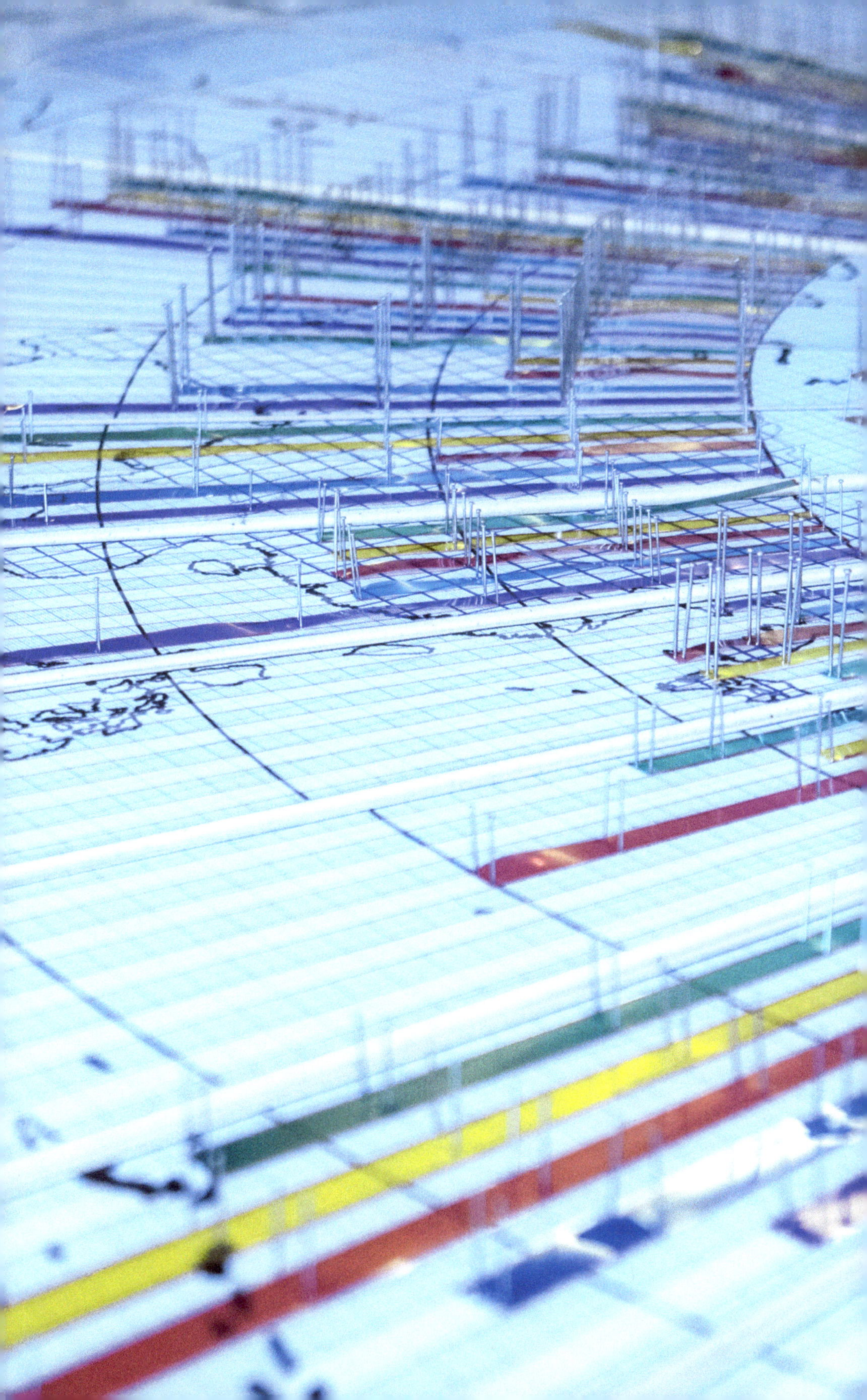

Diego Marcon
Esercizi di stile #1, #2
E-STRAORDINARIO 2015, 2016

Esercizi di stile is the title of the project conceived by the artist Diego Marcon (Busto Arsizio, 1985), proposed on two occasions: the first at the Paper and Watermark Museum of Fabriano, with a group of twenty entrepreneurs from the Marches region (2015); the second at the Mudec – Museum of Cultures of Milan, for thirty-six students in the Master in Economics and Management of Art and Cultural Heritage of the *Il Sole 24 Ore* Business School (2016). Both the workshops were produced with the collaboration of Luca Varvelli, president of the GRAM training company.

As suggested by the title, *Esercizi di stile* presents itself as an experiment in writing: taking its cue from the book of the same title by Raymond Queneau, the participants are given a short "base anecdote" from which to develop three variations, relating to the language register, the literary genre, and the physical medium on which to rewrite the text. Long-time managers and youth entrepreneurs from the Marches area, as well as the Master students, worked together in groups, and at the end of the working day all of the contributions, reworked by the artist, were collected to form a magazine/fanzine – an artist's book for all purposes – published in a numbered series, of which each participant received a copy. On the occasion of the project's stop in Milan, an eBook was also produced.

Esercizi di stile reflects on the importance of form in the creation of stories and language as a tool that determines their transmission, stimulating an analytic look and questioning the concepts of truth and reality. The idea of the workshop came from Marcon's interest in the possible combinations of stories and narration, regardless of the medium: static or moving images, as well as sounds and objects, are used by the artist to give life to a series of works in which the concept of filing and cataloguing play a fundamental role.

***Esercizi di stile #1*, 2015. A page from the artist's book**

ANEDDOTO DI BASE

In coda dal panettiere, verso sera. Entra una ragazza di circa venticinque anni, capelli lisci e biondi, lunghi fino alle natiche, gote arrossate. Sotto al braccio sinistro, una rivista arrotolata. Con brevi e veloci passi supera la fila, e arrivata alla cassa domanda quattro ciabatte e un trancio di focaccia alle cipolle.
Un signore sui sessantacinque anni, anch'esso in coda, la rimprovera, alzando la voce. La ragazza non lo degna di uno sguardo e, una volta pagato, esce dal negozio.
La rivedo la mattina seguente, mentre aspetto il pullman alla pensilina accanto alla chiesa: dall'altro lato della strada, assieme ad un bambino, dà da mangiare a dei colombi.

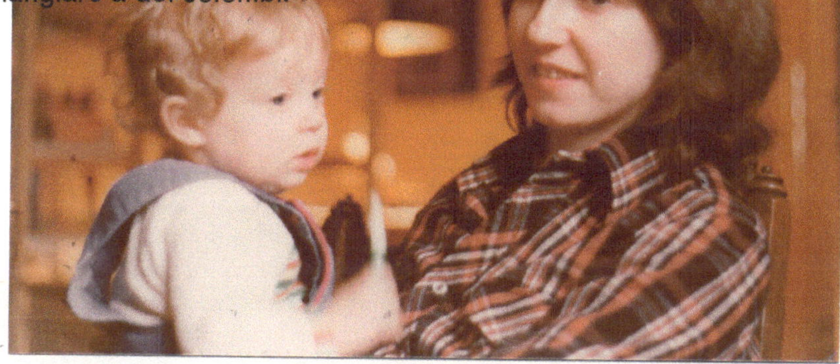

15/02/'89

IO E MAMMA COMPRIAMO
IL PANE DA DARE AI COLOMBI.

GRUPPO C: VARIAZIONI DI SUPPORTO
C.16 Riscrivere l'aneddoto sul retro di una fotografia fornita dall'artista

Ettore Favini
Sillage
FEC for Factories 2015

Sillage is the project by the artist Ettore Favini (Cremona, 1974) conceived for Elica and the Fondazione Ermanno Casoli on the occasion of EXPO Milan 2015 and presented in the Save the Children Pavilion, to support their initiatives of food education and safety.

The title of the project indicates the trace left by a scent, able to overcome barriers and spread in the surrounding environment. In line with this definition, *Sillage* was developed in different phases, the first in the community garden of the Save the Children Village inside EXPO, where three celebrated models of Elica hoods (*Audrey*, *Edith* and *Seashell*) were transformed into vases to plant barley, oats, almonds, fennel and anise; plants that are edible and easy to cultivate, linked to themes always focused on by Save the Children, and more in general to EXPO 2015, *Feeding the Planet, Energy for Life.* Once grown, the plants were transformed into essences, and subsequently, used for a fragrance specifically developed for *Marie*, the Elica fragrance diffuser. The limited-edition cover of the diffuser was also created by Ettore Favini, who refashioned the photograph of a still life formed by the vegetables that make up the fragrance, obtaining an abstract image. The project reflects the artist's interest for themes such as the environment and landscape, demonstrating how contemporary art finds deep connections with the possibility for environmental change.

Sillage was presented in the context of a performance/event at Palazzo Visconti in Milan. Part of the proceeds from the sales went to support the *Every One* campaign by Save the Children, aimed at combatting infant mortality in the poorest areas of the world.

***Sillage*, 2015**

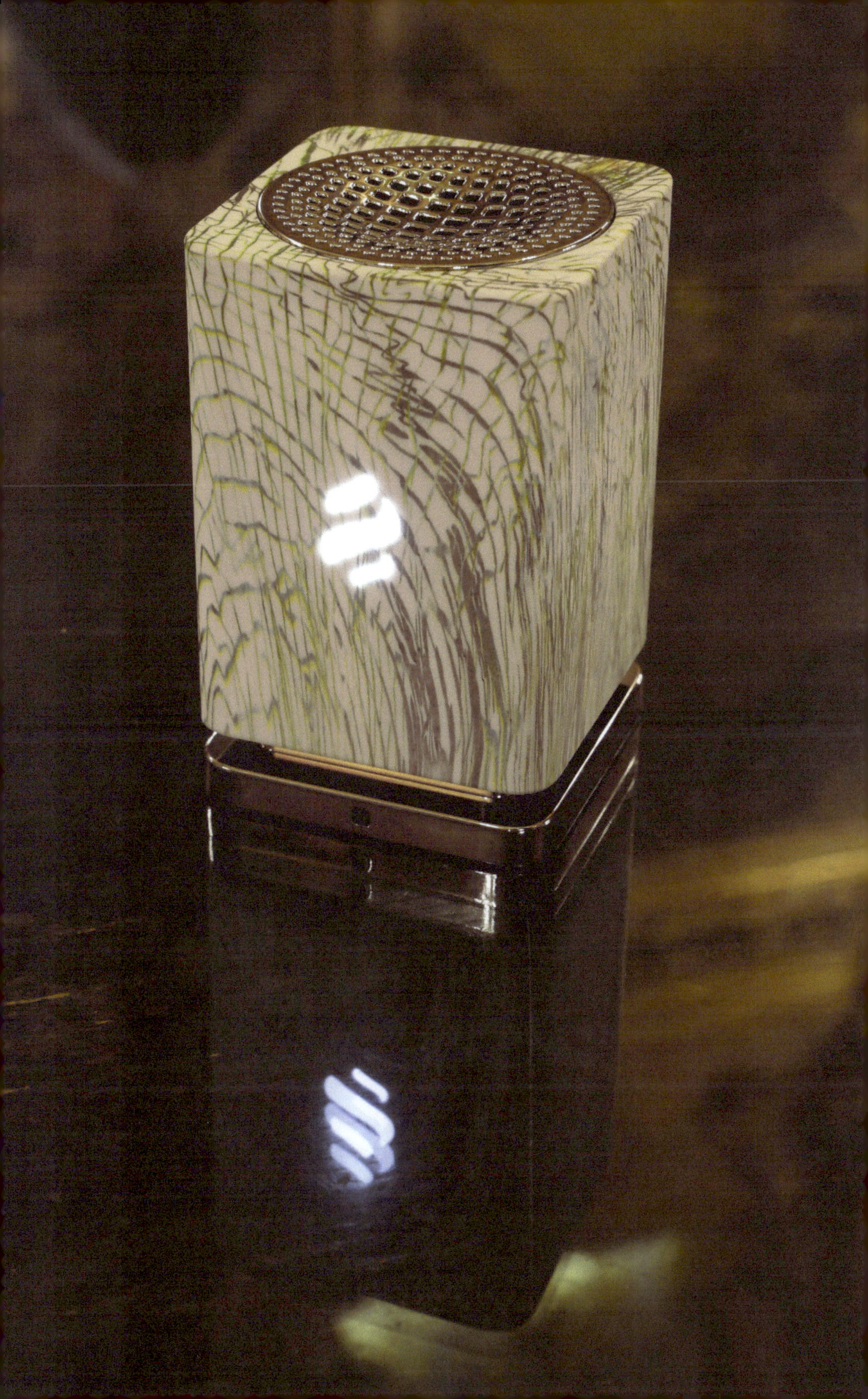

Yang Zhenzhong
Disguise
15th edition of the Ermanno Casoli Prize, 2015

The winner of the 15th edition of the Ermanno Casoli Prize was the Chinese artist Yang Zhenzhong (Hangzhou, China, 1968) with the project *Disguise*. Zhenzhong worked for over two months in the Elica plant in Shengzhou, actively involving dozens of employees.

The theatrical dimension of this edition of the Prize is evident from the title, *Disguise*. The project was in fact based on a performance by the Elica employees, invited by the artist to wear masks that reproduced their features, created through the use of the sophisticated technology of 3D scanning. During the regular shift, the workers – with the masks on their faces – performed their traditional duties; however, thanks to the alienating element of the mask, the employees' actions took on an unexpected form, appearing as a sort of "staging" of the production process.

The performance was then translated into a video consisting of dilated atmospheres and cinematographic solutions able to emphasize the employees' actions. With their faces covered with the masks, their movements acquired the grace of a liberating dance, transforming the work context into a sort of theatrical *pièce*. Thanks to the simple metamorphosis of their features, Zhenzhong was able to restore a lyrical character to the employees' work, offering a novel view of the assembly line and the company environment. The work is also a reflection on the concept of identity that the mask, instead of cancelling, amplifies in a surreal and alienating way.

Disguise represented a challenge for the artist, who had already authored videos, but until that time had never produced something with such a participative and shared dimension. The entire project was presented in the Elica showroom in Shanghai in May 2015, with an installation that, in addition to the projection of the video, included the masks worn by the employees and other objects from the scenes. The work was selected and exhibited at the 11th Biennial Exhibition of Shanghai.

***Disguise*, 2015. Still from the video**

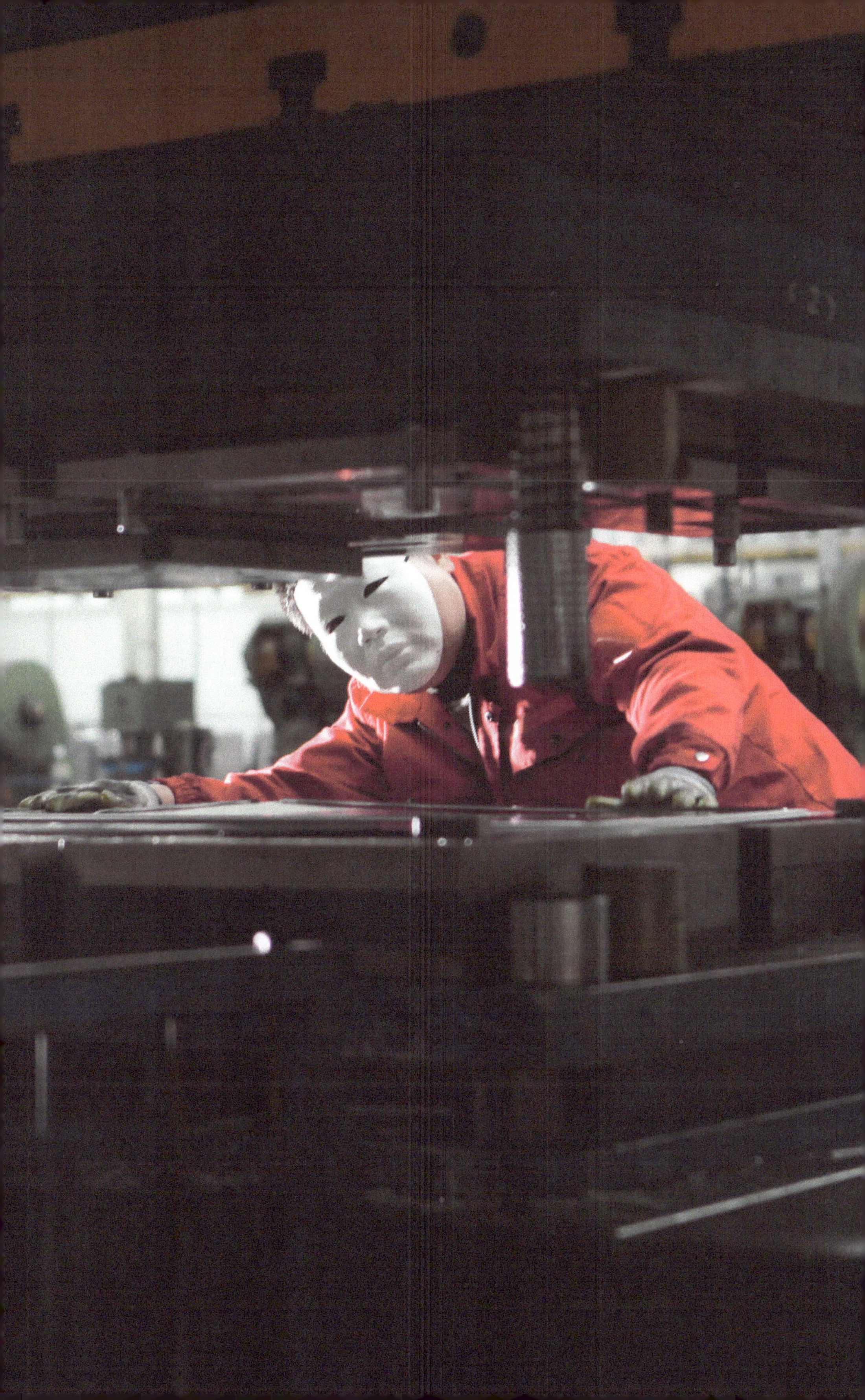

Marcello Maloberti
Mini Italia Kobra
E-STRAORDINARIO for Kids 2014

Mini Italia Kobra is the title of the performance conceived by Marcello Maloberti (Codogno, 1966) for E-STRAORDINARIO for Kids, created together with fifty children of Elica employees, on the streets of the city center of Fabriano. The preparatory phase of the workshop included a visit to the exhibit *From Giotto to Gentile* at the Bruno Molajoli Civic Art Gallery, followed by a practical workshop in which the little participants created special "backpacks." Produced with cardboard boxes decorated with drawings and collages, the backpacks depict people, objects, works of art, monuments and typical landscapes of the Italian collective imagination. The images and materials used were drawn from an archive prepared by the children, together with their families, in the months prior to the workshop. At the end of the workshop the performance was held in the city center: a colored, festive procession of children that enlivened the streets and squares accompanied by the Fabriano music band. For the occasion, the band performed a rearranged version of the song *Kobra* by Donatella Rettore, while the children paraded by with the "backpacks/archive" they had created, carrying an Italian three-colored flag extended with about twenty meters of red and white-checked fabric, typical of the tablecloths used on Italian tables, like a long snake or a Chinese dragon.

The activity represented a moment of reflection on Italian cultural heritage, both its "high" history and its popular traditions, that is a powerful bond and element of identity that cuts across all generations, in line with the philosophy of Maloberti, who has always been interested in the contamination between performance, urban context, kitsch aesthetic and mass culture. After walking through the streets of downtown, the festive procession reached the Elica factory, the moment that marked the inauguration of the segment of road that leads to the company, named after Ermanno Casoli, Elica's founder.

***Mini italia Kobra*, 2014**

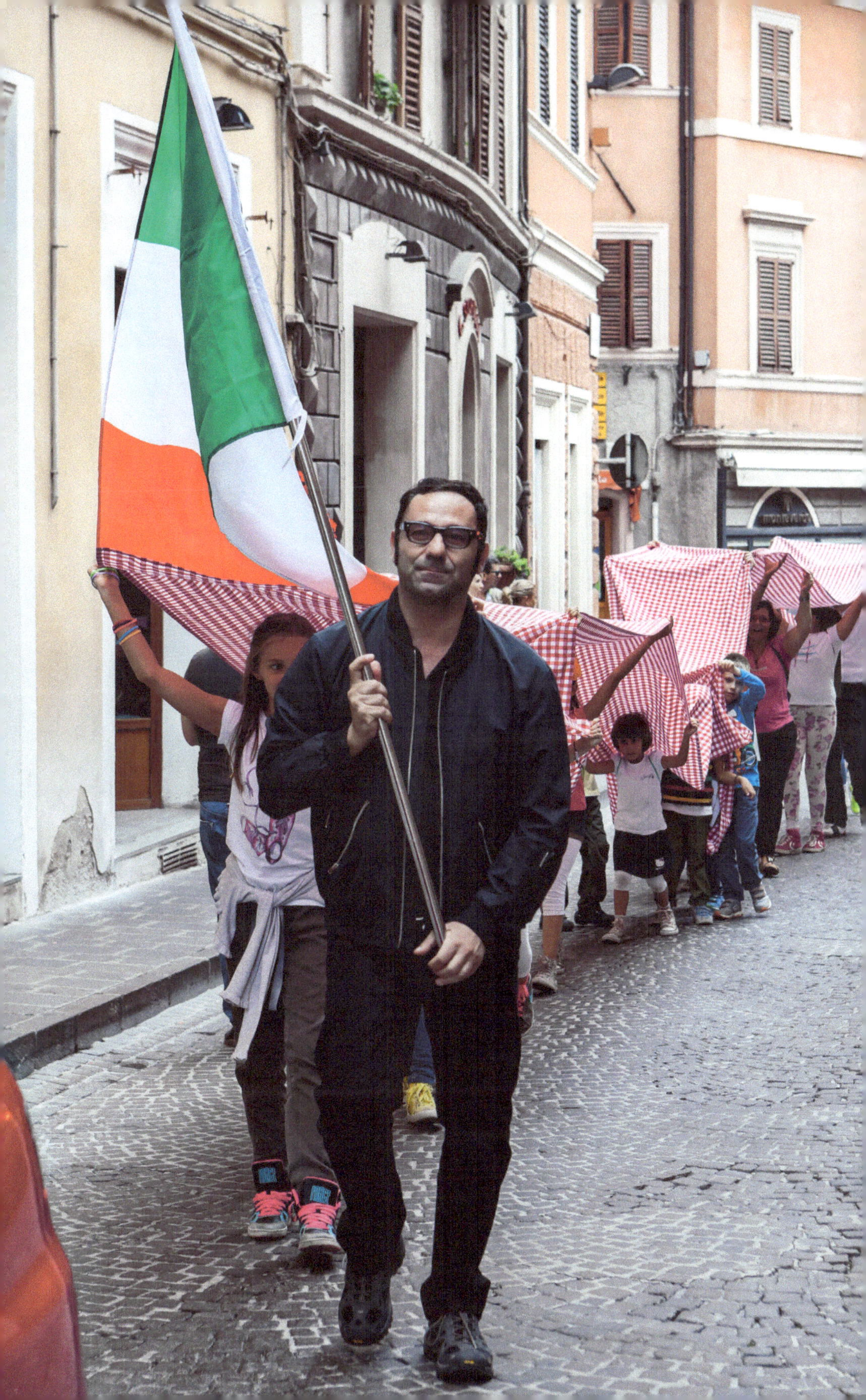

Danilo Correale
The Game – una partita di calcio a tre porte
14th edition of the Ermanno Casoli Prize, 2013-2014

Conceived by the artist Danilo Correale (Naples, 1982) for the 14th edition of the Ermanno Casoli Prize, *The Game – una partita di calcio a tre porte* saw the involvement of companies other than Elica for the first time. The protagonists were the employees of three companies in the territory of Siena: ColleVilca, PR Industrial and Trigano, who created an entirely unique game of soccer, midway between a sports event and a performance, a metaphor to read and interpret human relations.

In particular, Danilo Correale worked from the fundamental theories of three-goal soccer, a sport conceived by the Danish situationist artist Asger Jorn, used as a tool to overcome the spirit of competition that characterizes traditional soccer, promoting feelings of aggregation and cooperation among the participants, and stimulating and favoring the formation of elastic strategic alliances. In collaboration with dozens of employees of the companies, Correale gave form to the identity of three teams, (*GladiaTori*, *Real Cristal*, and *Esuberanti 301*, each with their own colors, jerseys, and fans): a temporary community founded on collaboration, playing and participation.

Correale's project took place over almost a full year and was developed in four phases: the first saw the artist gradually enter into contact with the employees of the single companies through meetings to prepare the birth of the teams and understand three-goal soccer; in the second phase, the group practices took place, where the participants not only learned the practical rules of three-goal soccer, but also made friends; the third phase was the actual game, in December 2013, at the Colle Val d'Elsa stadium; the fourth and final phase was the presentation in Siena in June 2014 of the documentary film that told the story of the whole experience, with all of the employees involved present.

The Game – una partita di calcio a tre porte was a project fully in line with the philosophy of Danilo Correale, who has always been interested in the behavioral and aesthetic dynamics of micro-communities in the context of capitalist society. The documentary film was subsequently acquired by the MADRE Museum of Naples for its permanent collection.

***The Game – una partita di calcio a tre porte*, 2013**

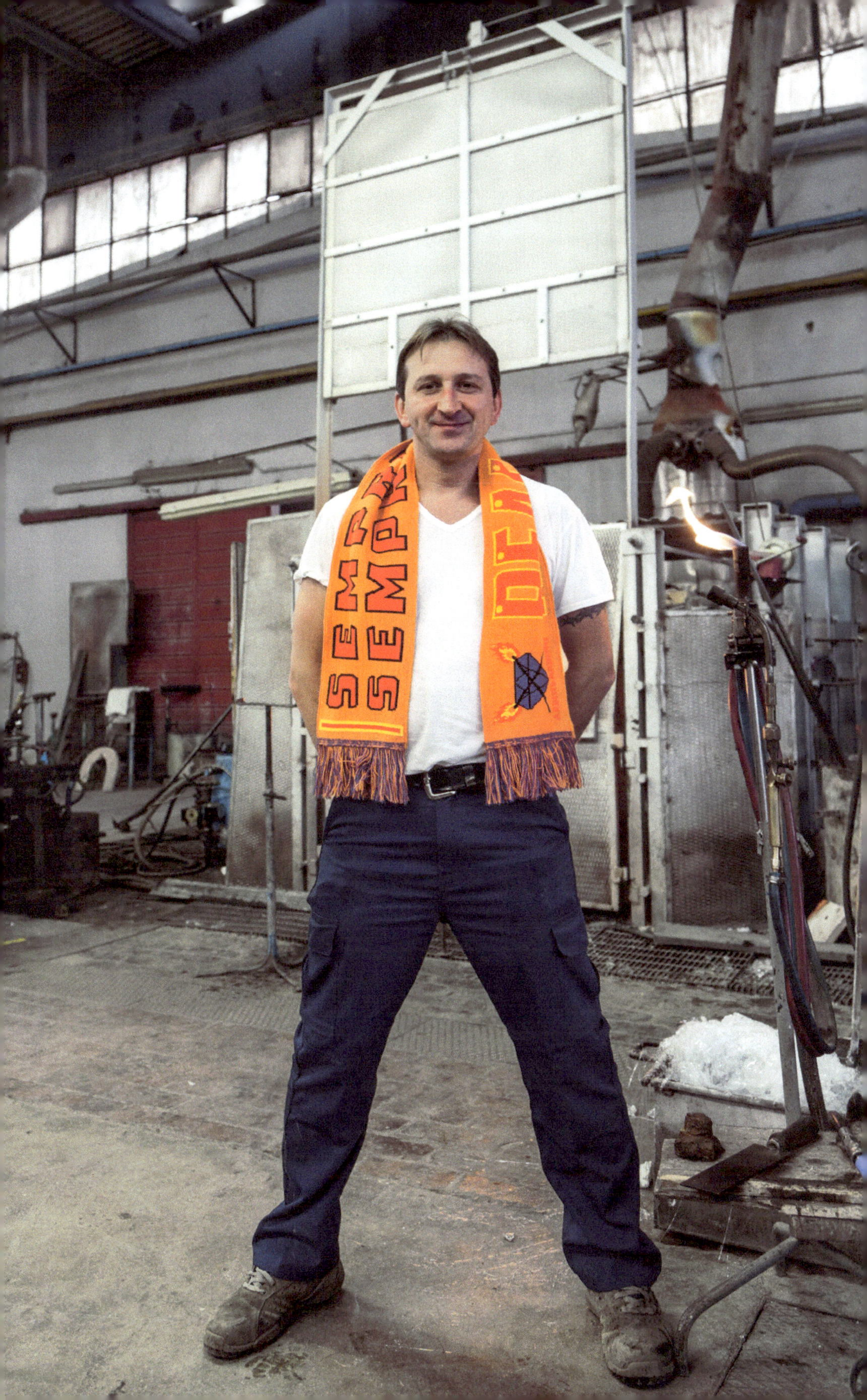

Fabio Barile, Francesco Neri
Middle-Earth. A Journey Inside Elica
FEC for Factories 2014

Middle-Earth. A Journey inside Elica is the title of the project created by the photographers Fabio Barile (Barletta, 1980) and Francesco Neri (Faenza, 1982) for Elica. For the occasion, the artistic director of the FEC, Marcello Smarrelli, was assisted in managing the project by Alessandro Dandini de Sylva, who specializes in contemporary photography.

This is a commission aimed at conducting a photographic campaign in three of Elica Group's facilities around the world – Querétaro (Mexico), Shengzhou (China), and Fabriano (Italy) – with the goal of recognizing the complexity of a multinational company that goes beyond the simple definition of "business"; a company formed by the people who work there, each with their own precious identity, investigated without any rhetoric by the photographers' lenses.

The thirty pictures show the faces, workspaces and landscapes that characterize the locations of the factories, documenting the continuous interaction and close dialogue between the photographers, the people and the environment, succeeding in the difficult task of describing the different faces of Elica: its local roots and international projection, the strength of the highest tradition of Italian design and its openness to the dynamics and cultures of the various countries where it works, the advanced technologies of production systems and the inclination to research typical of a laboratory.

The photographs were presented in an exhibit set up in the Elica showroom during the *Fuorisalone 2014* (a side event of the Milan Furniture Fair, with a set-up managed by the stARTT architecture and territorial transformations studio) and collected in an important publication in which they are accompanied by the interview with the photographers and the critical texts written by the curators. The participation of Barile and Neri demonstrated the FEC's desire to offer support for the most recent trends in photography, of which the two authors are among the most highly regarded-exponents. They seek to re-interpret in new terms a "line" represented by photographers such as Luigi Ghirri and Guido Guidi.

Fabio Barile, *Painting oven Mergo*, 2014

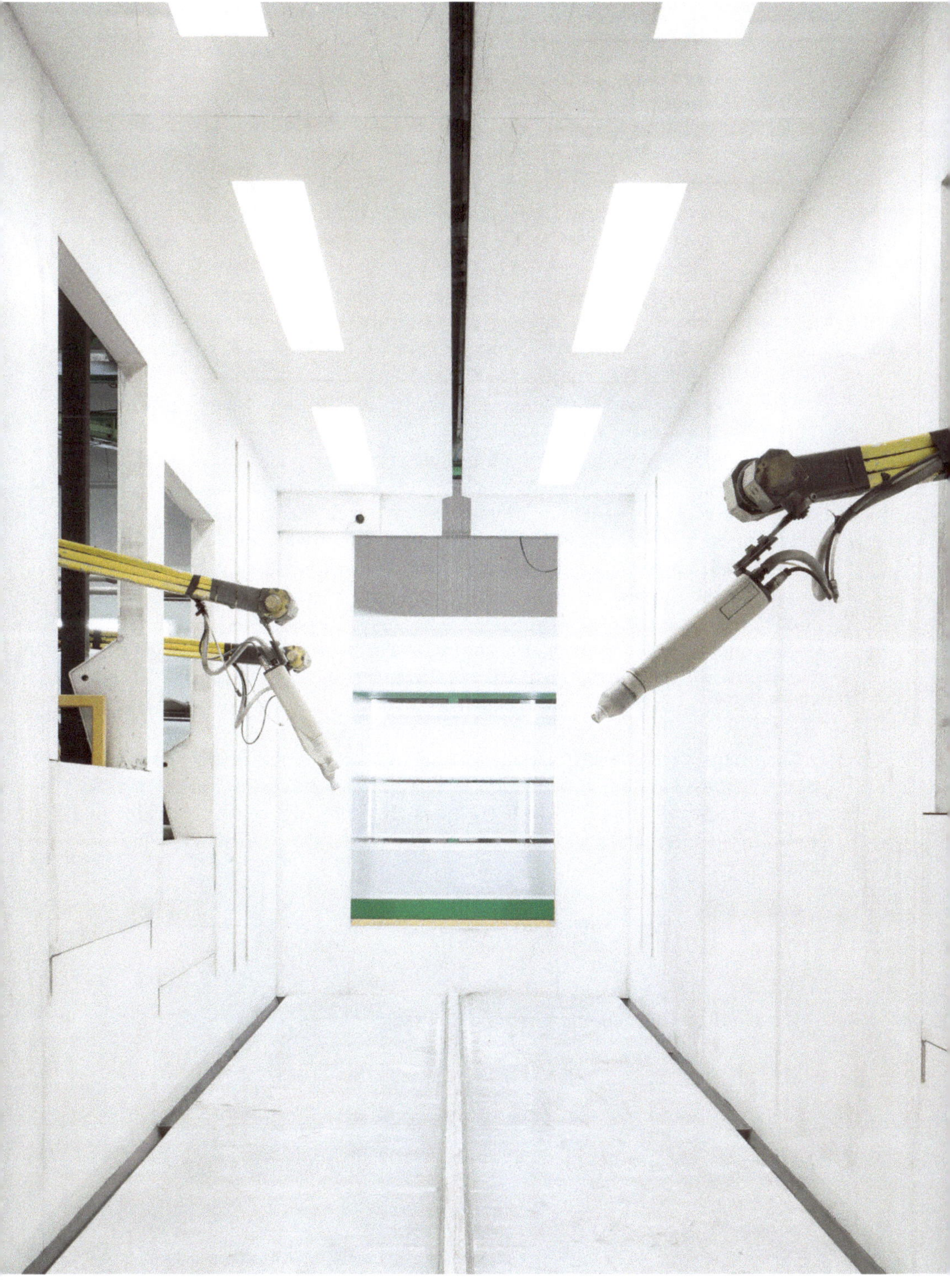

Marinella Senatore
Filming the process #1, #2
E-STRAORDINARIO 2011, 2012

Filming the process is the title of the workshop conceived and conducted on two occasions by the artist and film-maker Marinella Senatore (Cava de' Tirreni, 1977). The first was held in Milan at the the Documentation Center for Visual Arts (DOCVA) organized by the Careof and Viafarini associations inside the *Fabbrica del Vapore* cultural space, with the participation of twenty employees of Biotronik Italia spa (2011). The second was organized for thirty-five students in the Master in Economics and Management of Art and Cultural Heritage of the Business School of *Il Sole 24 Ore* (2012), once again in Milan. Both the editions of *Filming the process* were designed with the trainer Giovanni Boano, of the Hic et Nunc training company.

The workshop focused on the possibility to trigger and drive processes of participation and aggregation through the use of cinematographic practices, a method of expression that due to its choral structure is frequently used by the artist. In both of the editions of the workshop, the participants were involved in the production of a series of short films in which, divided by groups, they covered all of the phases of the work process: from writing to shooting, from direction to final editing.

The project thus stimulated the ability to address the work of the single participants towards a shared goal and a "collective thinking," where the areas of intervention and skills of each member were managed in favor of collaboration and teamwork. That method distinguishes and makes Marinella Senatore's activity unique: active participation, collaboration, and involvement of specific contexts and communities of people are in fact the salient features of the artist's work, recognized around the world for her ability to trigger processes able to give life to actions and performances with high rates of creativity and inclusiveness.

***Filming the process #2*, 2012. A moment of the workshop**

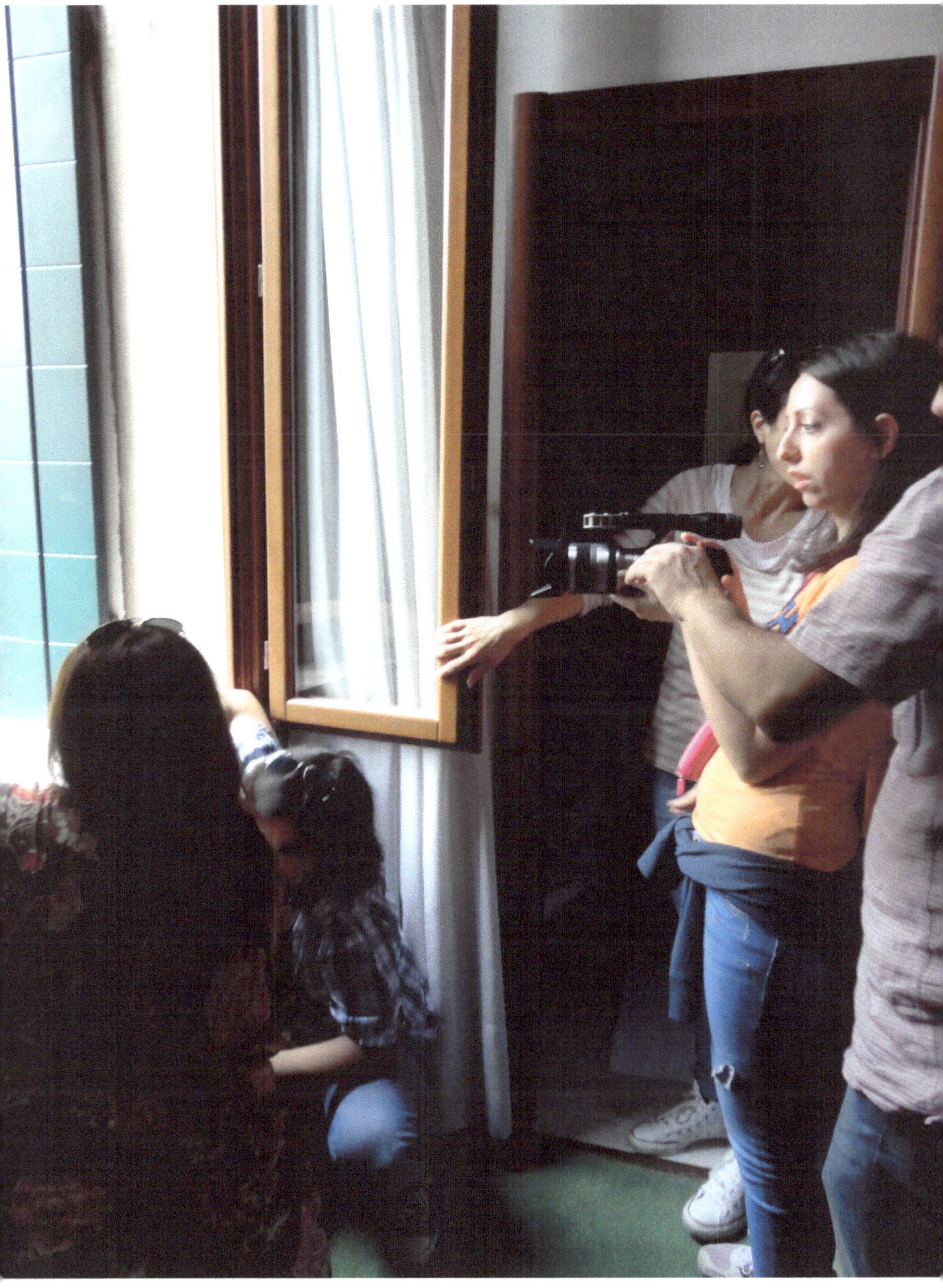

Anna Franceschini

Rock-Paper-Scissors

13th edition of the Ermanno Casoli Prize, 2012

The work conceived by Anna Franceschini (Pavia, 1979) for the 13th edition of the Ermanno Casoli Prize starts from the specific features of the territory of Fabriano, broken down and reinvented through study using the medium of film and the conceptualization of images in movement, that are part of the artist's approach. Franceschini concentrated on the quality of the landscape of the Marches region, as well as some aspects linked to the social and economic dimensions of the area, observed during a period of residence in Fabriano.

These characteristics were subsequently translated into a project entitled *Rock-Paper-Scissors*. The work consisted of film recordings transferred onto video media, divided and reformulated in a video installation on three spatially contiguous channels, with a rotation of images of the landscape of and around Fabriano (the mountains, the woods, the nearby Frasassi Caves), machines in action within the Elica factory in Mergo, and the ritual of the *Infiorata*, i.e. the creation of large floral compositions on the ground that takes place each year during the night of San Giovanni in the city. The images, recorded on Super8 film – without audio and with a quality that approaches the language of traditional experimental cinema – come in a dizzying succession, like the rotating symbols of a slot machine, in an infinite search for meaning through juxtaposition, constructing a cinematographic device that drives itself thanks to an intrinsic need to show to others and to show itself.

The title comes from a correspondence between the collection of images and their alternation, analogous to the Chinese game of rock-paper-scissors: the mountains represent the rock, the automated machines in the Mergo factory are the scissors, while the paper is represented, metonymically, by the floral designs, the preparatory sketches that precede the chromatic distribution of the petals in a city, Fabriano, known around the world for the production of quality paper.

Linguistically, the work reflects on the concept of *loop* in two different ways as regards internal topology: on the one hand, the loop is horizontal, with no starting or ending point, infinitely repeatable and executable; on the other, it is vertical, in the succession and replacement of the combinations of images on the three video channels.

Rock-Paper-Scissors was displayed at one of the warehouses of the Elica headquarters, in a pavilion designed by the Salottobuono architecture studio covered with mirrored steel slabs that reflected and absorbed the daily work performed in that context.

The edition of the Prize was accompanied by video projections and talks – aimed in particular at Elica employees, but open to the public – entitled *Images Moving Images*, held in Ancona with the involvement of the artists Dina Danish, Rebecca Digne, Diego Marcon and Jean Baptiste Maitre.

***Rock-Paper-Scissors*, 2012**

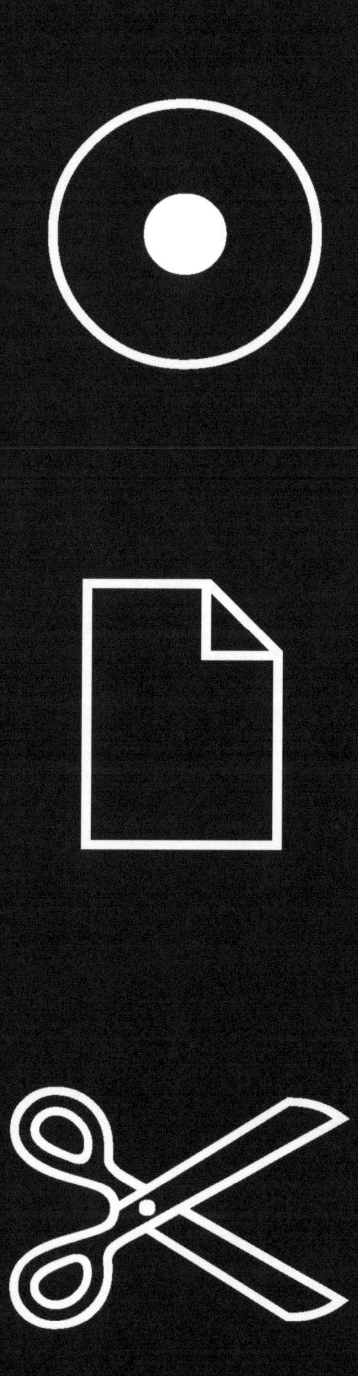

Sissi
Aspiranti Aspiratori
FEC for Factories 2012

Aspiranti Aspiratori is the project by the artist Sissi (Bologna, 1977), created for Elica. Entering the heart of the company with her constant presence and actions, the artist generated a continuous and incessant osmotic exchange which led to the birth of a new identity: the *Organindustry*, that is, the industry transformed in the very body of the artist.

Starting from this premise, Sissi got to work on the task of rethinking the concept of air purification, a central theme in Elica's research. To create the project, the artist constructed her own temporary atelier within the Prototypes Laboratory of the Fabriano headquarters. The "Cubator" – this is the name given to her workspace – appeared as a protected and limited place, but at the same time open to all types of interaction. In this space, the employees of the company could see the artist's works as they were born and grew, becoming participants and accomplices in this genesis. From that delicate process of contamination and exchange came drawings, collages, sculptures and thoughts, then translated into the ten *Aspiring Aspirators*: ten potential figures that aspire to become air purifiers, each with a well-defined identity and a name that indicates the key concept, consistent with its form and function.

Three of the ten *Aspiring Aspirators* designed were then produced and subsequently displayed, together with the animated video *Casting* that tells the story of the their birth, shown in the Elica showroom on the occasion of the Fuorisalone 2012, a side event of the Milan Furniture Fair, with an installation by the Salottobuono architecture studio.

The project was also the protagonist of two important events sponsored by the FEC in collaboration with Elica: the presentation of the artist's book published by Corraini that documents all of the phases of the work, presented at the MAMbo – Museum of Modern Art of Bologna, as part of the 9th Artelibro Festival of Bologna 2012; and at the artist's personal exhibit of the same name, held at the Aike-dellarco Gallery of Shanghai in 2013.

Aspiranti Aspiratori was selected by the Permanent Design Observatory of the AdI (Association for Industrial Design), to be included in the book *ADI Design Index 2012* in the "Research for business" area.

***Aspiranti Aspiratori*, 2012**

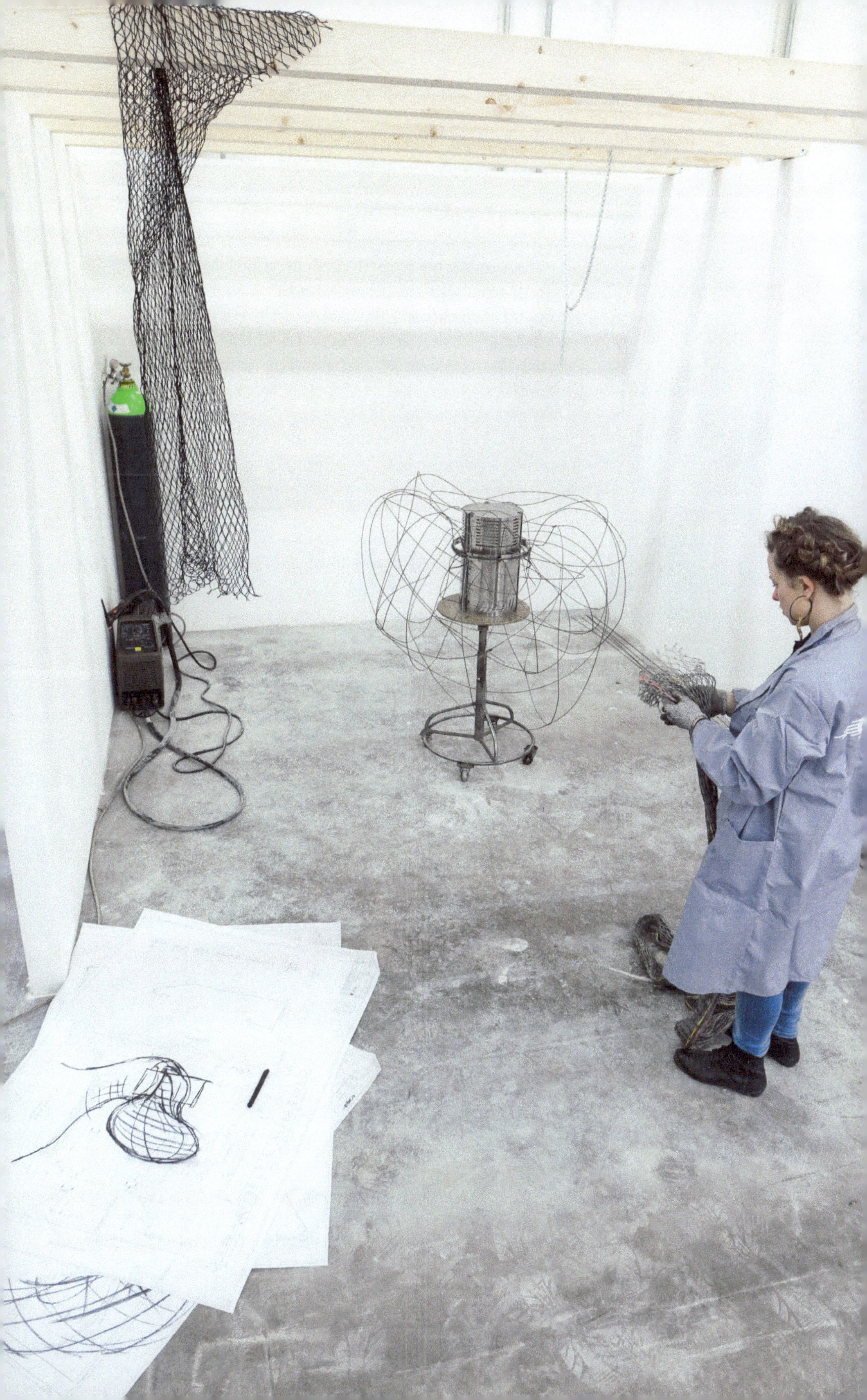

Francesco Barocco
I Saettatori
12th edition of the Ermanno Casoli Prize, 2011

I Saettatori is the title of the work created by Francesco Barocco (Susa, 1972) for the 12th edition of the Ermanno Casoli Prize, with the participation of forty-five Elica employees. The project refers to a drawing by Michelangelo which depicts nine archers without bows or arrows, emblems of a paradoxical action, lacking an evident aim but full of energy and tension.

The artist interpreted the involvement of the employees not as direct participation in the creation of the work of art (as is customary for the Ermanno Casoli Prize), but as conceptual and emotional sharing of the artistic experience. Barocco in fact structured his intervention in different phases (a workshop, an engraving exhibit, and the creation of some works for the Elica headquarters in Fabriano), presenting a process aimed at becoming acquainted with the ideas and references that inspire the artists, showing daily life, practice, the repetitiveness of artistic gestures, and the doubts that characterize creative work. This way, Barocco offered a practical demonstration of the possible similarities that can be found between the activity of the artist and that of other types of work, trades and professions.

The first phase of the project took place at the Paper and Watermark Museum of Fabriano, where the artist gave a series of lessons on engraving, showing how knowledge of tools and technical mastery, like in any other profession, constitute the basis of artistic work. Francesco Barocco then reconceived the Elica spaces in Fabriano, readapting them to create a permanent installation composed of his etchings (displayed using large wood stumps as supports) and by a selection of engravings by great authors from the history of art (Albrecht Dürer, Giovanni Battista Piranesi, Katsushika Hokusai, Edouard Manet, Louise Nevelson, Anders Leonard Zorn, Hans Bellmer and Carol Rama), training the participants so that they could guide their colleagues and guests who visit the company along the exhibit path.

***I Saettatori*, 2011. Detail of the installation**

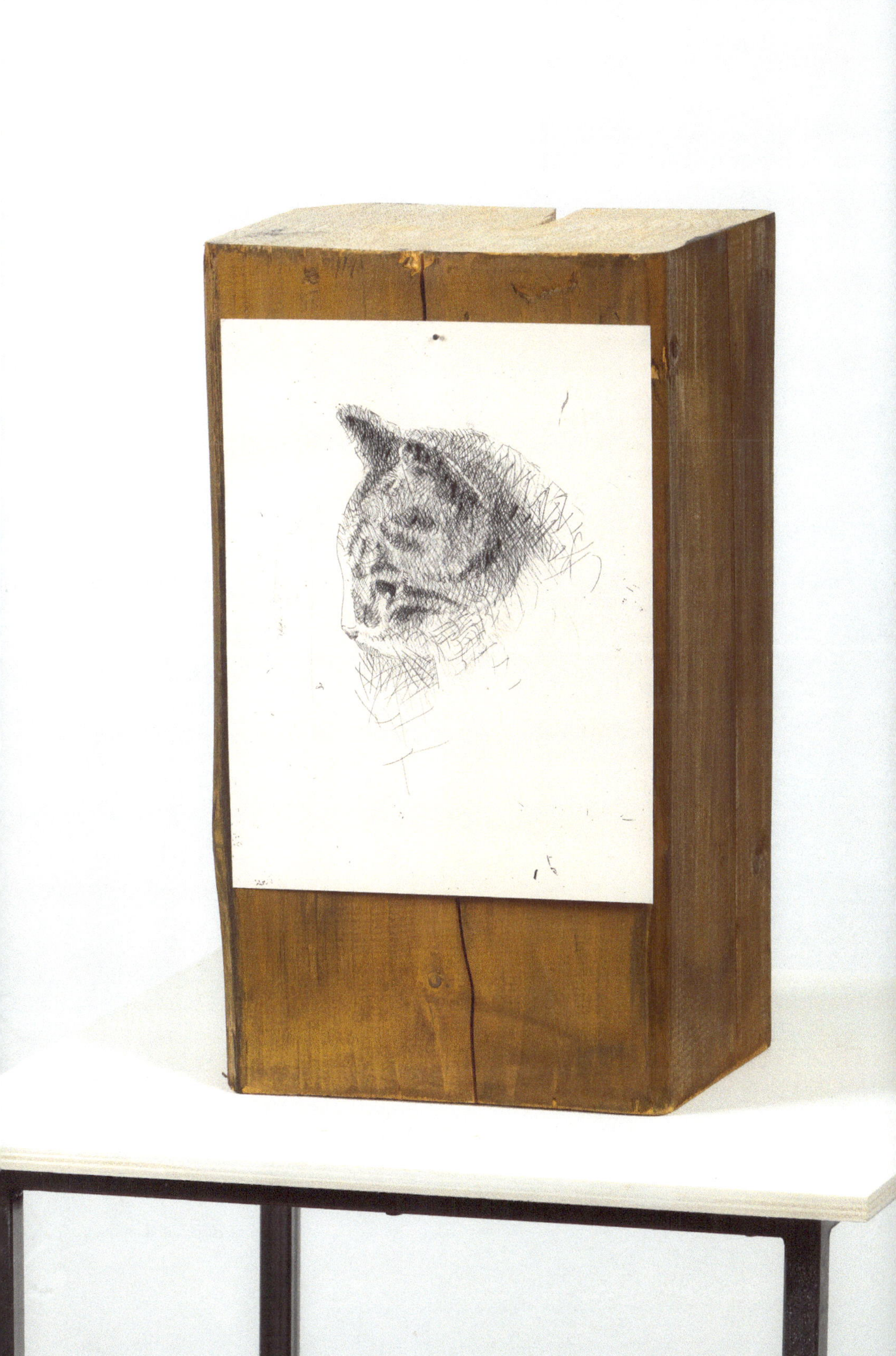

Grzegorz Drozd
Opera
E-STRAORDINARIO on tour 2010

Opera by Grzegorz Drozd (Warsaw, 1970) is the first E-STRAORDINARIO appointment organized outside of the borders of Italy (on tour, as per the title of the project). For the occasion, the artistic director of the FEC, Marcello Smarrelli, was assisted in curating the project by the Pole Stach Szabłowski (Center for Contemporary Art at Ujazdowski Castle, Warsaw). The workshop saw the participation of thirty employees of the Elica plant in Jelcz-Laskowice, Poland, assisted by the trainer Monica Schwertner.

Grzegorz Drozd is a careful observer of the reality he describes with his own language, creating disquieting and surprising situations that are often improvised and without screenplays, playing on stereotypes and rituals that call into question the conventions of the system of art.

The project that the artist conceived of for E-STRAORDINARIO, based on valuing each single intervention within a collective action, highlighted the creative potential of the community composed of the workers, introducing unusual elements in the daily life of the factory, despite maintaining the organization and distribution of work unchanged. Gregorz Drodz thus created a musical performance in which the participants had a toy musical instrument that they could play freely during the performance of their daily duties.

As happens in business environments, during the performance each individual became a part of a broader and more complex system, and the joint action of the participants was aimed at reaching a common goal: production, the *opera*, intended both in a musical sense and in the symbolic sense of *opus*, of material, of product that is born from a process.

***Opera*, 2010. Still from video**

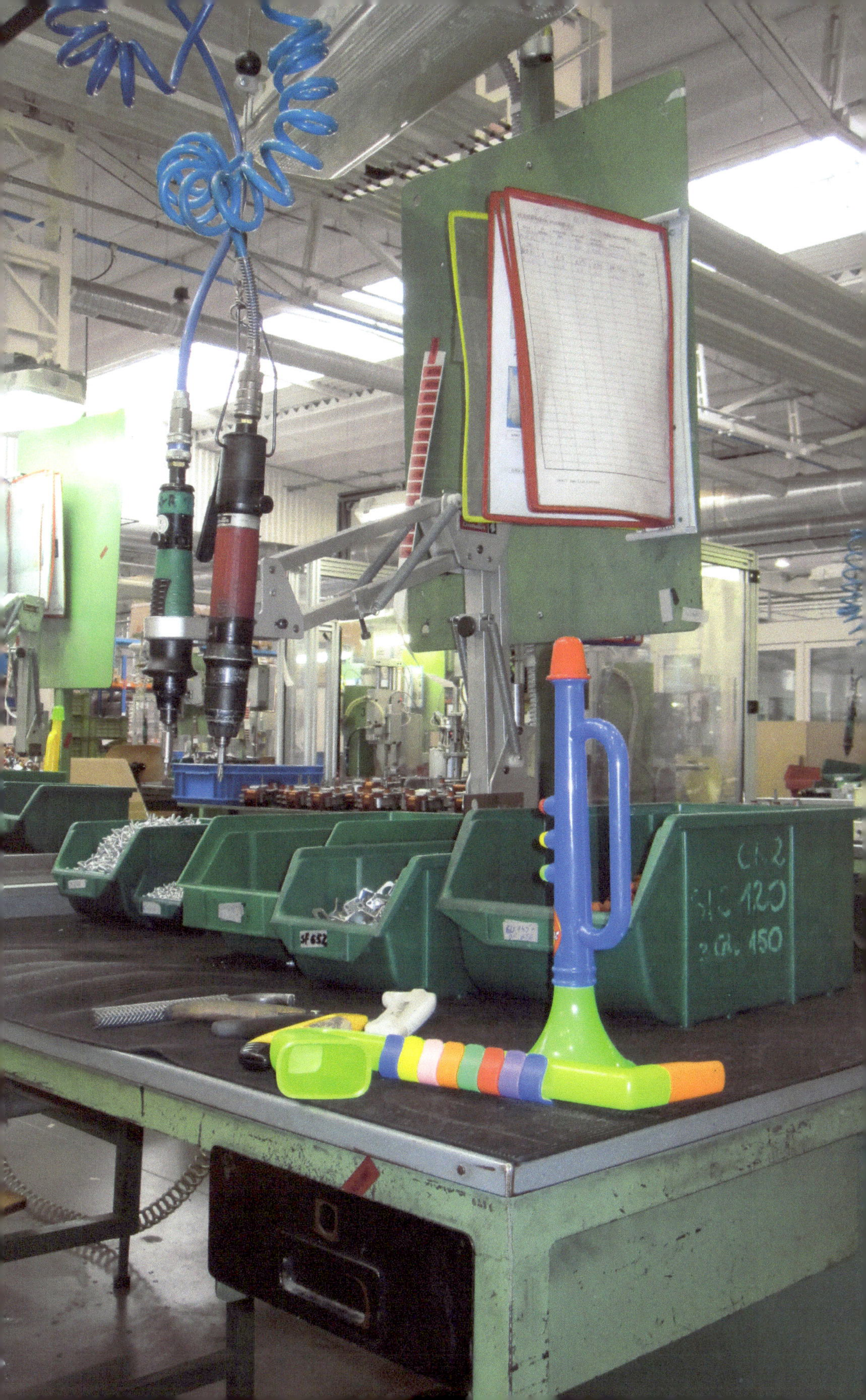
SF652

Francesco Arena
Teste
11th edition of the Ermanno Casoli Prize, 2009

Teste is the title of the work created by Francesco Arena (Torre Santa Susanna, 1978) with the participation of twenty Elica employees for the 11th edition of the Ermanno Casoli Prize. The project focuses on the value of the past as a source of reflection and iconographic inspiration. Since ancient times, artists have dealt with the question of time and history, the constant search for a language more suitable to represent and transmit the memory of certain crucial moments or make those people who have left their mark on human destiny immortal.

Starting from these assumptions, through a long process of reflection led by the artist, the working group identified six significant figures for the history of the Marches region (the artists Gino De Dominicis and Osvaldo Licini; the industrialist and politician Giambattista Miliani; the pedagogue and educator Maria Montessori; the Jesuit, mathematician, and cartographer Father Matteo Ricci; and the soprano Renata Tebaldi) and for each of them a clay sculpture portrait was created. The six busts were placed in various points inside and outside the Elica headquarters in Fabriano, and through an original hydraulic mechanism for the collection and dispersion of rainwater (obtained with the use of waste material from the production of hoods), they were subjected to a process of natural corrosion.

The intervention thus became a clear metaphor for the passage of time and the consequent corrosion and dispersion of memory, as demonstrated also by the other works produced by Arena in his career. Six years later, the artist again intervened on his work, placing small marble slabs in the places where the now completely worn-down sculptures had been located, with the names of the six people depicted in the first phase of the work engraved on them. Entrusting the names of the people depicted to the passage of time, greater clarity was given to the contrast between the ephemeral nature of memory and that of the work of art to make it current and lasting.

***Teste*, 2009. Detail of the installation**

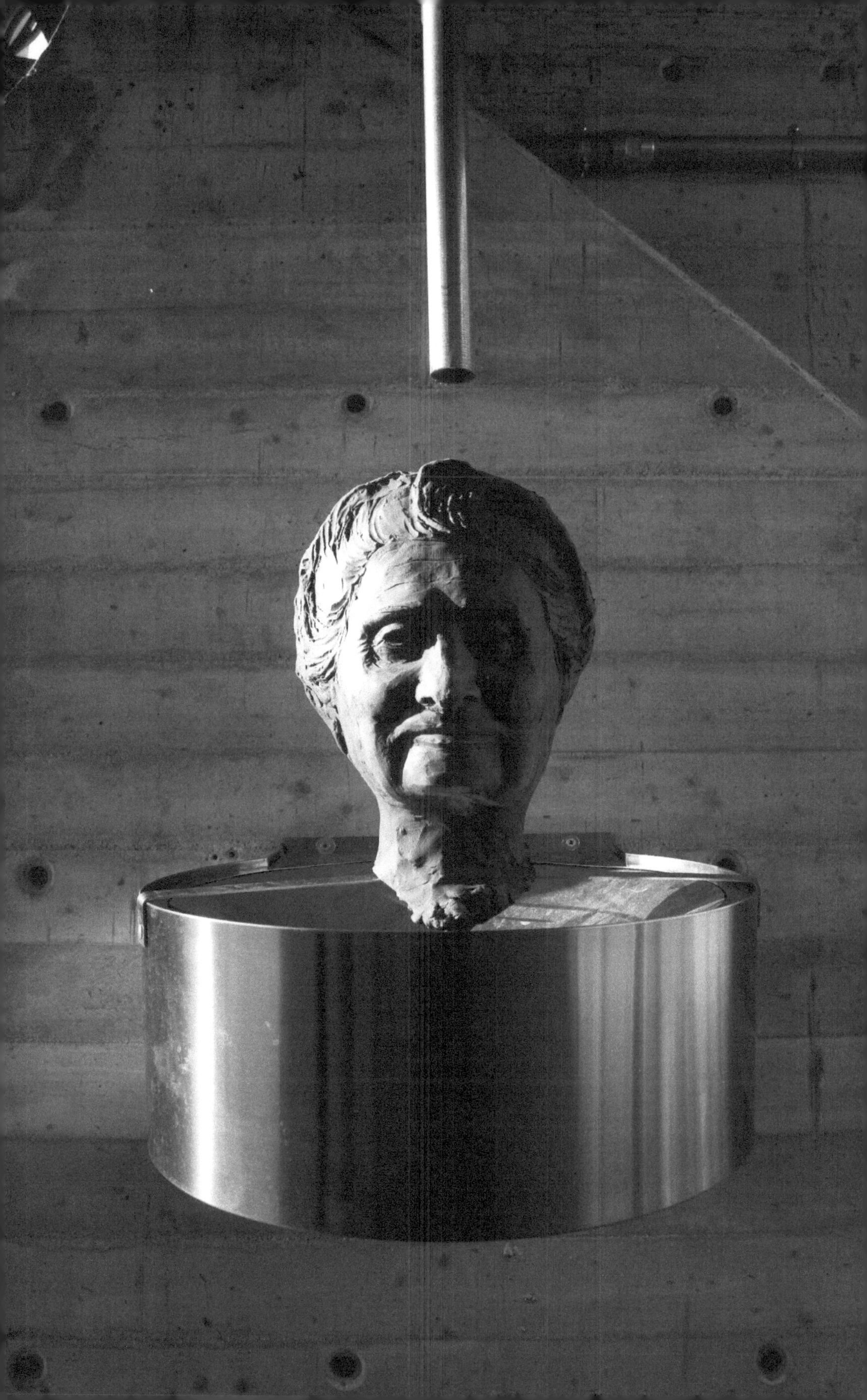

Cesare Pietroiusti
L'intelligenza del caso
E-STRAORDINARIO 2009

L'intelligenza del caso is the title of the workshop conceived and conducted by the artist Cesare Pietroiusti (Rome, 1955) with fifty-seven employees of Elica, held in the company premises in Fabriano.

The workshop, organized over two working days, aimed to investigate two specific themes: the error determined by chance, which can generate an unexpected resource, and the mechanisms linked to economic exchange – both at the center of Pietroiusti's studies. Initially, the artist involved the participants in a reflection on the themes proposed, to then shift on the next day to the creation of two thousand drawings using candle smoke (an element connected to the aspirating function of the hoods) and Rosso Conero red wine (typical of the Marches). These two elements, thanks to the interventions of the participating employees, produced unexpected and uncontrollable effects on paper (the high-quality product from Fabriano).

Duemila disegni da portare via is the title of the large installation created at the Fabriano headquarters and destined to be gradually dispersed. All of the people who come to the facilities (employees, clients, suppliers, visitors) are in fact asked to take a drawing, committing to respecting the instructions given by the artist and the participants that are printed on each page: those who get a drawing made with wine have to return it to the same place within a year, having used it in an experience that leaves a trace on the page; those who get one made with candle smoke, declared to be an incomplete work, must complete the process of its combustion, and may consider the ashes as the finished work of art.

The goal of the workshop was to learn to recognize chance and make creative use of chance, side effects and errors, reflecting on and playing with the rigidity of paradigms and the methods of economic processes, understood as the exchange of goods and money, typical of the worlds of both business and art.

***L'intelligenza del caso*, 2009. A moment of the workshop**

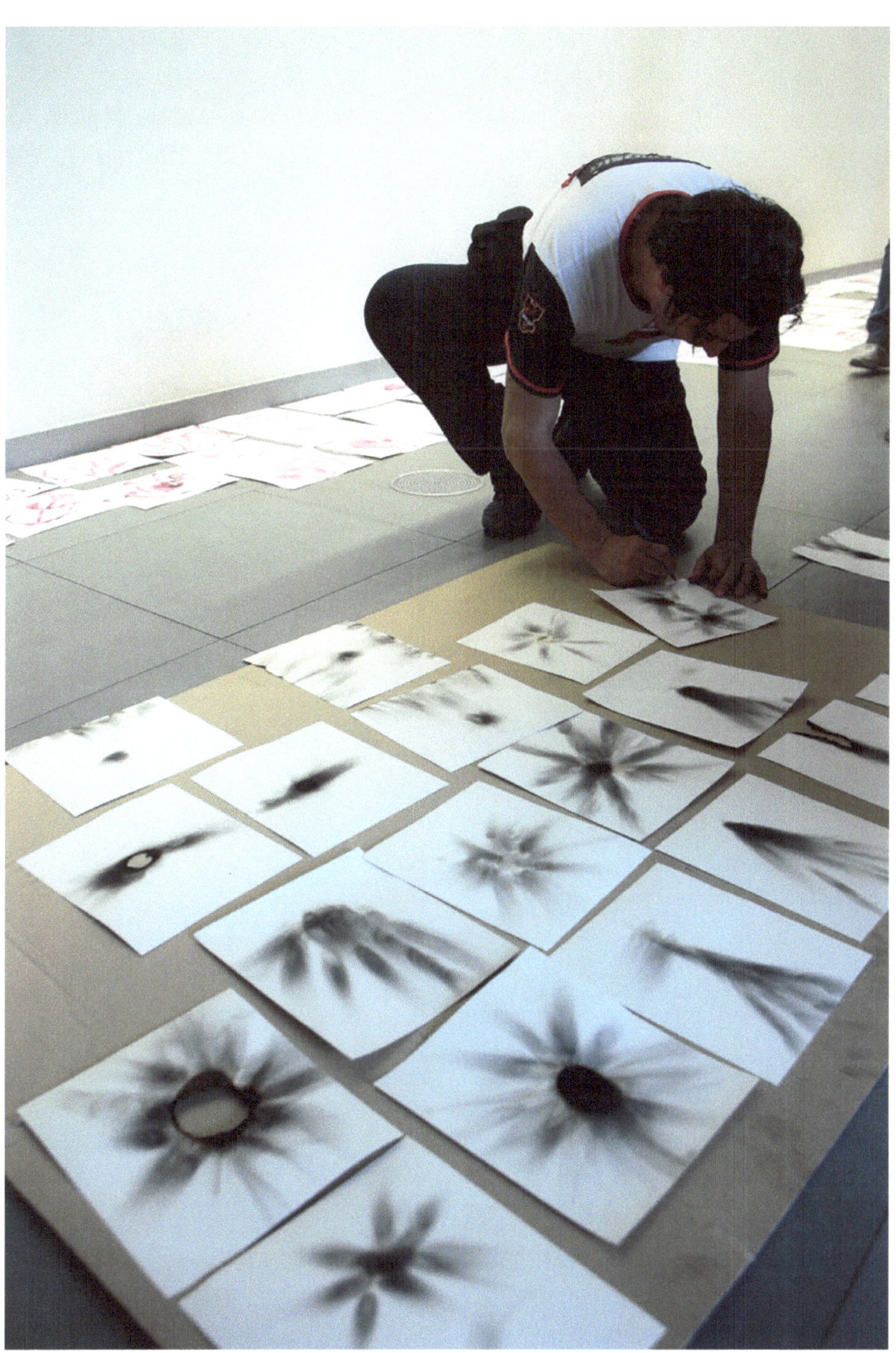

Acknowledgements

The authors wish to thank the artists who have worked and continue to work with the FEC, without whose generosity this book would not have the same depth and importance. We thank all of the companies that host the artistic interventions carried out by the FEC and the trainers that sponsor them, without whom all of this would not be possible.

We thank the Catholic University of Milan for the support given to the initiatives regarding the themes addressed in the book.

Particular thanks go to Daniela Aliberti, a doctoral student in Management & Innovation at the Catholic University, and Cristina Terzoni for their precious contributions to the research and coordination of this project.

Bibliography

Adler, N.J. (2015), «Finding Beauty in a Fractured World: Art Inspires Leaders – Leaders Change the World», *Academy of Management Review*, 40(3), 480-494.

Antal, A.B. (2013), «Art-Based Research for Engaging Not-Knowing in Organizations», *Journal of Applied Arts & Health*, 4(1), 67-76.

Antal, A.B., Strauß, A. (2013), *Artistic Interventions in Organisations: Finding Evidence of Values-Added*, Creative Clash Report, WZB, Berlino. Antal, A.B., Hutter, M., Stark, D. (Eds.) (2015), *Moments of Valuation: Exploring Sites of Dissonance*, Oxford University Press, Oxford.

Arthur, M.B., Hall, D.T., Lawrence, B.S. (1989), *Handbook of Career Theory*, Cambridge University Press, Cambridge.

Ashforth, B.E., Saks, A.M. (1995), «Work-Role Transitions: a Longitudinal Examination of the Nicholson Model», *Journal of Occupational and Organizational Psychology*, 68(2), 157-175.

Austin, R.D., Devin, L. (2003), *Artful making: What Managers Need To Know About How Artists Work*, FT Press, Upper Side River.

A.A.V.V. (1981-1991), *Microstorie*. Einaudi, Turin.

Barry, D., Meisiek, S. (2010), «Seeing More and Seeing Differently: Sensemaking, Mindfulness, and the Workarts», *Organization Studies*, 31(11), 1505-1530.

Barry, D., Meisiek, S. (2015), «Discovering the Business Studio», *Journal of Management Education*, 39(1), 153-175.

Bechky, B.A. (2003), «Sharing Meaning Across Occupational Communities: The Transformation of Understanding on a Production Floor», *Organization Science*, 14(3), 312-330.

Bell, B.S., Kozlowski, S.W. (2008), «Active Learning: Effects of Core Training Design Elements on Self-Regulatory Processes, Learning, and Adaptability», *Journal of Applied Psychology*, 93(2), 296.

Berthoin Antal, A. (2012), «Artistic intervention residencies and their intermediaries: A comparative analysis», *Organizational Aesthetics*, 1(1), 44-67.

Berthoin Antal, A., Debucquet, G., & Frémeaux, S. (2019), «When top management leadership matters: Insights from artistic interventions», *Journal of Management Inquiry*, 28(4), 441-457.

Bodega, D., Paolino, C. (2016), *Corporate Collections in Italy* (unpublished research report).

Bostrom, N. (2009), «Dignity and Enhancement», *Contemporary Readings in Law & Social Justice*, 1(2).

Bowker, G.C., Star, S.L. (2000), *Sorting Things Out: Classification and Its Consequences*, MIT Press, Boston.

Burke, P.J., Stets, J.E. (2009), *Identity Theory*, Oxford University Press, Oxford.

Carlile, P.R. (2002), «A Pragmatic View of Knowledge and Boundaries: Boundary Object in New Product Development», *Organization Science*, Vol. 13, No. 4, 442-455.

Carlucci, D., Schiuma, G. (2018), «The Power of the Arts in Business», *Journal of Business Research*, 85, 342-347.

Chemi, T. (2020a), «The Golden Path Towards the Arts/with Business», in Formica P., Edmondson J., *Innovation and the Arts. The Value of Humanities Studies for Business*, Emerald Group Publishing, Bingley, 43-58.

Chemi, T. (2020b), «It Is Impossible: The Teacher's Creative Response to the Covid-19 Emergency and Digitalized Teaching Strategies», *Qualitative Inquiry*, 1-8.

Collins, J., Hansen, M.T. (2011), *Great by Choice: Uncertainty, Chaos and Luck – Why Some Thrive Despite Them All*, Random House, New York.

Cook, T. (2009), «The purpose of mess in action research: building rigour though a messy turn», *Educational Action Research*, 17(2), 277-291.

Crowther, P. (2001), *Art and Embodiment: From Aesthetics to Self-Consciousness*, Oxford University Press, Oxford.

Darsø, L. (2004), *Artful creation, learning-tales of arts-in-business*, Samfundslitteratur, Frederiksberg.

Dewey, J., Bentley, A. (1949), *Knowing and the Known*, Beacon Press, Boston.

Eisner, E.W. (2002), «What Can Education Learn from the Arts about the Practice of Education?», *Journal of Curriculum and Supervision*, 18(1), 4-16.

Ferreira, F. A. (2018), «Mapping the Field of Arts-Based Management: Bibliographic Coupling and Co-Citation Analyses», *Journal of Business Research*, 85, 348-357.

Fisher, K.M., Lipson, J.I. (1986), «Twenty Questions about Student Errors», *Journal Of Research in Science Teaching*, 23(9), 783-803.

Formica, P. (2020), «Business Innovation and the Arts: The Golden Encounter», in Formica P., Edmondson J., *Innovation and the Arts. The Value of Humanities Studies for Business*, Emerald Group Publishing, Bingley, 1-42

Friedman, B.A. (2007), «Globalization Implications for Human Resource Management Roles», *Employee Responsibilities and Rights Journal*, 19(3), 157-171.

Furnari, S. (2014), «Interstitial Spaces: Microinteraction Settings and the Genesis of New Practices Between Institutional Fields», *Academy of Management Review*, 39(4), 439-462.

Gerdeman, D. (2021), «COVID Killed the Traditional Workplace. What Should Companies Do Now? », *Harvard Business School*: https://hbswk.hbs.edu/item/covid-killed-the-traditional-workplace-what-should-companies-do-now

Gergen, K.J. (1999), *An Invitation to Social Construction*, SAGE Publishing, Thousand Oaks.

Ghoshal, S. (2005), «Bad Management Theories Are Destroying Good Management Practices», *Academy of Management Learning & Education,* 4(1), 75-91.

Goldie, J. (2012), «The formation of professional identity in medical students: considerations for educators», *Medical Teacher*, 34(9), e641-e648.

Gombrich, E.H. (1999), *The Uses of Images: Studies in the Social Function of Art And Visual Communication*, Phaidon, Londra.

Hargadon, A., Sutton, R.I. (1997), «Technology Brokering and Innovation in a Product Development Firm», *Administrative Science Quarterly*, 716- 749.

Haskell, F. (1993), *History and its Images: Art and the Interpretation of the Past*, Yale University Press, New Haven.

Henderson, K. (1991), «Flexible Sketches and Inflexible Data Bases: Visual Communication, Conscription Devices, and Boundary Objects in Design Engineering», *Science, Technology, & Human Values*, 16(4), 448- 473.

Henriksen, D., Mishra, P. (2020), «Move slow and nurture things: wise creativity and humane centered values in a world that idolizes disruption», in Formica P., Edmondson J., *Innovation and the Arts. The Value of Humanities Studies for Business*, Emerald Group Publishing, Bingley, 43-58.

Jones, M.O. (1996), *Studying Organizational Symbolism: What, How, Why?* (Vol. 39), SAGE Publishing, Thousand Oaks.

Jorn, A. (1964), *The Application of the Triolectical Method in General Situology.*

Kreiner, G.E., Ashforth, B.E. (2004), «Evidence Toward an Expanded Model of Organizational Identification», *Journal of Organizational Behavior*, 25(1), 1-27.

Ladkin, D. (2008), «Leading Beautifully: How Mastery, Congruence and Purpose Create the Aesthetic of Embodied Leadership Practice» *The Leadership Quarterly*, 19(1), 31-41.

Lanaro, P. (2011), *Microstoria. A venticinque anni da L'eredità Immateriale*, FrancoAngeli, Milan.

Leonardi, P.M. (2012), «Materiality, Sociomateriality, and Socio-Technical Systems: What Do These Terms Mean? How Are They Related? Do We Need Them?», in: P.M. Leonardi, B.A. Nardi, & J. Kallinikos (Eds.), *Materiality and Organizing: Social Interaction in a Technological World*, Oxford University Press, Oxford.

Ligasacchi, G. (2017), «L'arte fa bene al business?», *Collezione da Tiffany*, Firenze.

Malchiodi, C.A. (1998), «Embracing our mission», *Art Therapy: Journal of the American Art Therapy Association*, 15, 2, 82-83.

McCarthy, K.F., Ondaatje, E.H., Zakaras, L., Brooks, A. (2001), *Gifts of the Muse: Reframing the Debate About the Benefits of the Arts*, Rand Corporation, Santa Monica.

McKinsey Report (2021), *COVID-19: Implications for Business*: https://www.mckinsey.com/business-functions/risk/our-insights/covid-19-implications-for-business#

Meisiek, S., de Monthoux, P.G., Barry, D., Austin, R.D. (2016), «Four Voices: Making a Difference with Art in Management Education», in: *The Routledge Companion to Reinventing Management Education,* Routledge, London.

Miles, S. (2017), «Stakeholder Theory Classification: A Theoretical and Empirical Evaluation of Definitions», *Journal of Business Ethics*, 142(3), 437-459.

Mirvis, P.H. (2005), «Large Group Interventions: Change as Theatre», *The Journal of Applied Behavioral Science*, 41(1), 122-138.

Montanari, F., Scapolan, A., Gianecchini, M. (2016), «'Absolutely free'? The Role of Relational Work in Sustaining Artistic Innovation», *Organization Studies*, 37(6), 797-821.

Nicholson, N. (1984), «A Theory of Work Role Transitions», *Administrative Science Quarterly*, Vol. 29, No. 2.

Paolino C, Resti, C. (2017), «Arte e Azienda: le corporate art collection in Italia», *Economia e Diritto Del Terziario,* ISSN: 1593-9464.

Paolino, C., Bissola R., Imperatori, B. (2016), *Practices combination and collections' configurations: a complementarity-based approach to corporate collections*, EGOS.

Paolino, C., Antal, A. B. (2020), «Sergio Rossi and Its Magic Kingdom: Artistic Interventions, Brand Identity Renewal, and Stakeholder Awareness», in Massi M., Turrini A., *The Artification of Luxury Fashion Brands*, Palgrave Pivot, Cham, 33-61.

Pless, N.M., Maak, T., Harris, H. (2017), «Art, Ethics and the Promotion of Human Dignity», *Journal of Business Ethics*, 144(2), 223-232.

Pratt, M.G. (2000), «The Good, the Bad, and the Ambivalent: Managing Identification Among Amway Distributors», *Administrative Science Quarterly*, 45(3), 456-493.

Purg, D., Sutherland, I. (2017), «Why Art in Management Education? Questioning Meaning», *Academy of Management Review*, Vol. 42, No. 2, 382-406.

Ravasi, D., Lojacono, G. (2005), «Managing design and designers for strategic renewal», *Long Range Planning*, 38(1), 51-77.

Richards, D. (1995), *Artful Work: Awakening Joy, Meaning, and Commitment in the Workplace*, Berrett-Koehler Publishers, San Francisco.

Scharmer, C.O. (2007), *Addressing the blind spot of our time. An executive summary to the new book Theory U: Leading from the Future as It Emerges*, Society for Organizational Learning, Cambridge.

Schein, E. (1978), *Career Dynamics: Matching Individual and Organizational Needs*, Addison-Wesley, Boston.

Schein, E.H. (2013), «The Role of Art and the Artist», *Organizational Aesthetics*, 2(1), 1-4.

Sköldberg, U.J., Woodilla, J., Antal, A.B. (Eds.) (2015), *Artistic Interventions in Organizations: Research, Theory and Practice*, Routledge, Londra.

Soda, G., Usai, A., Zaheer, A. (2004), «Network Memory: The Influence of Past and Current Networks on Performance», *Academy of Management Journal*, 47(6), 893-906.

Spear, S., Bowen, H. K. (1999), «Decoding the DNA of the Toyota production system», *Harvard Business Review*, 77, 96-108.

Star, S.L., Griesemer, J.R. (1989), «Institutional Ecology, 'Translations' and Boundary Objects: Amateurs and Professionals in Berkeley's Museum of Vertebrate Zoology, 1907-39», *Social Studies of Science*.

Stigliani, I., Ravasi, D. (2012), «Organizing Thoughts and Connecting Brains: Material Practices and the Transition from Individual to Group- Level Prospective Sensemaking», *Academy of Management Journal*, 55(5), 1232-1259.

Strati, A. (1999), «Putting People in the Picture: Art and Aesthetics in Photography and in Understanding Organizational Life», *Organization Studies*, 20(7), 53-69.

Strati, A. (2007), «Sensible Knowledge and Practice-based Learning», *Management Learning*, 38(1), 61-77.

Strati, A., de Montoux, P.G. (2002), «Introduction: Organizing aesthetics», *Human Relations*, 55(7), 755-766.

Strauss, A. (2009, July), *Context Is Half the Work: An Intercultural Perspective on Arts and Business Research* (Conference paper presented at SCOS, Copenhagen).

Sutherland, I. (2012), «Arts-based Methods in Leadership Development: Affording Aesthetic Workplaces, Reflexivity and Memories With Momentum», *Management Learning*, 44(I), 25-43.

Taylor, S.S. (2002), «Overcoming Aesthetic Muteness: Researching Organizational Members' Aesthetic Experience», *Human Relations*, 55(7), 821-840.

Taylor, S.S., Ladkin, D. (2009), «Understanding arts-based methods in managerial development», *Academy of Management Learning & Education*, 8(1), 55-69.

Taylor, S.S., Fisher, D., Dufresne, R.L. (2002), «The Aesthetics of Management Storytelling: A Key to Organizational Learning», *Management Learning*, 33(3), 313-330.

Vettese, A. (2012), *L'arte Contemporanea. Tra mercato e nuovi linguaggi*, il Mulino, Bologna.

Weber, K., Glynn, M.A. (2006), «Making Sense with Institutions: Context, Thought and Action in Karl Weick's Theory», *Organization Studies*, 27/11; 1639-1660.

Wrzesniewski, A., Dutton, J.E. (2001), «Crafting a Job: Revisioning Employees as Active Crafters of Their Work», *Academy of Management Review*, 26, 179-201.

Zan, L. (2002), «Renewing Pompeii, year zero. Promises and expectations from new approaches to museum management and accountability», *Critical Perspectives on Accounting*, 13(1), 89-137.

www.ingramcontent.com/pod-product-compliance
Lightning Source LLC
LaVergne TN
LVHW052250100826
845147LV00001B/6

* 9 7 8 8 8 3 1 3 2 2 3 7 9 *